Praise for *Shattered Innocence*

"Robert Scott shows that the Jaycee Dugard story is more compelling and more shocking than the news previously reported. *Shattered Innocence* is a fascinating account of a young girl's abduction by a monster who should never had been free to walk the streets. This is a groundbreaking book."

—*New York Times* best-selling author
Robert K. Tanenbaum

"Robert Scott's book zeroes in on many compelling but unreported aspects of the Jaycee Lee Dugard case. What happened to Jaycee Lee is equal parts fascinating and horrifying, and Robert Scott embraces both to tell this extraordinary story in a fresh way. The result is a fast-paced, informative read."

—Sue Russell, author of *Lethal Intent*

THE
LAST TIME
WE SAW
HER

ROBERT SCOTT

PINNACLE BOOKS
Kensington Publishing Corp.
http://www.kensingtonbooks.com

PINNACLE BOOKS are published by

Kensington Publishing Corp.
119 West 40th Street
New York, NY 10018

All Kensington Titles, Imprints, and Distributed Lines are available at special quantity discounts for bulk purchases for sales promotions, premiums, fund-raising, and educational or institutional use. Special book excerpts or customized printings can also be created to fit specific needs. For details, write or phone the office of the Kensington special sales manager: Kensington Publishing Corp., 119 West 40th Street, New York, NY 10018, attn: Special Sales Department, Phone: 1-800-221-2647.

Pinnacle and the P logo Reg. U.S. Pat. & TM Off.

ISBN-13: 978-0-7860-2037-9
ISBN-10: 0-7860-2037-7

First Printing: January 2012

10 9 8 7 6 5 4 3 2

Printed in the United States of America

ACKNOWLEDGMENTS

I'd like to thank the staff
at the Benton County Courthouse
for their help on this book.
And I'd also like to thank my
editors, Richard Ember
and Michaela Hamilton.

I heard a bloodcurdling scream.

—Nathaniel McKelvey

Joel Courtney is a bad dude.

—Spokesperson, Albuquerque PD

Brooke Wilberger became an icon for our community.

—DA John Haroldson

PART I

CHAPTER 1

TERROR ON A DARK STREET

Albuquerque, New Mexico
November 29, 2004

Natalie Kirov was a beautiful young woman. Twenty-two years old, blond, petite, and vibrant, she was very far from her native country of Russia. An exchange student at the University of New Mexico (UNM), in Albuquerque, Natalie had learned to love the area that was so different from her own homeland. Every morning colorful balloons rose from the fields around the Rio Grande and wafted aloft on winds that made them soar along the Sandia Mountains. Old Town, with its collection of historic buildings dating back to the early 1700s, was just down the hill from the campus. And as each day went by, Natalie's English skills improved, and she became more and more a part of the student life on campus.

Natalie worked part-time on campus to make ends meet, and on the evening of November 29, 2004, she left her job at a day care center at UNM, around 5:30 P.M. She took a shuttle bus to an area near the duck pond on campus and then started walking home through a neighborhood where many students lived. This was an area that Tony Hillerman had written about on several occasions in his series of Navajo mysteries. As Hillerman noted in *Coyote Waits: It was a neighborhood of small frame stucco bungalows left over from the 1940s with weedy yards and sagging fences.* By 2004, some of the homes in the area were newer, with well-kept yards, but there were also empty lots filled with weeds and overgrown shrubbery, and still those that had "weedy yards and sagging fences."

The residential area below campus may not have been the most luxurious in the city, but it was filled with plenty of students returning to their residences and commuters arriving home from work at 6:00 P.M., so Natalie felt safe as she walked along. There was one drawback to this illusion of safety, however. Much of the street upon which she walked was unlit, and at this time of November, it was already dark. There were also gaps in the rows of houses with screens of dark vegetation. As Natalie neared the intersection of Harvard Drive and Garfield Avenue, there was even an old barn sitting on a wooded lot next to the street, which made that locale look more like country than city.

Suddenly, as if in a nightmare, a shadowy figure came up behind Natalie. Without warning his hands clasped around her waist and throat. In a rough voice the stranger whispered into her ear, "Come with me! Get in my car! I have a knife!"

For a brief moment Natalie thought it was all a joke. After all, this was the heart of the city, just a little after six o'clock. She thought it was someone she knew from school who was playing a prank on her.

That perception quickly disappeared as the man pulled a knife out of his pocket and placed the sharp blade against her neck. Its cold steel dispelled any more thoughts that this was a prank.

Knowing that she had to comply, or die right there on the street, Natalie allowed herself to be manhandled toward the assailant's vehicle. She was thrust into a small red Honda and told not to move or scream.

Her assailant got into the car right behind her through the passenger door. He climbed over her, moved behind the steering wheel, and started the engine. As the car began moving down the street, she could see in the dim light that her attacker was about thirty years old and scruffy-looking. She also noticed that he was very agitated and his eyes had a wild look.

Even though the car was now moving, Natalie decided to take her chances. She grabbed the passenger-door handle and jerked on it, deciding it was better to throw herself from a moving car than to end up wherever this man was taking her. But to her surprise and horror, the door would not open.

The man growled at her and flashed his knife. "Don't do that again!" he snarled. "Or I'll hurt you!"

Extremely frightened now, Natalie complied. She even obeyed him when he said, "Take off your clothes and put them on the backseat." He pointed the knife at her once more with his free hand. Natalie disrobed, item by item, until she was completely naked. He glanced at her momentarily and then kept driving.

Even under these extreme circumstances, Natalie kept her wits about her. She told the man, "Please don't take me far away. I don't know the area."

Surprisingly, the man agreed, and replied, "I won't take you far."

True to his word, he drove only a little farther down to an area near Princeton Drive. Natalie had no illusions about what was coming next. Even as he drove, the man reached over and let his free hand roam all over her naked body. He inserted one of his fingers into her vagina and then into her anus. It's not exactly clear at what point this happened, but he soon parked in a dark area. He then unzipped his pants and told her to "go down on it."

Natalie cried out, "I don't know how! I've never done that!"

"I'll show you how," he replied, and forced her head down.

But it wasn't working. The man became more and more angry and agitated. "We need another spot," he said, perhaps worried that they might be seen on Princeton Drive.

He started the vehicle again and drove away. As he did so, he told Natalie not to look out the window. She disobeyed him, however, wanting to know where he was taking her. She thought she was being cagey about this, but he spotted her. Her captor snarled, "I told you not to peek!"

Natalie's memory of what occurred next became jumbled in its images of this nightmarish ride. It might have been on the side of a street, but more likely the man stopped in the parking lot of an apartment complex. He pulled out a small item, which, at first, she thought was a pen. It was, in fact, a small crack pipe. The man loaded the pipe with some crack cocaine, lit it, and then blew smoke into her nostrils. He told her to open her mouth and inhale. But Natalie didn't want to do that.

"What is it?" she asked.

"Shut up!" he replied. "Just do as I say! This will relax you."

But it didn't relax her. It only made her more frightened about the whole situation.

Natalie cried, "Can't I just go home?"

The man answered, "If you make me happy, you have a better chance of going home."

He climbed on top of her and kissed her neck and breasts. Despite fondling her some more, inserting his finger once again into her vagina and anus, the man could not stay erect. Frustrated and angry, he made her lie on her stomach as he searched around for something to tie her up with. Eventually he bound her wrists together with laces from one of her shoes and bound her ankles with her scarf. Then he stuffed her panties into her mouth and bound it to her head with another shoestring. He draped a coat over her head and fastened it there with a belt. Then he told her, "Don't move. I'm watching you."

Satisfied with his handiwork, the man suddenly and unexpectedly exited the vehicle and went walking away toward a row of apartments near the parking lot where they were now situated. Once he was out of sight, Natalie began thrashing, twisting, and wiggling with all her might to loosen her restraints.

She said later, "The scarf was kind of loose, and I got that off easily. Then I loosened the shoestring that bound my wrists." She pulled the panties out of her mouth as well, but she was in such a hurry, she did not remove them from around her neck. That accomplished, Natalie didn't even bother dressing. She just grabbed her coat, managed to unlock the car door, and vaulted out into the open. Then, without a backward glance, she took off running.

Clad only in socks and a coat, which barely covered her naked body, Natalie went running down the street until she came to the vicinity of Louisiana Boulevard SE. But this wasn't the best part of town, and as she tried to flag cars down, they must have thought she was some whacked-out druggie or prostitute. No one stopped to help her.

Natalie was eventually able to speak to one group of people in a car near a stoplight. She begged, "Please help me! Let me in!" But the people stared out at her in dismay. One of them said, "Our car is too full." And then they took off.

Natalie ran across the street to a small Mexican restaurant. There were people inside there, but they, too, were reluctant to help her. Perhaps they had limited English, and the Russian-accented words pouring out of Natalie's mouth were hard to understand. And then, unexpectedly and almost by a miracle, a car with a woman and some children pulled over near the restaurant. The car was driven by Dara Finks, and one of Dara's daughters was in the front passenger seat. Seeing the strange young woman running down the street, clad only in socks and a coat, Dara nonetheless had decided to pull over in the dark to see if she could help.

Dara and one of her daughters went into the restaurant and spoke with the strange girl, who was so scantily dressed. Natalie's story came tumbling out; she spoke of how she had been attacked by a man with a knife and was forced to disrobe. Dara offered to call 911, while Dara's daughter offered Natalie an extra pair of pants, which were in the car.

All three women got into Dara's car; and as they took off, Natalie could see her attacker across the street getting into his red Honda and starting the car. She was afraid he might follow them, but he took off in another direction.

Natalie got on Dara's cell phone and spoke to a 911 dispatcher. Natalie told the dispatcher what had just occurred and gave a description of her attacker and the car he had been in. Natalie was given instructions where to meet a police officer, who would then handle her report.

The first law enforcement agent to arrive was Officer Aragon of the Albuquerque Police Department (APD). Officer Aragon spoke with Natalie and Dara and began a report on the incident. Natalie told about being abducted at knifepoint, driven away in the car, forced to disrobe, and then sexually molested. She also spoke of the last location she had been when she'd managed to escape. Because she knew from what area she'd started running to seek help, Officer Aragon was able to take Natalie back to the exact block of Louisiana Boulevard SE. With any luck the red Honda might have returned to the lot, and an arrest could be made.

The car wasn't there, but Natalie's description of the vehicle was very good. She told Officer Aragon that it was a red Honda with a red-and-gray interior and a stuffed-animal monkey in the back window. The monkey had suction cups on its hands and feet, which allowed it to be attached to a vehicle window. The Honda had been in the apartment complex parking lot at the location where they now were. It was there that the man had tied her up and then exited the vehicle, looking for something or someone.

Soon other officers arrived on the scene, including APD detective John Romero. Detective Romero had his crime scene technicians spread out and search the area. One of them found a shoestring that most likely had been used to bind Natalie. And then a real piece of luck occurred. Officer Aragon went to an apartment close to where the red Honda had been parked. He contacted a woman there named Zoraido Oviedo. Oviedo told Officer Aragon that she knew a man named "Joe" who owned a red Honda. In fact, Joe had just left her apartment in a hurry, saying, "I gotta get outta here!" He had been very agitated and afraid of something.

Oviedo didn't know Joe's last name, or where he lived. But she thought it was somewhere in the area of Yale and Gibson boulevards. In fact, she didn't even know if Joe was really his name. It's just what he called himself.

Natalie was transported to a hospital for treatment by Officer R. Sanchez. Meanwhile, Officer E. Taylor drove to the area of Yale and Gibson where Oviedo had indicated Joe lived. As Officer Taylor cruised up and down the streets, he spotted a red Honda with a toy monkey in the back window. And as Taylor got out to inspect the vehicle, as if by magic, a man who matched the description that Natalie had given approached the Honda.

Officer Taylor detained the man and asked if his name was Joe.

The man corrected Taylor and said that his name was Joel.

By the incredible survival instincts of Natalie Kirov, the timely and brave intervention of Dara Finks, and the good police work by the Albuquerque Police Department, a chain of events was about to go into effect. A chain of events that would lead back through a man named Joel to a kidnapping, rape, and murder of a young woman in Oregon months prior to that November evening. Just like with Natalie, Joel had snatched the young blond woman off a "safe street." That young woman was a college student as well. Joel drove her to a remote location, made her disrobe, sexually molested her for more than a day, and then killed her in a patch of lonely dark woods. What had begun to unravel in New Mexico in November 2004 had only started to transpire in Oregon in May 2004.

CHAPTER 2
CLOSE CALLS

Corvallis, Oregon, May 24, 2004

The man named Joel was in a bad mood on the morning of May 24, 2004. He'd spent a long night of drinking and snorting cocaine at a party in Portland, Oregon. Now overdue for a DUI court appearance more than 150 miles away on the Oregon coast in Newport, Lincoln County, he was tired and hungover. There were no direct freeways from Portland to Newport, and he knew he was going to be late for his "driving under the influence" charge.

Joel called the court and left a message on their answering machine about his late appearance. Then he decided to drive down Interstate 5 to Albany and cut across to the coast on Highway 20. This highway would take him through the college town of Corvallis, on the Willamette River.

Corvallis was a city of fifty-five thousand residents and nineteen thousand college students at Oregon

State University (OSU) in 2004. Corvallis went by the title "The Pacific Northwest's Most Beautiful College Town." Noble Prize–winner Linus Pauling had been an OSU graduate, and inkjet printing and the computer mouse had been invented there. In fact, Corvallis had one of the highest per capita number of computer users in the nation. Up until the year 2004, Corvallis had one other statistic: It was the twentieth safest city of its size in the United States out of a list of 344. But all that was about to change.

As Joel drove through Corvallis around nine-twenty on Monday morning, May 24, he began to spot more and more young college girls walking toward campus. They were just the kind of girls he liked. And even better, as far as he was concerned, these girls were walking alone on the residential streets beneath the shady trees.

In some areas there were no other people around, or even passing traffic. All of this was just too tempting for Joel. He'd been in similar situations in the past when he'd spotted a young woman walking alone on a street. He'd taken advantage of the situation in the blink of an eye, forcing them into his vehicle and making them disrobe, before having sex with them. And besides, now he was driving a mini-van with tinted windows. Even in the daytime no one could see into the back of the van. He could hustle a girl into the van's interior, threaten her, and then drive to some remote location. Then he could do whatever he wanted with her.

Joel started cruising the streets of Corvallis, closer and closer to campus. On the southwest side of campus, he spotted a young woman walking into the parking lot of the Oak Park Apartments, about a block away from OSU's Reser Stadium. There was no one else around that he could see. Here was his chance.

Diane Mason was twenty years old in May 2004, and a student at OSU. She lived not far off campus, and on that morning she began her usual walk to class by cutting through the Oak Park Apartments complex. As she did so, she noticed a green minivan enter the parking lot from a side street. As the van drove in, Diane exited the parking lot and crossed Western Boulevard, walked past the Reser Stadium parking lot, and headed for Thirtieth Street, on the edge of campus. There were a few cars going by on Western Boulevard, but no people or cars at all on Thirtieth Street.

Suddenly the green minivan she had seen at the Oak Park Apartments pulled up and actually blocked her path. Diane had to walk out into the street to move around it. The van's engine was still running; and as she approached the driver's side of the vehicle, the driver rolled the window down. As soon as Diane was adjacent to the window, the man inside spoke to her.

"I'm lost," he said. "Can you help me?"

Diane asked where he was going and he mentioned the name of some fraternity she had never heard of. Diane told him, "It's probably on Greek Row, near Twenty-fifth and Harrison."

Diane noticed that the man was in his late thirties or early forties, had light-colored hair, a goatee, and light-colored eyes, which were probably blue. He was wearing a casual shirt and had two earrings in his left ear. One of them was a gold hoop-type earring.

Diane recalled later, "When I gave him directions,

he seemed a little confused. He had an Idaho map in his hands, but he said he also had a Corvallis map in the back of the van. He wanted me to point out directions on that map. At that point he opened the driver's-side door to get out and I had to back up about three feet into the street to let him out. I thought this was odd, since most people don't get out of their vehicles to ask directions.

"I began to get a really uneasy feeling about all of this, since I was alone on the street. There was no traffic. There was no noise. And this person I didn't know had just gotten out of his vehicle."

When the man got out of the minivan, Diane judged his height to be between five-nine and five-eleven. He had a medium build and seemed average in most respects. He walked to the side of the van, opened a sliding door, and began rummaging around inside the van behind the driver's seat. Diane could see that there were several boxes inside and items of clothing and blankets.

Diane said later, "He slid one box in the back, which I thought was odd, since there was nothing behind it and it wasn't heavy." She wondered if he didn't want her to see what was inside the box.

The man said to her, "Let me look for another second."

But by this point Diane was becoming very nervous. Things just didn't seem right about this situation, and she was aware that no one else was around. Diane told the man, "I've got to get to class"; she started walking away.

Soon after she began walking toward campus, she heard the van begin to move. It turned around toward Western Boulevard once again. Diane walked on, and the van did not return.

Joel became even more irritated. This ruse had not worked, but he was persistent. Now that he was determined to have a young woman, he was in prime "trolling grounds," near a university campus. He drove back on Western for a short ways, doubled back, and soon spotted another young woman walking alone in the Reser Stadium parking lot. This was a wide area of dirt and gravel, and there was no one else around.

Jade Bateman was a student at OSU and very athletic. In fact, she worked part-time at the athletic office on campus. As Jade walked along, she noticed a green minivan cruising through the Reser Stadium parking lot. The minivan cruised by her very slowly, and the man inside was staring at her. It made her very uncomfortable. Instead of walking away, Jade decided to confront the driver. She moved toward the van and said to the man, whose driver's-side window was rolled down, "Can I help you?"

The man seemed to be in his thirties or early forties. He was wearing a baseball cap and had a goatee. He also wore dark sunglasses. The man said to Jade, "I'm looking for the athletic offices."

Jade replied, "Are you looking for the football office or one of the other sports offices?"

He said he was looking for one of the sports offices, and Jade told him that he should drive up to Gill Coliseum and they could help him there. All during this conversation Jade was on a cell phone with her mother, who lived in Portland.

Jade said later, "I asked my mom to stay on the phone. I was very serious about this. It was more of a demand than a suggestion. I was nervous. I felt that I was in a situation that wasn't good."

Jade's mother, Phyllis, recalled that phone call very well. She said, "I knew that Jade lived not far off campus. From my daughter's apartment you could see the football stadium. That morning I was getting some things ready for the recycle center, and Jade's friend was coming over with his pickup to get it. I was on my cell phone with Jade and she was giving someone directions to someplace. I told her, 'Jade, I'm going to hang up and let you talk to that person.' She told me, 'Do not hang up the phone!' She said it fairly strongly. She normally didn't speak to me that way."

Jade was indeed nervous. A green minivan with a stranger at the wheel—in a large parking lot, with no one else around—was very unsettling.

And then, as luck would have it, another individual drove out onto the parking lot. The individual was Bob Clifford, an athletic director at OSU. Clifford knew Jade by sight, and what he saw now in the Reser Stadium parking lot disturbed him enough to make him drive over and see what was going on.

Bob said later, "I noticed a girl I knew named Jade, standing by a green Dodge minivan out in the Reser Stadium parking lot. It just didn't seem like a normal situation. I drove over and noticed that the van had Minnesota plates. I pulled up to the passenger side and tried to get the driver's attention. But he kind of ignored me. He kept his hands attached to the steering wheel and would not acknowledge my presence. He was wearing a baseball cap, sunglasses, and a light spring coat.

"So I pulled in front of him and put my car in

park. I turned around and looked at Jade. Then he and I exchanged quick glimpses of each other. I looked at her again, and she started to walk away."

Jade was glad that Bob Clifford had arrived on the scene. She wasn't sure if the man in the van was up to something, but the whole situation just didn't feel right to her. Jade started walking toward campus, and the man in the van just sat there.

Bob noted, "At that point everything seemed okay. I pulled away, and the van followed me. I took a right onto Twenty-sixth Street, and the van turned onto Western."

By now, Joel was "really pissed." Two situations that should have worked for him had now been foiled, but he wasn't giving up. He remembered a pretty young woman in the parking lot of the Oak Park Apartments who was cleaning lampposts when he had first followed the other girl to Thirtieth Street. The young woman cleaning the lampposts was petite, blond, and pretty. With any luck she would still be out there all alone, cleaning light fixtures.

CHAPTER 3
VANISHED

As luck would have it, the young woman cleaning light fixtures was nineteen-year-old Brooke Wilberger, who was on summer break from where she attended college at Brigham Young University (BYU) in Utah. Brooke was born on February 20, 1985, in Fresno, California, to Greg and Cammy Wilberger. The family soon moved to La Grande, Oregon, and then to Veneta, Oregon, a town in the Willamette River Valley, about forty miles south of Corvallis. Brooke had several older siblings, brothers Bryce, twenty-five, and Spencer, twenty-two, and sisters Shannon, thirty, and Stephanie, twenty-seven. Sister Jessica was six years younger than Brooke.

Although Brooke was bright, she had trouble with her speech as a child. Even though she spoke, many of her words were unintelligible. Cammy, who was a third-grade teacher, told Brooke's siblings not to tease her. Cammy said later, "I took her brothers aside and said, 'I don't care what you say or do, but never tease Brooke about her speech.' And they never did."

Eventually, with the aid of a speech therapist, Brooke did just fine in learning to speak. In fact, by high school, she was carrying nearly a 4.0 average. Very bright in academics, Brooke also did well in extracurricular activities, especially tennis and track. By then, she had a long blond ponytail, a trim figure, and was very pretty. Since the Wilbergers lived out in a rural area, Brooke joined 4-H and loved horses. And even though Brooke was quiet, she wasn't afraid to stick up for herself, and she joined in a high-school play, *The Pirates of Penzance.*

It was at Elmira High School that she met a boy, Justin Blake, and soon she and Justin were going to dances. Eventually they became girlfriend and boyfriend. Brooke's mom recalled later, "The church had dances in Eugene, and when Brooke came back, I'd say, 'Who did you dance with today?' Pretty soon she started telling me about this boy named Justin. In high school they did most things together. She really liked him."

After high school Justin, who was a member of the Church of Jesus Christ of Latter-day Saints (LDS), more commonly known as Mormons, went on a mission to Venezuela. Brooke and her entire family were also Mormons, and Brooke was well aware that many young men in the Mormon Church went off on a mission at about that age in their lives. Brooke wrote him at least once a week. She even thought about going on a mission herself when she turned twenty-one, the minimum age that females could go on missions for the church.

Brooke's parents, who had atteded nearby OSU,

along with all of Brooke's older siblings, thought that Brooke would go there as well. But Brooke was very-independent, and she told them she wanted to go to Brigham Young University in Utah. Her parents told Brooke that she would have to save up money to do that, and she did, taking on jobs during the summer months. Brooke wanted to go to BYU because they had a department that specialized in early childhood speech problems. She was very grateful to her own teachers when she was young, and she wanted to specialize in that area as well. That was a constant in Brooke's life. She was always giving back to individuals and to the community.

As far as being safe while walking to and from classes at BYU, Cammy later said, "She was a cautious kid. One of the concerns she had about her little car was that it did not have automatic locks on the doors. She even took a class in self-defense, because there had been some issues at BYU."

In May 2004, classes were over at BYU, and Brooke came home to Veneta, Oregon. She stayed for a short while with her parents and younger sister, Jessica, and then decided to go and help her sister Stephanie and Stephanie's husband, Zak Hansen, who managed the Oak Park Apartments in Corvallis.

On May 24, Brooke got up about six-thirty and had a bowl of cornflakes for breakfast at her parents' home in Veneta. Soon her parents were off to work, and Brooke asked Jessica if she needed a ride to school. Jessica said no, so Brooke packed a few bags and took off for Corvallis. In a short while, she arrived at her sister Stephanie's apartment around eight-thirty. Brooke and Stephanie talked for a bit and then Brooke went outside to clean lamps and lampposts around the apartment complex. It was a job she didn't relish, since many of the lampposts had spider webs on them. Brooke didn't like spiders; but as in all of the tasks that she performed, she cleaned them well.

Brooke was wearing a BYU Soccer T-shirt, FreshJive sweatshirt, blue jeans, and flip-flop sandals. Around 8:45 A.M., Brooke started cleaning lampposts at the Oak Park Apartments on the west side and completed those around nine. This area could clearly be seen from vehicles driving along Philomath Boulevard.

Brooke continued working eastward, where trees and twenty-foot shrubs on the back side of the property blocked views from the street. Around 9:30 A.M., a tenant named Mark Wacker spotted Brooke in the parking lot by a light fixture. Wacker saw that the girl was at the third light fixture from the east side of those set of apartment buildings. She was cleaning the bottom of the light fixture with a rag and a bucket of water.

At 9:45 A.M., Brooke's cousin Kris Horner saw Brooke working on a light fixture, and around ten o'clock, Brooke's sister Stephanie spied Brooke cleaning near the number 1223 unit. Stephanie took her children to preschool and was gone for a while from the apartment complex.

Sometime after ten, Corvallis Disposal truck driver Jim Kessi drove into the Oak Park Apartments parking lot to pick up material from the recycle bin. As he did so, he spotted a young blond woman cleaning lampposts. He waved at her, and she waved back. He noticed that she was cleaning the third light fixture from the east end of that area. She had its round plastic cover in her hand.

Kessi picked up his load of cardboard from the recycle bin and backed out into the parking lot once again. As he did so, he could see that the blond girl was still cleaning light fixtures. There were no cars in the parking lot near her, and no people around as well.

Sometime after ten o'clock, Nathaniel McKelvey, who lived in the 1229 unit at Oak Park Apartments, heard a loud, piercing scream. He would later describe it as "short in duration and bloodcurdling." At that same moment Carina Howrey, who also lived in the same unit, heard a female's scream. She later described the scream as "short in time." Howrey looked out her back door, then out her front window. But she didn't see anyone.

Nathaniel McKelvey and Carina Howrey were the last people to hear anything escape from Brooke Wilberger's lips. All except for the man named Joel, in the green minivan. After two failed attempts he now had what he was looking for: a pretty young woman abducted into his van, and restrained there. Now all he had to do was get her out of town, unnoticed.

As the minivan headed west, out of Corvallis, the only things left in the Oak Park Apartments complex testifying that Brooke Wilberger had been there were two flip-flop sandals, a few wet rags, and a bucket of sudsy water.

CHAPTER 4
SEARCHING

Brooke was supposed to come to her sister Stephanie's apartment for lunch at twelve-thirty. When she didn't show, Stephanie went to investigate. What she discovered in the apartment parking lot was unnerving—there was a bucket near a light fixture, but no Brooke anywhere.

Stephanie Hansen and Kris Horner began searching the entire apartment complex for Brooke. It was not like Brooke to change plans without telling anyone. And why would she just leave a bucket of water near a lamppost and a job unfinished? That was not like her as well. Around one o'clock, Horner found Brooke's blue-and-white flip-flop sandals in the parking lot. They were about eight feet apart from each other as if she'd suddenly lost them in haste. The thong on the right sandal had been pulled out.

Stephanie and Kris kept on searching all throughout the complex, until around three o'clock. At that point they were so upset by no signs of Brooke, Stephanie phoned the Corvallis Police Department (CPD). A dispatcher took Stephanie's statement and notated it as a missing person. What may have helped convince the dispatcher of the seriousness of the situation was Stephanie's description of Brooke as being a devout member of the Church of Jesus Christ of Latter-day Saints. It was common knowledge that Mormons did not generally drink alcohol, take drugs, or engage in illegal activities. Stephanie later said of Brooke, "She's a very responsible girl. She doesn't drink, doesn't smoke, doesn't party. She has a longtime boyfriend, who is off on a Mormon mission."

With other college-age girls at OSU, it's possible the dispatcher might have been less convinced that something was amiss. There might have been many other possibilities—a sudden change of plans, going to meet a boyfriend or friends at school, an argument with her sister, or any number of things. But none of those factors seemed to apply to Brooke Wilberger. And the state of Brooke's sandals was taken into account as well. Why would anyone leave them strewn in the parking lot like that, unless something out of the ordinary had occurred? The dispatcher agreed with Stephanie that something was wrong, and a CPD officer was dispatched to the Oak Park Apartments.

Cammy Wilberger didn't learn about Brooke's disappearance until after she had finished teaching school for the day. Cammy called Brooke's cell phone from class and was surprised when Brooke's brother Spencer answered it.

Cammy recalled, "So I chatted with him, and he

didn't say much. Finally I said, 'Is Brooke there?' And he said, 'We can't find her.'"

"Spencer, don't tease me!" Cammy replied to her son.

"Mom, I'm not! We can't find her!" Spencer responded.

"I knew that something was horribly wrong! My arms, everything in my body, just drained out," Cammy noted later.

Cammy soon contacted her youngest daughter, Jessica, who was at home, and told her, "Something's going on in Corvallis. We need to have a bag packed. I'm coming home now."

Then Cammy phoned her friend Cheryl Blake. Cheryl was the mother of Justin Blake, Brooke's boyfriend, and also the wife of the bishop in the LDS ward in which the Wilbergers attended church. As soon as Cheryl heard about Brooke, she put the LDS network of families into action. One person called another, and soon the news had spread amongst LDS members all over the region.

Greg Wilberger, who worked for the Borden Chemical company in Springfield, Oregon, was on his way to a business trip in San Francisco on that day. He was at the Portland International Airport when his family contacted him with the news. Greg immediately canceled his flight, got a rental car, and drove down to Corvallis, as fast as he could, in a daze. None of this seemed real. Corvallis was supposed to be a safe city. What had occurred there that his daughter would suddenly end up missing?

It was around 4:00 P.M. when the first CPD officer arrived at the Oak Park Apartments complex and spoke with Stephanie Hansen and Kris Horner. He noted the vital statistics about Brooke—her age, height, weight, and what she had been wearing when last seen. Around this same time Brooke's sister Shannon Cordon also arrived to join in the hunt for Brooke. Shannon later said, "It wasn't like Brooke not to tell anyone where she was going. She just wouldn't disappear on her own." This fact was soon amplified by finding Brooke's purse, car keys, and other personal items in the Hansens' apartment. Brooke's car was also still in the parking lot. Shannon told authorities, "She didn't have anything with her except the clothes on her back."

More and more officers began arriving at the Oak Park Apartments in the search for the missing girl. They were taking this seriously and already starting to look at the situation as an abduction rather than just a missing person. Mike Morrow and his team of Benton County Emergency Services (BCES) workers joined the hunt at around 6:00 P.M. By six-thirty, they were setting up a staging area in the Oak Park Apartments complex parking lot to take in and coordinate volunteer searchers. It was amazing how quickly the word spread to people in the area—OSU students and especially members of the local LDS Church.

Terry Malaska was a member of this latter group and she soon told a reporter, who had gotten wind of the situation, "When something like this comes up, we call the ward and say, 'Help!' And at that point we've got what are called home teachers, so it's kind of like an automatic phone tree. Every household has a home teacher that contacts them, and within a few minutes you can talk to a lot of people."

Jared Cordon, Brooke's brother-in-law, agreed, saying, "What happened was just amazing. We soon had several hundred people doing search-and-rescue work on Monday night. We had every local and regional law enforcement agency there. We got people taking two and three days off from work to help." Cordon added that LDS members started using the Internet and ham radio to spread the word about Brooke. They also started passing out "Missing Person" flyers, which were coming off copiers at an incredible rate.

Thousands of black-and-white copies of flyers showing a photo of Brooke were soon being distributed around Corvallis. The Kinko's in town donated free color copies of a "Missing Person" poster as well. The poster had a photo of Brooke and in large red letters at the top, the word *Abducted*. It noted that Brooke was five-four, weighed 105 pounds, was nineteen years old, with blond hair and blue eyes. She had a scar on her right forearm, which ran from her wrist to her elbow. This was from a gymnastics accident. She was last seen wearing a gray BYU Soccer T-shirt, a blue FreshJive sweatshirt, and had a ring engraved with the letters *CTR*.

The poster related: *Brooke Wilberger is believed to have been abducted on 5/24/04 at approximately 10:50 AM from the 1200 block of SW 26th Street in Corvallis, Oregon. Evidence suggests that Ms. Wilberger was alone, working in the parking lot of an apartment complex when she was abducted.*

A Corvallis Safeway grocery store provided free food to the hundreds of citizen volunteers, who had arrived at the Oak Park Apartments staging area, and the nearby Hilton Garden Inn provided free coffee and restrooms for the throng. Domino's Pizza started donating free pizzas for the searchers.

Peggy Pierson, of BCES, told a reporter, "The response is phenomenal. More than three hundred volunteers signed in. And those were just the ones who signed in." The volunteers fanned out through the Oak Park Apartments complex, into the neighboring streets and the OSU campus. They searched parks, wooded areas, and along streambeds. Before long, the true number of searchers was probably around five hundred. Flyers began being distributed in other towns besides Corvallis, such as Philomath, Lebanon, Monroe, and Albany.

Citizen volunteers weren't the only ones on hand. By the night hours of May 24, there were law enforcement officers from the Corvallis Police Department, Benton County Sheriff's Office (BCSO), and the Oregon State Police (OSP). Soon the Mary's Peak Search and Rescue (MPSR) unit was there as well. These were the professionals in search-and-rescue missions. In their first foray, they went out with twelve volunteers, showing them how to do a grid search where every nook and cranny was thoroughly searched in an area. When MPSR came back from the first round of searching, there were seventy new volunteers waiting for them at the staging area. Jerry Smith, of MPSR, said of the volunteers, "They searched around Avery Park. They did phenomenally well."

Dean Carlozzi, of MPSR, related, "My group found scraps of shoelaces and every hair-tie scrunchie that's ever been dropped in that park." Everything of possible evidentiary value was gathered for later analysis to see if it belonged to Brooke Wilberger.

A disabled volunteer rode a motorized scooter, back and forth, relaying messages and handing out water. A local woman showed up with a bag full of flashlight batteries. Every item and contingency that came up was handled in one way or another by volunteers.

Flyers went out, in ever-widening circles, to Salem, Newport, and Lincoln City. Every corner of the neighborhood and the OSU campus was searched in a thorough manner. It seemed that wherever someone looked on the night of May 24 through May 25, there were flashlight beams and volunteers looking under bushes, under cars, and over fences. It was almost surreal as flashlight beams danced around in the dark, like so many fireflies.

Despite all of the search efforts, by the afternoon of May 25, there were still no tangible clues as to where the missing young woman was. CPD captain Bob Deutsch told reporters, "We've come up with nothing so far, which is disappointing. As time goes on, the distances and places to look are greater." Deutsch noted that 70 to 80 percent of the CPD resources were being used in the search at this point.

More news about Brooke started filtering into the media around this time as well. AP reported that she attended BYU in Utah and was in her second year there. She lived in an all-female residence hall and was studying speech pathology. She intended to work with children with speech impediments after she graduated.

Once again, family members said that Brooke wouldn't just leave the area without telling someone first. Jared Cordon noted, "She's a great person. She's a bubbly, beautiful girl. It's extremely out of character for her to disappear."

By Tuesday afternoon, May 25, even the FBI was involved. An FBI spokesperson from the Eugene FBI office said that their agents were assisting the other law enforcement agencies in any way they could. One of their main tasks was in profiling who the abductor might be—his possible characteristics and the way he operated. This could help the other law enforcement agents focus on high-priority suspects first, since time might be of the essence. And already, hundreds of tips were pouring in.

By Wednesday, May 26, more than twenty detectives from local and regional offices of law enforcement agencies were involved in Brooke's case. This did not count the numerous patrol officers and sheriff's deputies who were involved as well. By that point more than three hundred tips had come in from as far away as New Mexico, Illinois, and even Maine. CPD lieutenant Ron Noble told reporters, "None of the tips have led to suspects. But we're looking for someone who might have something, hoping they give us a call."

Reporter Jesse Sowa, of the Corvallis *Gazette-Times,* interviewed volunteer Bob Carleski to get an idea of what it was like for volunteers out in the field. Carleski's regular job was a data consultant doing contract work in Albany, Oregon, about eleven miles from Corvallis. He took time off from his job to join one of Jerry Smith's MPSR search teams. Carleski's team consisted of eleven men and one woman, and their area of search was in foot-high ivy in the woods near Philomath Boulevard. Carleski spoke of how thorough the search was and the spirit of the crew he worked with. Everyone took their work very seriously.

Steve Calton, an LDS volunteer, was a Hewlett-Packard employee. Calton told Sowa, "They (Hewlett-Packard) could do without me today. I can't imagine what the family is going through." About why he was there, Calton said, "It's about helping your brothers and sisters."

The LDS Church members were not the only ones concerned about Brooke's welfare. *Gazette-Times* reporter Carol Reeves looked into this aspect of the case with various other churches and religious institutions on campus and in Corvallis. College minister Mark Troncale, of OSU's Calvary Chapel, spoke of a Tuesday meeting where they prayed for Brooke Wilberger. He related, "We prayed for her, for her family, and for the authorities."

Beth Crawford, of Westminster House at OSU, said that students in that institution were praying for Brooke and her family as well. Beth stated, "Her disappearance has left members of the campus community feeling vulnerable and has reminded people how fragile life is." She added that Westminster House was open to any student who wanted to share their thoughts or concerns about Brooke.

Not only were the campus religious communities involved, but the wider religious community in the area as well. Reverend Ron Johnson, pastor of the Corvallis Evangelical Church, said, "The people in our church are deeply concerned for this young woman and her family, and many have been praying for her return. Our leaders began to pray for her almost as soon as we heard the news about her."

The main religious-based effort, however, still remained with the LDS members of the area. Much of the effort was being coordinated at the stake level. A "stake" in the LDS Church is a combination of several churches in an area. In the Corvallis stake headquarters, located on Hamilton Street, there was a coordinating center for the volunteers, who were pouring in. Many of these volunteers had young children, and a child care center was set up for the kids while their parents went out on search missions. Along with the child care center, there was a general information table, a table full of flyers, and another table with volunteers handling incoming phone calls.

The main effort at the center was sending new volunteers out to the search-and-rescue teams in the field, which were being coordinated by the professionals, such as MPSR. Terry Malaska at the stake center related, "They (the professionals) direct all of the search-and-rescue operations. They tell us what time and how many and where, and we try to give it to 'em."

Those who didn't go out on actual ground searches were sent all over the area distributing flyers with Brooke's photo and pertinent information. Terry related that by the afternoon of May 26, more than ten thousand of these flyers had been distributed in an ever-widening circle.

Despite all of the prayers, and despite all of the massive searches by volunteers, there were no valid clues as to where Brooke had been taken or by whom. And although the legions of volunteers were very welcome, it was the law enforcement personnel who were vital in the massive operation. The heart of their coordination by May 26 was the "incident room" in the Law Enforcement Center on Fifth Street in Corvallis. Up to ten people in there were manning the phone lines and taking in a flood of tips about Brooke Wilberger. Many of these tips were useless, but all of them had to be taken seriously until rejected as not being valid or helpful. Nothing could be overlooked at that point.

Corvallis Police Department captain Bob Deutsch told reporters, "Most of the tips are from people who think they saw her somewhere. Some are from self-styled psychics. A lot of unfounded tips have no validity whatsoever."

Besides being a command center for the incoming tips from the general public, the incident room also coordinated the efforts of the detectives from the CPD, BCSO, and Linn County Sheriff's Office (LCSO), Albany Police Department, and OSP. Deutsch said that a lot of these detectives were checking out the criminal records of known sex offenders in the region. They were contacting these individuals and those who were on probation or parole. Deutsch called these people, "the usual suspects" in a crime of this nature. He added, "It's basic, traditional, old-fashioned detective work. That means checking backgrounds, checking alibis, interviewing people, reinterviewing people, looking at criminal histories, and checking out leads."

On top of all of that, some law enforcement officers were going door-to-door in Brooke's neighborhood, talking with people there and asking if they could check out their homes and backyards. And if that wasn't enough, the Corvallis PD had the task of keeping the regional media and national media informed about the progress of the case.

Lieutenant Ron Noble was handling most of the media contacts. Besides individual interviews with news stations and reporters, he was conducting three press conferences per day as well. The

CPD knew that the more people who watched the press conferences in outlying areas, the better were the chances that Brooke would be found. By now, national early-morning television news shows had aired several segments about Brooke as well. The news about her spread far beyond the confines of Oregon's Willamette River Valley to every corner of America.

Besides fear in the Oak Park Apartments complex about what had occurred to Brooke, there was now a sense of unease on the nearby OSU campus as well, especially for female students. A reporter for the *Gazette-Times* interviewed several female OSU students on this issue. Connie Folse, who was an OSU student, and lived three blocks away from where Brooke had last been seen, spoke about her concerns. Connie was a student and a special-events coordinator for the Women's Center on campus. Connie said, "I was shocked by the apparent abduction in broad daylight. Honestly, I felt so safe in Corvallis. But am I really that safe? It puts things in perspective. When I'm walking around, it's in the back of my head."

On the same theme of surprise that an abduction had occurred in Corvallis in daylight hours, OSU graduate student Debi Stabler related, "It seems so out of the blue. It has changed my assumption about Corvallis. It made me think it can happen anywhere."

Other female students spoke of carrying Mace, air horns and whistles with them whenever they walked alone to and from campus. Many made sure to walk in pairs at all times. And Alisha Bickett, from the small nearby town of Lebanon, said that she was even concerned in that outlying community. Alisha declared, "It's scary to know someone could be doing yard work, minding their own business, and be abducted."

Marisa Birky and Michelle Raethke were two typical female roommates and friends at OSU. They lived in Bloss Hall and were studying nursing on campus. More than ever, they made sure to walk in each other's company whenever they could. Birky said, "I'm more paranoid than normal. I used to feel so safe, and now I feel unsafe. Any little noise will set me off."

What really made the reporter's ears perk up was a story told by Marisa and Michelle. They said that a friend of theirs, three days before Brooke went missing, had a scary encounter of her own near campus. According to this friend, she had been walking on Twenty-sixth Street at night when a strange man suddenly came up from behind her. At the same moment a car drove up near her. The strange man told the young woman to get into the car. Instead, she bit his hand and fled into the bushes. The man didn't follow her, but rather jumped into the nearby car and it sped off. This friend of Marisa's and Michelle's hid in the bushes, and apparently had a cell phone. She called a male friend, who eventually arrived on the scene.

Captain Bob Deutsch, of CPD, addressed this story, saying that it was being checked out. In fact, the Corvallis PD had first heard about this incident after it was printed in the newspaper. At present, Deutsch didn't know if it was true or not, or if it had anything to do with Brooke's abduction. Deutsch said that there were a lot of tips coming in every hour, and some of them were eventually discounted.

A short time later, Ron Noble told a reporter for the Salem *Statesman Journal,* "We unfortunately do not have any good solid leads at the moment. We are waiting for one lead that will give us something solid to go on." Noble added that more than five hundred tips had come in by this point.

Then Noble told reporters about a gravel pit on private property that had been thoroughly checked on the previous day. The gravel pit had been searched because a tip had come in about disturbed soil there that looked suspicious. Searchers had not only discovered freshly dug earth, but also what they described as "odors of oil and decay."

The gravel pit was owned by the Morse brothers in neighboring Linn County. A team of OSP forensic experts were called in and they noticed fresh footprints and tire tracks around the disturbed soil. The team used a cadaver dog to sniff around the area, but it gave no "hits" that the ground had any connection with Brooke Wilberger. Despite the dog's reaction, the team members dug four feet down at the area of the disturbed soil. Lieutenant Ron Noble related, "They found nothing. We are discouraged and disappointed."

Noble went on to say, at a press conference, that CPD had identified five persons of interest in the case. These individuals had a pattern of behavior with women who matched Brooke Wilberger's description. Noble added, "We are not calling them suspects. We do, however, have knowledge of a history that makes them more interesting to us."

Then Noble told a reporter for the *Statesman Journal,* "As we're looking at backgrounds, history, behavior, we are finding things that make us somewhat concerned. These may be important to this case, or just people who treat blond white women poorly. None of the five we're looking at had previous contact with Brooke Wilberger, that we know of."

Noble was, of course, keeping many details of the investigation out of the media. He did admit that law enforcement authorities were constantly in touch with an FBI profiler, and Noble related that polygraph tests had been used with several persons of interest. Just what the polygraph questions were or the results of the tests had been, he did not divulge. Nonetheless, the CPD was looking at these individuals very closely. In fact, before long, several persons of interest would pop right up to the top of the chart. And once they did, their names and stories were all over the region's newspapers and on television news channels as well.

CHAPTER 5
VOLUNTEERS

The frenzied activity at the LDS stake center did not abate by the fourth day of Brooke's disappearance. Parties of forty volunteers were still assembling every few hours at the stake center and were being sent out on search missions. While one worn-out team came in from the field, another fresh team went out to replace them. By now, more than two hundred businesses were donating food and drinks to the volunteers. Chambers Construction, of Eugene, where Brooke had once worked, paid for thirteen thousand flyers distributed in the Thursday edition of the Corvallis *Gazette-Times*. Tammy Crafton, a Chambers Construction Company spokesperson, said that many workers personally knew Brooke and were saddened by her disappearance.

Many, many more volunteers who had never met Brooke Wilberger considered her to be one of their own by now. One of these volunteers was Janelle Wikel, of Albany. She told a reporter that she was eating breakfast on the morning of May 26 and saw a news report about the missing girl. Janelle said, "There was something about it that touched me." So Janelle and her young daughter went to the stake center in Corvallis and volunteered. There she saw pink ribbons that were being constructed. The pink ribbon idea was the brainchild of Shannon Reich. Reich had been on volunteer duty for a lengthy period of time; the others finally told her to go home and get some rest. Shannon went home, but she didn't rest. Instead, she started making bows out of pink ribbons to show support for Brooke Wilberger and her family. Soon ribbons started showing up on members of the Wilberger family, volunteers, and even law enforcement personnel.

When Janelle Wikel arrived at the stake center, she got an idea of her own. She began making buttons with Brooke's photo in the center of the button. It would not only show support for Brooke, but also give an idea of what the missing girl looked like to anyone who saw it. Before long, Philomath Elementary School donated button supplies for the construction of hundreds of such buttons, and a button-making machine was donated from Adams Elementary School. Heidi Neuffer, LDS relief society coordinator, noted, "The schools are really supportive."

By May 26, all age groups were helping out in the massive effort in Corvallis and its surrounding area. Two Philomath High School students were among the throng of teenagers out in the field and at the stake center. Shelby and Ashley Sparks were just a few of the many students who cut classes, with administration approval, so that they could donate their time. The sisters helped construct "support ribbons" out of pink ribbon and safety pins. They were LDS members who personally knew the Wilberger family, and they said that keeping busy helped them deal with the situation.

Teachers were involved in the outreach as well. Bob Baker, Brooke's high-school Spanish teacher, joined a search team on May 27. He described Brooke as being quiet in class, but not shy or afraid to speak her mind. Baker related, "If I had to make a list of people this would happen to least, Brooke would be at the top of that list."

Brooke's parents, Greg and Cammy, were incredibly appreciative of all the outpouring of support from the community. They shook hands with volunteers and hugged others when they went to Corvallis. On May 27, Greg told a reporter, "We're holding up pretty good." By late Thursday afternoon, nearly one thousand acres had been thoroughly searched in an arc spreading out from the Oak Park Apartments. But not one substantial clue as to what had happened to Brooke—or where she was—had been found. Once again it seemed amazing that Brooke could have been abducted in broad daylight in the middle of Corvallis.

That same Thursday afternoon, eleven members of Brooke's extended family held a press conference at OSU. They not only were there to thank all the people searching for Brooke, but to tell more about her as well. Brooke's brother-in-law Zak Hansen said of Brooke, "The sisters and their mother are very close. They do a lot together. I used to take Brooke snowboarding. She picked it right up."

Brooke's mother, Cammy, spoke about Brooke's

language skills, which had developed later than most children. Brooke was four or five years old before she said any words that were comprehensible. Despite this late start in that area, it did not hold her back later in school. By the time Brooke was in high school, she was getting almost all A's. Cammy related, "I'm a teacher, so I keep track of this stuff. She had one B in high school in Advanced Placement American history. That was very frustrating for her."

Brooke wasn't good just in academics; she had fun in extracurricular activities as well. During Spirit Week in high school, Brooke dressed up with Superman children's underwear over her black tights and wore a cape. She was a foundation board member in the Children's Miracle Network drive and helped raise $20,000 that year for the charity. On another occasion she got her parents to drive her to Seattle, Washington, to pick up one thousand Krispy Kreme doughnuts, which she then brought back to Elmira, Oregon, and sold at a fund-raiser.

In high school Brooke coached a soccer team of seven-year-olds, and she competed in soccer and track. Erin Shankle, one of Brooke's classmates, spoke of how good Brooke was in track, especially the long jump. And Erin added about the relationship between Brooke and her mother, "I remember her mom would always be right there. She was like a volunteer coach. She was definitely there every single track meet."

Brooke's father, Greg, addressed Brooke's decision to go to Brigham Young University in Utah. He said, "We were really kind of surprised when she picked BYU. All the other kids went to Oregon State University." It came as even more of a surprise to

Greg when his daughter took up country line dancing in Utah. Brooke had never shown any interest in that while she lived in Oregon. She was always open to trying new things.

Cammy related that the family wasn't rich, and Brooke had to save up her money to go to college so far away from her hometown. Cammy noted that Brooke had jobs every summer and was doing dining service at BYU. Part of Brooke's responsibilities in that job was to make food deliveries. She had to drive a large truck, and Brooke was very proud of that fact. She once called her mother and said, "Mom! I drove it in the snow!" For petite Brooke, this was quite an accomplishment.

Zak Hansen added that at BYU Brooke "definitely had goals. Schooling is very important to her." Then Zak spoke of Brooke's boyfriend, who was also an LDS member. Her boyfriend was on a mission in South America, and Greg noted that Brooke had spoken of going on a mission herself.

The family members concluded the press conference by stating that they wanted Brooke to know that they loved her and were going to keep looking for her. Cammy Wilberger said, "We would do anything to bring Brooke home. We feel that families are forever. We know that we will see her again."

It's important to note that Cammy Wilberger didn't say that she knew they would see Brooke again soon or even in this life. Families are very important in the LDS faith. It's believed that when a person died, he or she would meet up once again with other family members in the afterlife.

After the Wilberger press conference, Lieutenant Ron Noble told reporters that no substantial clues had been discovered as of yet. He said, "We'll continue to follow up on tips from the phone calls to determine if we have a potential suspect."

Soon thereafter, Greg Wilberger told a reporter for the *Statesman Journal* that his family was in constant touch with Elizabeth Smart's family in Utah. Elizabeth Smart had been abducted by a crackpot zealot in 2002 and had been held captive for several months. To some degree, her abductor had brainwashed Elizabeth into believing that he was a prophet. Elizabeth probably did so, in part, as a survival mechanism often known as the Stockholm syndrome. The abducted person becomes grateful to her kidnapper for not killing her; as a result, she starts to identify with the abductor. The victim will do anything to please the abductor. One prime example of this was Patty Hearst, who, after being "brainwashed," identified with her captors in the Symbionese Liberation Army (SLA), and eventually joined them in their criminal activities, such as robbing banks.

Elizabeth Smart was reunited with her family in March 2003. Elizabeth Smart's parents were giving the Wilberger family invaluable advice about how to cope and stay positive under extremely difficult circumstances. Authorities in Utah who had worked on the Elizabeth Smart case let the Wilbergers know that in three days of searching around Corvallis, the Oregon volunteers had accomplished what it took three weeks to do on the Smart case in Utah.

Greg said, "People have been asking, 'How do you feel?' You don't feel. You don't think. You can't have any feelings. You just go forward."

Cammy added that she and her daughters had

planned a "girls-only trip" to San Francisco in the summer months. All of that was, of course, on hold now. The primary thing in everyone's mind was getting Brooke back.

Despite the statement by Cammy Wilberger in which she didn't mention if they would see Brooke again soon, the Wilberger family did not give up hope that Brooke would be found alive. During another press conference, Greg Wilberger sounded more optimistic than in previous days. He said, "If she wasn't alive, we'd have found her already."

In fact, Ron Noble seconded this feeling of Greg's by saying, "We're a little more optimistic. We're approaching that time if she wasn't alive, we'd have found her." The implication was that if someone had kidnapped Brooke and intended to kill her, he would have done so in a matter of days after the initial abduction. And because traveling with Brooke very far would have been risky, her body should have been found in the area surrounding Corvallis, if she was dead. Since the search had been so thorough, with literally thousands of volunteers, the odds were that Brooke's body would have been discovered by now, even in a remote location.

Not that the search effort was abating at all. Zak Hansen told a reporter, "Hope comes from seeing five hundred people out there looking. No matter how long it takes to find her, we'll keep looking. This is our life right now."

Jared Cordon did admit that the family was working until they were sleep-deprived. When he finally crashed on May 27, Cordon slept right through his alarm clock and missed the appointment for an interview on a national television morning show.

Nonetheless, Cordon, as well as the others in the family, was still upbeat. "We think we're going to find her soon," he said.

Over the weekend of May 29 through May 30, many students in the area didn't spend their time relaxing or partying. Instead, they were out on one of the search teams or working at the stake center. This huge effort had even spread to other cities in the area, where it was deemed Brooke might have been taken. There were searches going on around Albany, Salem, and Eugene. In Eugene, a particular wooded area on the southwest side of the city was the focus of an intense search. A *Times-Gazette* reporter spoke with some of the people there, including Jim Webb and his son. Jim said, "We're looking for anything suspicious—tracks, abandoned vehicles. It just touches the heart."

Members of Corvallis's bicycle clubs were out that weekend as well, looking for signs of Brooke during their usual rides. They picked up search area maps and instructions at the main headquarters before taking off. Being on bikes, the riders could cover a lot more area than someone walking. They were instructed to look for anything unusual on their journeys, and they kept their eyes open as they pedaled down the back roads of Benton County and beyond.

Bikes weren't the only conveyances besides motor vehicles and foot traffic that weekend. On Sunday, May 30, the first large-scale organized horse team of searchers took off into the outlying areas. Being on horseback had several advantages over being on foot. Obviously, the rider could cover more ground than someone walking; and in addition to that, a rider had a height advantage over someone on foot.

While on horseback he or she could peer down into vegetation that might be missed by someone walking down a trail.

And there were the intangibles as well. Heidi Kinkade, who was one rider on a horseback team, noted, "We were told to really pay attention to our horses. Horses can smell and sense things and see things better than we can."

The main horse team search that Sunday was conducted by the Benton County Sheriff's Mounted Posse. These were all volunteers trained in riding and search techniques in rough country. They covered an area known as Bald Hill Natural Area and then down into the McDonald-Dunn Research Forest. Meanwhile, searchers on foot scoured rural areas, such as William L. Finley National Wildlife Refuge, Peavy Arboretum, Willamette Park and Natural Area, and E. E. Wilson Wildlife Area. The CPD was also asking landlords to check any vacant apartments and houses they owned—especially in outlying areas or properties that were heavily wooded.

Not even psychics were being dismissed at this point. Lieutenant Noble admitted that more than four hundred of the one thousand tips that had come in were from people who had "psychic visions" about where Brooke might be discovered. Some of these tips were way off base, but others had given specific names of people they thought might be involved.

Noble said, "We believe if we find the person responsible, we will find Brooke. So we're using those names."

Besides the ordinary folks some of the searchers were professionals, halfway between ordinary citizens and law enforcement. Such a group of volunteers worked for a private company called the Simpson Wildland Firefighters. In the previous few years, these types of private-company wildland firefighters had sprung up all over the West. In conjunction with firefighters who worked for government agencies, these firefighters worked in often steep, rugged terrain. The Simpson Wildland Firefighters of Salem were one such group of individuals, highly trained and used to working in steep, brushy terrain.

At the moment, however, they weren't up in the mountains, but rather were on boggy flatlands in the Willamette Valley. John Harding, a crew boss, said that the current condition was much different from what they were used to. Nonetheless, they knew how to search thoroughly through heavy vegetation. At one point in Brooke's search, the team had to cross chest-deep water of the Marys River. Harding said, "It was a challenge. It woke us up. It doesn't matter to us about the terrain. We just want to find her."

Corey Fox, another member of the Simpson team, noted, "Mostly, we're in high altitudes fighting forest fires. This is flat ground. It's pretty easy for us by comparison. We have experience in the bushes. We have experience in finding stuff."

And yet, crew member Brandon Thrasher expressed what was on a lot of volunteers' minds that day. Thrasher had experience in searching for missing persons, and he said, "Time is short. I just know more and more the likelihood of finding her alive is growing slim and slimmer."

Carol Reeves, a reporter for the *Gazette-Times*, explored this theme of mental and physical fatigue, which was plaguing all of the searchers. She spoke with Benton County chaplain Todd Pynch about this matter. Pynch had been at Ground Zero in New York City after the terrorist attack on the World Trade Center. Pynch said that many volunteers of the Wilberger search effort were like those whom he'd seen at Ground Zero. They couldn't turn it off, even when they left the area. He related, "It's more of a twenty-four/seven thing than you realize."

Pynch spoke of the searchers not getting the rest they needed and not being able to shut off thoughts about the lost girl, even when they went home. After days of searching, the mental strain and physical strain began to take its toll. Pynch added that in a terrible car accident or even with suicide, there was a finality about those things; people moved on, in dealing with the event. But in a case like Brooke's, there were only questions, anxiety, and tension from there being no finality. After a while frustration began to take hold in many searchers. They began asking themselves, "Why are we out here?"

Pynch stressed to searchers that they had to take care of themselves, or they would be useless in the search effort. Their bodies would become too tired to function properly, and their minds would become numbed by the continued strain. And as far as frustration went, he assured searchers that even when they searched an area and came up empty, it was still valuable. It was one more plot of land that the command center could scratch off the map as having been searched.

Pynch noted, "Any case that involves a child is more stressful. Everybody has empathy for a young girl being taken away. One of the stressors that came out of nine/eleven was the feeling that this couldn't happen in America. The same is true now—this isn't something that happens in Corvallis."

But it did happen in Corvallis, and no amount of perceived safety was going to change that fact. The emotional toll was starting to tell, even amongst trained personnel. By the ninth day of the search, Lieutenant Noble admitted that no items had been found that were linked to Brooke's disappearance. And Noble admitted something else after nine grueling days: the amount of volunteers was starting to taper off.

There were unforeseen factors, beyond the emotional and physical toll, that had to be dealt with as well. Much of the terrain being searched was wooded and filled with poison oak. In fact, four searchers had such bad reactions to an especially virulent patch of poison oak, they had to be treated by emergency medical technician (EMT) personnel. Peggy Pierson, of Benton County Emergency Services, related, "These were extreme reactions to allergies. The reactions included upper-respiratory problems, skin rashes, and swelling of the face."

One thing that law enforcement was taking a very close look at were the registered sex offenders in the area. Benton County had 140 of these, and all but nineteen were contacted the first week after Brooke's disappearance. Neighboring Linn County had five hundred registered sex offenders, and these were checked out, too, as well as some in Lane County. There was even one individual from Linn County who became a person of interest when he tried to elude officers. When he was caught, it turned out that he had nothing to do with Brooke's abduction.

Of more interest to authorities was the alleged

abduction attempt of another young woman in Corvallis on May 21, 2004, just three days before Brooke went missing. The young Asian woman in question had not initially talked to police about the incident, but rather told her friends at OSU, Marisa Birky and Michelle Raethke, about it.

Diana Simpson, a spokesperson in the investigation, said that initially no one in law enforcement had spoken to this young woman. Like everyone else, they had read about it for the first time on May 27 when Birky and Raethke mentioned the incident in the *Gazette-Times*. It was only after that, that law enforcement was able to contact the young woman.

CPD captain Bob Deutsch told reporters, "If indeed there was some connection between the two cases, especially if the vehicle had some connection to one of our persons of interest, then we'd have some really hot leads." Deutsch did not say who the particular person of interest was or why the type of vehicle mentioned was important. But he did add that as of June 1, there were five persons of interest whom they were still looking at. And then he admitted that the detectives were starting to shorten their hours of working on Brooke's case. About this aspect, Diana Simpson said, "It's a bad situation, but there are still good motivated spirits. They want to work hard and be successful at this."

So did Brooke Wilberger's parents. On the afternoon of June 1, Brooke's family members and close to five hundred people gathered in front of the Benton County Courthouse in Corvallis for a prayer vigil. Larry Blake, bishop of the Veneta Ward of LDS, prayed for Brooke's safe return. He thanked

God for the good weather that helped searchers and thanked all the volunteers for their efforts. Blake declared, "We are so grateful for the blessing of unity. We have felt this week the oneness in searching for Brooke. So much has been donated. So many of the communities have given so much."

Ron Noble noted on that same day that the number of volunteers on June 1 had shrunk to around two hundred. At its peak there were well over a thousand people searching at any given time. Hope may have been waning in the community at large, but the Wilberger family was still staying strong in this regard. Cammy Wilberger told the volunteers, who had shown up at the stake center in Corvallis that day, "We feel the love."

In fact, help came in from multiple directions. By that time two regional cable companies were airing public service announcements about Brooke. These announcements reached 1.5 million cable viewers in Oregon, Northern California, and Southern Washington. A website on the Internet about Brooke's case had 120,000 hits in the previous week.

The newest areas searched were along the southern border of Highway 20/34, east of the Willamette River, and on some private property near Payne Road and Highway 99W. The reason that property was being searched was because of a tip phoned in by a psychic. Like many of the other tips by psychics, however, this one also came up empty, as far as anything relating to Brooke Wilberger.

Despite their optimism, the Wilberger family knew that the search effort could not go on forever. On Friday, June 4, the Wilbergers asked for one last major search over the upcoming weekend. They asked landlords to search vacant buildings, vacant lots, and backyards. Greg Wilberger declared, "We really need your help. Then we can be at peace. We'll let the Lord take care of it after that."

Even the Wilberger family was trying to get back to some degree of normality by that point. Cammy had spent the previous day correcting her third-grade students' papers and writing report cards. It was one small attempt to bring some ordinary structure to her life. She said that she missed her students and they missed her. One little boy in her class told her that he'd been a good boy while she was away.

In this last rush of searching, two hundred tips came in over a twenty-four-hour period. And it was learned by the media that one "person of interest" had gone beyond that designation. His name was Sung Koo Kim, a thirty-year-old unemployed microbiologist who lived in Tigard, Oregon. Kim had recently been arrested for stealing female students' panties at George Fox University in Newberg, Oregon. Additionally, he had also been arrested for stealing female students' panties from Sackett Hall on the Oregon State University campus in Corvallis. When Kim was arrested, officers seized more than one thousand items of evidence. What they found absolutely stunned them and they began to wonder if at last they had found the person who had abducted Brooke Wilberger.

CHAPTER 6

KIM

The incident with Sung Koo Kim came to light when a student named Beth observed an Asian male entering Macy Residence Hall on George Fox University in Newberg, Oregon, on April 22, 2004. Macy Hall was a female-only dormitory on campus. Beth saw the Asian male, who appeared to be about thirty years old, walk up to the third floor of the dormitory and then down the hall. Beth later told police, "The man was acting suspiciously and would not look at anyone in the face."

Detective Todd Baltzell, of the Newberg Police Department (NPD), contacted Beth and she told him of her concerns. Around the same time Baltzell contacted other female students who attended George Fox University. One of these was a young woman named Lacey, and she, too, spoke of an Asian man who had been at Macy Hall on April 18, at about 5:00 P.M. Lacey had gone to the laundry room in the dorm and saw an Asian man kneeling down looking into a dryer. When he caught a glimpse of her, he immediately stood up and left the building in a hurry. Lacey didn't notify police about this until two other female students reported some of their undergarments missing.

Because of the missing undergarments and reports by Beth and Lacey about a strange Asian man who seemed to be prowling around the women's dormitory, Detective Baltzell went to George Fox University to talk in person with these women. He eventually contacted Beth and Lacey, along with female students named Jenna, Whitney, Stephanie, and Meredith. Whitney told him that on April 18, at around five o'clock, she noticed that her track uniform and two bras were missing from her laundry load. She checked the laundry basket and the washer and dryer, to no avail. Whitney was sure that she had not misplaced them somewhere, and the last time she saw them they had been in the dryer. She said that the top of her track uniform was a blue spandex top with *GFU* in gold lettering on the front. The bottom part of the uniform was blue spandex with a white stripe down the side. She was missing two new bras, size 32A, with a bow in the middle.

Jenna told Baltzell that she was sure she was missing a Victoria's Secret black strapless bra, size 36C. She was also missing a pair of hot pink Victoria's Secret panties and a beige pair of Victoria's Secret panties. She was confident that she hadn't misplaced these items.

Stephanie reported that three weeks previously she had noticed that she was missing three brandnew white bras, size 36B, a black spandex thong-type pair of panties, and a beige spandex thong-type pair.

Beth told the detective that on April 22 she'd spied the Asian man walk into Macy Hall behind a group of female students. She was pretty sure the man was not a student at the university, so she followed him. She walked behind him up a stairway and then all the way down a hallway. He was acting so strangely that she decided to call security from the room of a fellow student she knew.

Security requested that Beth keep watching the man to see where he was going. She went out the door of the hallway and down some stairs, but she didn't see him anymore. She stood outside the building for about a minute and a half, when suddenly the man came into view. She called out to him, "Hey!" But he just grunted and walked right past her.

Now Beth was very alarmed. She went up to a dorm window of a student named Meredith and rapped on the window. When Meredith went to investigate what was happening, Beth told her about the strange man, and they both were soon on his tail. Beth and Meredith followed him through campus and out to a parking lot, where the Asian man got into a black Honda Accord and then drove away. Beth memorized the letters on the license plate, while Meredith memorized the numbers. Then they repeated to themselves what they recalled. It was after this incident that Beth contacted the Newberg PD.

Detective Baltzell had the various young women walk him through every location where they had spotted the strange man. Baltzell asked Beth if the man had asked her for directions. She said no. Baltzell asked if he seemed to be lost. Once again she said no, and added that he seemed to be "walking purposefully."

Lacey took Detective Baltzell to the laundry room in the dorm and showed him the dryer where the man had been kneeling down, looking inside the dryer. When she first spotted him, she thought he might have been a repairman. His hands were actually in the dryer. She passed him and threw something into a garbage can nearby. When she did so, he immediately got up and hurried out of the laundry room.

It was this strange behavior that made her think that he wasn't a repairman, after all. She followed him down the hall to see what he would do next. He left the hall in a hurry. Her description of him was an Asian man about five-ten, 175 pounds, clean shaven, no glasses, and no noticeable scars or tattoos.

After interviewing these students, Detective Baltzell got the identity of the owner of a Honda with the license plate that Beth and Meredith had memorized. It turned out to be Sung Koo Kim, born on April 17, 1974, and now living in Tigard, Oregon. Baltzell requested a photo of Kim from the Department of Motor Vehicles (DMV). Baltzell later arranged this photo with five others in what he termed a "throw down." (More commonly known as a photo lineup.)

On May 7, 2004, Detective Baltzell showed the photo lineup to Beth. Within five seconds of looking at the photos, Beth picked out the photo of Sung Koo Kim as the man she had seen on campus. On May 11, Baltzell showed Lacey the photo lineup. She wasn't certain if the man she had seen was in the photo array.

Because of what he'd learned from these women,

especially Beth picking out Sung Koo Kim from the photos, Detective Baltzell contacted Detective Hocken, of the Tigard Police Department (TPD). Hocken looked through records and discovered a report from the Portland Police Department (PPD) about Sung Koo Kim. Kim was a suspect in a daytime burglary on the Lewis & Clark College campus. Security found him there with some female undergarments, and they escorted him off campus. He wasn't arrested at the time, merely told to leave the area.

On May 12, 2004, Detective Baltzell drove to Kim's address and noticed a black Honda in the driveway—with the license plate that Beth and Meredith had memorized. Baltzell also wrote down pertinent information about the house in preparation for requesting a search warrant. When he made the request, he noted that he had been a full-time officer with the TPD for nine years, and had over eleven hundred hours of training. His current duties included narcotics and sex abuse crimes. In that regard he had investigated over one hundred sex-related crimes.

Baltzell stated that he knew from his experience and training that an individual who was into fetishes would often take panties, bras, lingerie, or stockings. Baltzell wrote: *A person who does burglary to obtain undergarments to satisfy an arousal is known as a fetish burglar and is often considered extremely dangerous because in many circumstances the fetish burglary is a prelude to a sexual assault or lust murder.*

It was this combination of burglary and female intimate items that made Sung Koo Kim appear potentially dangerous in Detective Baltzell's eyes. He wanted something done about the situation before a serious crime occurred. Baltzell put in his search warrant request to a judge and was eventually given the go-ahead to search and seize items at the Kim household. Within the warrant Baltzell was to look for the specific items mentioned as missing by the George Fox University female students.

When the Tigard police searched Kim's residence on May 13, they were stunned to find that he was in possession of more than one thousand pairs of women's undergarments. This evidence was collected and Sung Koo Kim was arrested on burglary charges. At that point it was a fairly minor crime.

Things were about to change, however. Once the news about Brooke Wilberger broke, the Tigard PD sent information on to the Oregon State Police, which then contacted the Corvallis Police Department. Lieutenant Phillip "Phil" Zerzan, of the Oregon State University Police Department (OSUPD), was also contacted about Kim. Zerzan informed CPD on May 28 that one of the undergarments in Kim's possession was a pair of underwear with a label that said, *Sackett Hall, OSU, First Floor.* The underwear had belonged to a young female student named Stacey. She had noticed that some of her underwear had gone missing from the laundry room earlier, so that's why she had made a tag about Sackett Hall. And then those underwear had been stolen as well.

On May 28, Trooper Timothy Gallagher, of the OSP, contacted Stacey. She told him that a month previously six pairs of her panties had disappeared from a laundry load. Her roomate, Ashley, also had some underwear that disappeared. Detective Todd Baltzell contacted Stacey and Ashley, and they were able to identify underwear that Sung Koo Kim had possessed.

Trooper Gallagher then spoke with Detective Kenneth Pecyna, of the OSP. Pecyna had been a detective since 1986 and had investigated major crimes, including murders, rapes, sexual assaults, and burglaries. He informed Gallagher that in cases involving the theft of women's underwear, many times trace evidence on the underwear could identify the owner. This evidence included hairs, body fluids, and secretions. All of these could be traced by DNA back to the rightful owner.

Detective Pecyna also told Gallagher that women's undergarment thieves would often clandestinely observe their victims by use of cameras, video recorders, and cell phones that had camera capability. These images were often downloaded to a computer so that the thief could then connect the victim to the undergarments he had stolen. These types of photos were also stored on CDs and DVDs. It was a way of keeping a permanent record of items and victims, and also of reliving the scenario.

Gallagher learned from Detective Eric Ronning, of the NPD, that Kim's computer had been seized during the implementation of the search warrant. Gallagher also learned that other computers in the house had not been seized, nor had items in Sung Koo Kim's Honda.

Gallagher learned one more thing as well. Law enforcement had seized receipts, tickets, credit card information, and ATM slips, and a few of these proved that Kim had taken trips to Corvallis. Gallagher noted on one report that in his experience a person often would keep more receipts in his vehicle, especially in the glove box. Also, trace evidence might be found in a vehicle as well.

With that in mind Gallagher wrote up a probable-cause report, asking for a new search warrant on Sung Koo Kim's residence: *I believe that evidence of the crime of burglary in the second degree and thefts will be found at Sung Koo Kim's residence in Tigard, Oregon. Also evidence may be found in a vehicle; to wit, a 1991 black Honda Accord.*

Then there was one more chilling notation. Gallagher wrote, *Detective Ronning indicates that when they executed their search warrant, Mr. Kim had substantial rifles and pistols, all of which were loaded and ready for immediate use.* Gallagher said that based on that, he requested a nighttime search and seizure by officers, because Kim might either be asleep or very drowsy. This might aid in keeping the officers safe during a raid upon the house.

In the early-morning hours of Saturday, May 29, 2004, the search and seizure in Tigard took place, and it wasn't by just a few uniformed officers going in with a search warrant. An entire SWAT team descended upon the Kim residence and arrested Sung Koo Kim. His parents and sister, who had no idea what was taking place or why, were absolutely traumatized. Luckily for everyone involved, Sung Koo Kim did not pick up any weapons before being handcuffed and taken to jail.

The actual items seized were as varied as the list was long. From the top shelf of the entertainment room, a box full of bras and panties was seized. From the top of a refrigerator, the officers got a digital camera, and from a bedroom table, a laptop computer. From Sung Koo Kim's parents' room, they seized a computer tower. Other items included a black spiral notebook, twenty CDs, seven floppy disks, three commercially packaged videos, twenty-three unmarked videotapes, a cell phone with a camera, and a Sony Handycam. There were various receipts seized as well from all over the house, and a pair of female panties taken from an outdoor garbage can. Two items were of particular interest. One was a book, *The Beginners' Guide to Lock Picking;* the other was what appeared to be a bloodstain on the garage floor.

Sung Koo Kim's vehicle also came in for search and seizure. The officers took the floor mats and the mat from the trunk as well. A screwdriver was taken, various gas receipts, a pair of scissors, and a blue surgical mask. Prints were lifted from the dashboard, seat backs, and side windows.

The Salem *Statesman Journal* soon began tying Kim's arrest to the Brooke Wilberger case. In headlines the newspaper proclaimed POLICE ARREST MAN IN 19-YEAR-OLD'S DISAPPEARANCE. Beneath the headline was a photo of Brooke Wilberger. The *Statesman Journal* also related that a SWAT team consisting of the Oregon State Police, Newberg PD, and Corvallis PD were in on the early-morning arrest of Kim. And yet it was with a note of caution that CPD lieutenant Ron Noble stated that Kim was "only a person of interest" in Brooke's disappearance, and not under arrest for that incident.

After Sung Koo Kim was arrested, he didn't stay behind bars for very long. Even though his bail was set at $1.5 million, his parents were able to raise over $150,000 in bond money to spring him from jail. This covered the bail amount for the charges in

Yamhill and Benton counties. Kim was now free until trial.

Sung Koo Kim obtained an attorney, Michael Greenlick, of Portland. Because of the possible ties to the Brooke Wilberger abduction, there were plenty of reporters interested in Kim now. Greenlick told the media that Sung Koo Kim had been born in South Korea, but he had moved with his family to the United States when he was very young. Greenlick added, "Mr. Kim had nothing to do with Brooke Wilberger's disappearance. He is just a target of police speculation."

Michael Greenlick was not Kim's attorney for long, however. Since Kim's parents, Joo and Dong, had spent so much money on bailing him out of jail, they didn't have enough now to pay for Greenlick's future attorney fees. Sung Koo Kim had to take on public defenders Janet Lee Hoffman and Joseph O'Leary as his lawyers.

When Sung Koo Kim made his first court appearance at the arraignment in Benton County for the alleged theft of women's underwear at Oregon State University, he pled not guilty to all charges. His new attorneys told reporters after the arraignment that there was no evidence that Kim was even in Corvallis when Brooke Wilberger disappeared.

Lieutenant Ron Noble had something to say about this as well. He told the media that "Kim is a *significant* person of interest in the Brooke Wilberger case. We haven't been able to verify yet, his alibi."

Benton County chief deputy district attorney (DDA) John Haroldson weighed in on this issue as well. He said, "There have been a number of people who have drawn the interest of investigators, and certainly media interest. We really have to be careful not to overreact."

Sung Koo Kim's days of freedom were very short-lived. Four days after his arraignment in Benton County, he was arrested once again—this time on charges coming out of Multnomah County, where Portland was located. This time Kim was accused of having stolen women's undergarments from at least three universities and colleges in the Portland area. His bail was set at $10 million—an insurmountable total for his parents to bail him out this time.

Part of the reason the bail was set so high was the discovery of certain very disturbing things found on Sung Koo Kim's computer. He had over forty thousand images of women being tortured, whipped, burned, and branded. He had also made two videos of young women at a Laundromat. The women did not know they were being videotaped. Even more important, law enforcement had discovered that Kim had looked up on the Internet about countries that did not have extradition to the United States.

Because of these revelations Noble, of the CPD, told the media that the Wilberger family expressed "concern at the contents of the police affidavits. Overall, it's disturbing information."

Once again Kim's lawyer declared, "We've provided substantial evidence that he was not involved with the Wilberger disappearance in Corvallis." The so-called "substantial" evidence was that Sung Koo Kim was making online stock trades via Ameritrade on the morning that Brooke went missing, and then he went to a Circuit City store with his father in the Portland area. Hoffman declared that a surveillance camera at the Circuit City store backed up Kim's claim.

Multnomah County district attorney Michael "Mike" Schrunk, however, stated that Kim's alibi was not iron-clad. DA Schrunk related that Sung Koo Kim had been at Circuit City, as he said, but he was there at 12:52 P.M., nearly three hours after Brooke may have been abducted. The drive from Corvallis to Tigard generally took about an hour and a half. That still gave Kim time either to deposit her alive somewhere, or kill her and dispose of her body in an isolated area. According to Schrunk, the Ameritrade deal and being at Circuit City could have just been attempts by Kim to create an alibi. And Schrunk noted that the Ameritrade situation occurred on Kim's sister's laptop computer and not on his own. She could have easily been the one online, not Sung Koo Kim.

Schrunk then added something very interesting. He said that the lint from a dryer in the Oak Park Apartments complex that was in Kim's possession matched lint coming from an OSU student named Lynsey's undergarments. Lynsey was a swimmer on the OSU team and she had gone to the Oak Park Apartments on occasion. In fact, she was scheduled to move into the Oak Park Apartments in late May. Not only that, Lynsey had a resemblance to Brooke Wilberger, and Sung Koo Kim had downloaded information about Lynsey onto his computer. He not only had information about her, but a photo as well. Schrunk said, "There is significant evidence to connect Sung Koo Kim to Brooke Wilberger."

The next day, Kim's lawyer was right back with statements of her own on the matter. Hoffman said that Kim's alibi was good in the Brooke Wilberger situation. She stated, "The state affidavit puts the Wilberger disappearance as early as ten A.M., whereas the Corvallis Police Department states she went missing at ten-fifty A.M." If that was the case, then Sung Koo Kim did not have time to abduct Brooke, get rid of her, and make it back to the Portland area to be at a Circuit City store at 12:52 P.M. Hoffman added, "The DA (Schrunk's) document stretches the bounds of reality."

Despite Hoffman's remarks, the Multnomah County District Attorney's Office was sticking by its statements. Deputy DA Norm Frink told reporters that Sung Koo Kim was still a very viable suspect in Brooke Wilberger's disappearance. DDA Frink stated, "Even if he didn't do that, the facts that make him a suspect are deeply disturbing in themselves."

Janet Lee Hoffman carried on more than just a war of words. She wrote a document to the presiding judge in Multnomah County, trying to get Sung Koo Kim's bail reduced. Hoffman wrote: *It is inappropriate to allow the Wilberger disappearance to drive the determination as to whether Mr. Kim should be detained in custody.* Hoffman claimed that Kim's family members corroborated his statements that he had been the one to make the Ameritrade transactions at 11:14 A.M. on May 24. Kim often used his sister's laptop, Hoffman said. Then she added that Sung Koo Kim answered a phone call a short time later at the Kim residence from one of his sister's friends. This was at 12:10 P.M. and on a landline. And then at 12:52 P.M., a surveillance camera proved that he was at the Circuit City store with his father. He was there until at least 1:30 P.M.

Hoffman even backed up her claims with a polygraph test that Kim had taken after his initial arrest, concerning the Brooke Wilberger matter. The test was administered by an FBI-certified polygrapher named H. Hadley McCann. McCann had begun duty with the FBI in September 1972, and from 1989 to 1998, he was a regional polygraph examiner for the FBI. By 2002, he went into private practice and often conducted polygraph tests for local and state law enforcement agencies.

McCann noted that in the case with Sung Koo Kim, he met Kim at the Yamhill County Jail. He advised Kim that the polygraph test was strictly voluntary, and that he could refuse to take one. Kim said that he understood, and decided to take a test.

Kim was asked, "Did you abduct that girl from the apartment complex in Corvallis?" Kim answered, "No."

Then he was asked, "Did you have any contact with that missing girl on May 24, 2004?" Once again Kim answered, "No."

McCann's conclusions were: *It is the opinion of the examiner that the recorded responses to the questions were not indicative of deception.*

Polygraph tests can be a useful tool in investigations, but the Multnomah County DA's Office knew they weren't infallible. And adding to Sung Koo Kim's woes was a new development with the Benton County District Attorney's Office. District Attorney Scott Heiser wanted Kim's bail in that county raised from $25,000 to $100,000. Heiser said that Kim posed a flight risk and danger to the community. Judge Locke Williams took Heiser's request under advisement and then increased the bail amount to $100,000. Even if Kim was able, by some miracle, to raise the bail to spring him from Multnomah County, he now had a higher bail amount in Benton County to contend with.

Wanting to know more about who Sung Koo Kim was, a reporter for the McMinnville *News-Reporter* spoke with a person named Richard Johnston, who had known Kim at Washington State University, where they had both been students. Richard and Kim had gone target shooting on occasion, and Richard related that he and some other guys at college had tried to include Kim in their activities. But according to Johnston, Kim was very reclusive, and his fascination with guns and porn began to turn the others off.

This off-putting tendency only increased when Kim's behavior started becoming more and more erratic. Kim told the others that he thought the Columbine school massacre was justified because the shooters had been teased and bullied. At another time, according to Johnston, Kim stated that he could kill at will because he was an "angel of Jesus Christ." They absolutely shunned him after Kim brought an AR-15 semiautomatic assault rifle to the dorm.

None of those things looked good for Sung Koo Kim as the days progressed in June 2004. But even the DAs in Yamhill, Multnomah, and Benton counties agreed that there was still not enough evidence to charge him with the disappearance of Brooke Wilberger. And all while the Kim/Wilberger possible connection percolated along, there were other events happening in the Wilberger case as well. Some of them were just as surprising as the Sung Koo Kim angle, and before long, both detectives and reporters were running in several different directions about possible Brooke Wilberger abductors.

CHAPTER 7
A TRAIL OF BLOOD

While the Sung Koo Kim investigation and charges in various counties occurred, the search for Brooke Wilberger continued, although in a much diminished form. Yet even with less numbers of volunteers searching, it didn't mean that the conveyances being used were any less novel than the horseback riders and cyclists. Members of the Corvallis to Portland Regatta (CPR) decided to chip in their efforts as well. Allison Titus, a member of the Willamette Rowing Club, had heard about Brooke's disappearance and thought that rowing members might be of help as they rowed on their 150-mile journey on the Willamette River during the regatta.

Allison told reporters, "I knew our course would take us through areas that hadn't been searched." Before long, many of the rowers in the single, double, and quad competition were signing up to search along the river banks as they made the journey on the river. One of these included three-time Olympian

Tiff Wood. He and the others were given laminated posters with information about Brooke. These posters were personally given to them by members of the Wilberger family. The Wilbergers also gave them pink ribbons to tie to their oar handles.

And if there weren't as many people at the second prayer vigil for Brooke as at the first, the energy level of the two hundred-plus people who attended was just as committed. Not even the steady drizzle seemed to dampen their spirits. Among the gathering was Corvallis mayor Helen Berg, Corvallis police chief Gary Boldizsar, and Benton County sheriff Jim Swinyard. They and the others gathered in Corvallis's Central Park.

Chaplain Todd Pynch told the crowd, "On May twenty-fourth, evil entered our community and took Brooke. When bad things happen, it causes people to turn to a Higher Power. Psalm 46:1 has been a place I look for answers. The verse says, 'God is our refuge and our strength.' We cannot give up hope. We will not give up hope."

The prayer vigil was very ecumenical and included pastors and reverends from many different denominations. Reverend Marc Anderson, of Calvin Presbyterian Church, said that it was hard to comprehend that God knew where Brooke was, and *yet* she could not be found by the searchers. Anderson prayed for the Holy Spirit to surround Brooke and change the heart and mind of her abductor. And Anderson prayed, "Lord, will you lead someone to her. Break these bonds and release her."

Steve Rydin, worship leader of Kings Circle Assembly of God Church, led the gathering in singing, "How Great Thou Art" and "I Stand in Awe." And

John Dennis, of Corvallis's First Presbyterian Church, addressed the matter of fear that had entered the area with the kidnapping of Brooke. Reverend Dennis said, "We pray for those who are frightened. We pray for those forces they fear. We pray that they will be eradicated by forces that are higher."

The Wilbergers were very grateful for the support from so many different denominations and people of different faiths. Cammy Wilberger said, "We've been amazed. The initial search was from people in the church we go to, but this has crossed over."

Even a couple of days after the prayer vigil, the Wilberger family said that it was their faith that kept them going. Greg related, "We don't have any energy for negative things right now. The family needs all of its positive energy to find Brooke."

Cammy added, "I think God is a very loving God. But if something like this happens, it's their free agency (the abductor's) that took Brooke."

Even though the major search effort was over, it did not mean that Corvallis or the surrounding area had forgotten Brooke. On Saturday, June 12, a large concert was held in Corvallis's Central Park. It was labeled as a "Thank You Concert" to all the volunteers who had helped over the previous weeks since May 24.

Lori Moss, a musician with the group Silvergirl, told reporters, "Sometimes we need something that's not serious, to relax and just have a little joy." Cherie Gullerad, another member of Silvergirl, actually wrote a song for the occasion about Brooke. The beginning words were that they were all here waiting for Brooke's return and would keep the home fires

burning. Gullerad said, "I think everyone can identify with Brooke in some capacity."

Besides Silvergirl, other local bands and musicians
included Dave Cudo on saxophone, Heart of the
Valley Children's Choir, Jon ten Broek playing American folk songs and Hawthorne doing Celtic music.
At the end of the program was a slide show of Brooke
growing up. Once again there were a lot of regional
companies that offered free items to people at the
concert. Great Harvest Bread Company gave away re-
freshments, while the Teddy Bear Fudge store sold
small bars of fudge for the Find Brooke Fund.

Becky Nielsen, a co-owner of Curves for Women
fitness club in Corvallis, got together with friends and
created a large quilt for the Wilberger family. People
could purchase squares that would go into the quilt,
and all the money would go to Brooke's fund.

Theresa Hogue, a reporter for the *Gazette-Times,*
spoke with one concert attendee named Hana Hirat-
suka. Hana was a thirteen-year-old girl whose Spanish
teacher was Jared Cordon, Brooke's brother-in-law.
Hana spoke of how much her life had changed since
Brooke's abduction. She said, "Mom won't let me and
my friend walk home alone now. I don't mind. I don't
want to get stolen."

Hana's mother, Priscilla, said that she now constantly scanned crowds when she was out with her
daughter. Sudden noises made her jump, and lone
men caught her attention. She was not only vigilant
for her daughter, but for herself as well.

As the search continued for Brooke in the area
around Corvallis, events elsewhere had a major

impact upon the case. One of these concerned a man named Richard Wilson. Wilson, thirty-nine, of Walla Walla, Washington, suddenly went on a spectacular crime spree in the Northwest. Wilson had raped a young woman in Vancouver at knifepoint in 1995, had been arrested, and had served prison time. Paroled after his prison term, he lived with his parents in Walla Walla until May 17, 2004, when he stole some items from a house in the area and then took off. Before leaving, he had told an acquaintance that he was not going back to prison—no matter what.

For the next two weeks, Wilson committed crimes throughout Washington, Oregon, Idaho, and into Utah. Sheriff Frank Rivera, of Sherman County, Oregon, said, "Wilson had every law enforcement agency in the Columbia River Gorge looking for him."

By June, Wilson most likely had committed the rape of a girl in Biggs Junction, Oregon, and murdered seventeen-year-old Teresa Garcia in Mountain Home, Idaho.

On June 9, in Grantsville, Utah, seventeen-year-old Kimberli Lingard, who worked at a laundry there, was found shot in the chest and head. Patrons coming into the laundry at 7:30 P.M. found her lying on the floor. Wilson had just robbed the place of $50 from the register and shot Lingard. She was rushed to University Hospital in Salt Lake City, where she underwent brain surgery.

Around 9:30 P.M. that same day, Wilson robbed a gas station in Delle, Utah, and shot fifty-nine-year-old Dee Jensen. Jensen was able to call 911 after Wilson left and described the shooter and his vehicle. Soon an all points bulletin (APB) was out for Wilson's car.

Around 10:30 P.M., a Utah state trooper spotted a car matching the description Jensen had given, going at speeds of one hundred miles per hour on Interstate 80 toward Nevada. About six miles from the border, highway patrol officers threw down spikes, which blew out the vehicle's tires. Trapped and unable to move, Wilson fired a shot out the car window and then turned the gun on himself. True to his word, he was not going back to prison. He committed suicide, instead. He had left a trail of blood from Washington State through Oregon, Idaho, and Utah.

And then Corvallis PD learned that Wilson might have been driving on Interstate 5 in Oregon between Corvallis and Medford at one point during his crime spree, around the time Brooke Wilberger disappeared. Lieutenant Noble told reporters that they weren't sure if Wilson had anything to do with Brooke's disappearance, but it was being checked out. They already knew he had raped a girl in Biggs Junction. After much investigation it was determined that Wilson had not been in Corvallis on May 24.

This Richard Wilson angle had barely died down when another "person of interest" shot up the charts. On the afternoon of Friday, June 11, a seventeen-year-old girl was walking down Seventh Avenue in Lebanon, Oregon, about twenty miles from Corvallis. A man in a Honda Accord pulled up beside her and ordered her into his car. She complied because she thought he had a weapon. The man drove for a few blocks and then received a call on his cell phone. This made him very upset; and after taking the call, he pulled over and let the girl out. Then he drove away without uttering a word.

Eight hours later a woman on a bicycle was riding along a street in the same area when a Honda Accord pulled up beside her. The man inside tried talking to her. He seemed to be asking for directions, but she couldn't understand him. He eventually got frustrated and took off.

A couple walking their dog in the area noticed what had just occurred, and they knew about the earlier incident with the seventeen-year-old girl. These people told the girl on the bicycle about what they had seen earlier and then the couple phoned the Lebanon Police Department (LPD). The young woman on the bicycle went to the police department a short time later and made a report as well.

LPD detective Kim Hyde noted that both the seventeen-year-old's and the bicyclist's description was of a white male between the ages of thirty and forty. He had light-colored hair and a light-colored goatee. He was wearing blue jeans and a gray sweatshirt with long sleeves. He also wore a red-and-blue baseball cap, which may have had the letter *A* on the front.

The car he had been driving was a Honda Accord, silver in color with gold tints. It had an automatic transmission, electric windows, and door locks. Detective Hyde discovered from a Honda dealer that this type of Accord was sold between 1998 and 2002 and the color was called "heather mist."

The police put out an alert, and a story and a description ran in the local newspapers. Then around 2:00 A.M., on Monday, June 14, a bartender at Ma's Dairy Farm, in Albany, called the Albany PD to report a man, who had been at her bar, who matched the description of the suspect in the newspaper. Even more than that, he drove a Honda Accord.

According to the bartender, the man had been sitting at the bar reading an article in the *Albany Democrat-Herald* about the suspect and his vehicle. The man started commenting to her that he looked a lot like the person in the drawing and his car resembled the image in the paper, too. It made the bartender very uncomfortable and she asked him to leave. He asked if he could finish reading the article first, and she let him do so. After he was done, he left without any trouble. As he was driving away, the bartender tried to get the license plate number of his Honda, but all she could remember was an *S.*

The man and his Honda didn't turn up, but something else did within days. A sixteen-year-old girl in Albany reported to the police department that she had been walking on Eighteenth Avenue when a man in a blue pickup truck pulled up next to her. With the passenger window rolled down, he ordered her into his car. She refused and took off.

The man continued driving slowly, with his window rolled down, and asked if she needed a ride. She said no and took off running, hiding in some bushes. The pickup turned around and drove away. This man was described as being between thirty and forty years old. According to the girl, he was white, of medium build, clean shaven, with short "marine-style" haircut. Whether it was the same man, with his goatee shaved off and a short haircut, the police didn't know. This man was obviously driving a different vehicle. The sixteen-year-old said it was a small pickup, dark blue with a lighter blue interior. There was a child's seat in the passenger seat, and that child's seat was multicolored.

Because of Brooke Wilberger's abduction, and all the attempted abductions in the region, women and girls all up and down the Willamette Valley were concerned about their safety. Beth Rietveld, with the OSU Women's Center, said, "Women should always let people know where they are going to be when they go out. Bad things like this happen all over the country all the time to women. We are just more aware of it here, right now."

Karen Roberts, of Corvallis, told a reporter that she walked three times a week and always told people where she was going. She added, "I have really become aware of where people are, and if they are following me. I have learned to keep my eyes on people."

Chris Merrill, who ran in the area, told the same reporter that she always carried a can of Mace with her when she ran in isolated wooded areas. The runner admitted that the Brooke Wilberger kidnapping and other attempted abduction incidents in surrounding towns had "really shaken her up. You just don't think that will happen in your little safe haven."

Even the Corvallis High School girls' cross-country running team was taking more precautions. Coach Meghan Arbogast said, "I make sure that no one on my team runs alone."

Some women wanted more protection than just being with someone else, or carrying Mace. In Elmira, where Brooke had gone to high school, Laurie Forbes, a pastor at Fern Ridge Faith Center, contacted the school district superintendent, Ivan Hernandez. Forbes asked Hernandez if a self-defense class for women and girls could be set up in one of the schools. Hernandez agreed and offered free use of the Elmira High School gym. Soon other ministries, the chamber of commerce, and the city of Veneta were promoting the program. Two instructors of martial arts volunteered their services.

As June turned into July, walking searches, horseback searches, cycling searches, and riverine searches had not turned up one viable clue as to where Brooke Wilberger was. Law enforcement began asking people in the area to look at the task force website concerning Brooke, which contained photos, statistics, and information. CPD captain Jon Sassaman told reporters, "We want people to use all their senses. We're asking people to be alert to their surroundings for anything that could potentially lead us to Brooke. If you think there is something important, call the line."

Lieutenant Ron Noble admitted there had never been anything like the search for Brooke Wilberger in CPD's history. And he also admitted it had caused great strains on the department. This was only exacerbated by budget cuts and the fact that two CPD officers were now serving with the military in Iraq. Noble said, "The officers on the search have spent more time at the office and in the field than at home." Obviously, the case was wearing on law enforcement officers, volunteers, and especially Brooke's family. One of the most draining things that almost all parents of kidnapped children expressed was the fact of not knowing what had happened or where their child could be found.

Asked if things now looked bleak for Brooke, because of how much time had gone by, Noble said, "We do know the statistics. We're refusing to label her a statistic. That's his daughter," and Noble pointed to Greg Wilberger, who was standing nearby.

In fact, both Ron Noble and Greg Wilberger at the moment were standing in the Reser Stadium parking lot at OSU when the reporter asked the question. Noble and Wilberger looked across Western Avenue at the Oak Park Apartments complex, where Brooke had been abducted on May 24. They were in the same parking lot where Jade Bateman had been stared at by the strange man in the green minivan, the same parking lot where Bob Clifford had been so concerned that he drove up to see what was going on.

But on July 10, 2004, neither Lieutenant Noble nor Greg Wilberger knew anything about Bateman's and Clifford's concerns. Both Bateman and Clifford had sent in tips to the hotline, but these tips were buried under a mountain of other tips. And on July 10, 2004, the most viable suspect in the case was looking more and more to the CPD to be Sung Koo Kim.

Not only had Kim stolen an undergarment from Lynsey at the Oak Park Apartments, he had labeled lint taken from a dryer there: *The OSU swim apts*. This lint and label had been found in Kim's possession when he was arrested. He had accessed the OSU website and typed *rape, torture, genital mutilation of women* in relation to female students there. He had also written on a file: *hood, mirrored glasses, video camera, digital camera, six nylons and bring panties and bra to put on her.* All of this made the CPD believe Kim had either done a violent rape or he'd been planning to, when arrested. Whether Brooke Wilberger had been a victim of Kim's remained to be seen.

The Benton County DA's Office wanted Kim to take another polygraph test. They were concerned that on the initial polygraph test, Brooke Wilberger's name had not been used. The questions on that test only referred to "that girl" from the Oak Park Apartments, and "that missing girl on May twenty-fourth." CPD captain Sassaman added that Kim's family had not cooperated with police.

And yet, there was a note of caution about Kim, if anyone had been listening. It came from the FBI to local law enforcement. The FBI warned them that at this stage of the game, they should not focus on any one individual concerning the abduction of Brooke Wilberger. Putting all their eggs into one basket could come back to haunt them later.

In an attempt to depict what Brooke Wilberger might look like now, if her abductor had tried to alter her appearance, the National Center for Missing & Exploited Children (NCMEC) created computer-generated images of Brooke's changed appearance. In addition, the Wilberger family handed out ID kits at the da Vinci Days Festival in Corvallis. Da Vinci Days was put on by students at OSU, and was replete with creative floats that they had made. These floats wound around Central Park in a parade in front of the citizenry lining the streets. The Wilbergers knew that da Vinci Days was a good way to reach a lot of out-of-town visitors to Corvallis, who poured in over the length of the festival. While many people in Oregon knew about Brooke's case in a general way, the Wilbergers wanted to give them specifics about Brooke and about keeping children safe in general.

Over the weekend of July 16 through July 18, the Wilberger family passed out over one thousand ID kits, which contained useful information about how to keep children safe. The kits also had a card where the child's fingerprints could be embossed and a DNA collection sub-kit. On the back side of one card, statistics showed that more than eight hundred thousand children were reported missing in the United States. Of those, 450,000 were runaways, 350,000 were abducted by family members, and 4,600 had been abducted by strangers. Brooke was, of course, in this last category.

Despite the FBI's warning not to zero in on any one individual, Sung Koo Kim began looking more and more in Benton County's eyes as the perpetrator in Brooke's abduction. Mark Posler was a CPD detective and had previous work as a policeman in Manhattan, Kansas. In an affidavit in support of yet one more search warrant on Kim, Posler wrote that he'd recently been in contact with Trooper Timothy Gallagher, of the Oregon State Police. New information had come to light from forensic efforts on one of Kim's computers, and what they had found there sent up red flags all over the board. On that computer Sung Koo Kim had looked up topics on the Internet: *asphyxiation, strangling, whores, killers_anonymous, female strangulation, faces of death fan club, and Corpse of the week.* These topics, in conjunction with his penchant for invading the private lives of young women, put Kim in a very bad light, as far as law enforcement was concerned.

In his request for a new search warrant, Posler wrote, *I believe there is evidence at Hotmail.com which will aid in corroboration or contradiction of Sung Koo Kim's statements regarding his online purchase of stolen underwear.*

By now, Kim was saying that he hadn't personally stolen the female underwear, but he had bought them on an Internet auction site.

Posler was granted the search-and-seizure warrant, and he soon had some new evidence of words that had been typed into Kim's computer as well: *hairpull, tit pull hang, slap hard, hogtie, fist pussy ass, cut off blood to head for ten minutes, needles in tits, cut off tits.*

All of this was disturbing, to say the least, and DDA John Haroldson, of Benton County, amended a document of charges against Sung Koo Kim to be more harsh in nature. Count 1 now read: *Burglary in the First Degree—A Felony—Defendant did unlawfully and knowingly enter and remain in a dwelling located at Sackett Hall, with the intent to commit the crime of theft therein.* Count 2: *Theft in the Third Degree—A Misdemeanor— The defendant on or about May 2, 2004, did unlawfully and knowingly commit theft of women's underwear of Ashley M.* Count 3: *Theft in the Third Degree—A Misdemeanor—The defendant on or about May 2, 2004, did unlawfully and knowingly commit the theft of women's underwear of Stacey R.*

Sung Koo Kim's lawyers weren't taking all of this lying down. Kim's original lawyer, Michael Greenlick, had hired an investigator very early on in the proceedings named Michael Hintz to try and discover evidence that would corroborate Kim's claim that he was nowhere near Corvallis on the day Brooke Wilberger disappeared. And Kim and his new lawyers had no doubt that the incredible bail amounts that ran over $10 million were because the authorities were trying to tie Kim to Brooke Wilberger.

Hintz wrote in a report that he contacted various people who would back up Kim's claims. First off was a meeting with Sung Koo Kim's father, Joo W. Kim, who said that his son had been home all night on May 23, and didn't leave the house all morning on May 24. Sometime around 12:30 P.M., both he and Sung went to a Circuit City in Tigard, because they wanted to look at laptop computers. They drove to the Circuit City, looked at laptops for a while, bought one, returned it, and then bought another one at a different store. It essentially took all afternoon for them to buy, return, and get a new laptop computer.

Hintz went to the Circuit City in question with Sung Koo Kim and Joo W. Kim. The Kims pointed out an employee there whom they said they had dealt with on May 24. Hintz had a copy of the receipt from the store and it was printed as being at 1:11 P.M., May 24, 2004.

Hintz described the employee at Circuit City as a "tall white female, wearing a name tag—Cameron." Hintz noted that the last name "Oulette" was written on the receipt and Hintz went up to Cameron and showed her the receipt that he had. She said that her full name was indeed Cameron Oulette.

Hintz then pointed out Sung Koo Kim and Joo W. Kim, who were standing nearby, and asked Cameron if she recognized them. Cameron was hesitant to answer and asked Hintz, "What is this about?"

Hintz replied that he was an investigator, and Sung Koo Kim had been accused of something. Hintz added that he was just checking out Kim's alibi.

At that point Cameron called her supervisor, a woman named Michelle, to come over. Hintz asked Michelle if the store had a security camera that would have been functional on May 24. Michelle said that there were cameras functional that day, and they would have recorded everything that went on in the store. Then Michelle added that the Loss Prevention Department had the authority to search their video database and release sections to law enforcement. However, since Hintz was not an officer, she couldn't just hand a copy over to him. He would have to go through the Circuit City legal department to get a copy of the tape.

Right around that time Joo W. Kim spoke up and asked Cameron if she remembered him. Cameron replied, "I remember both of you." Then she referred to an ad that Sung Koo Kim was holding in his hand. Cameron said she remembered the Kims coming into the store with that very ad.

After that investigation Hintz contacted a woman named Jamie about her recollection of events on May 24. Jamie told Hintz that she was a friend of Sung Koo Kim's sister Jung. On May 24 in the morning hours, Jamie, who was a nursing student at Oregon Health & Science University (OHSU), was taking a clinical exam. At around 11:45 A.M., she was through with the exam and believed that between that time and noon she phoned the Kim residence asking for Jung. Sung Koo Kim answered the phone, instead, and said that his sister was out. Jamie told Hintz that she didn't have the bill as yet from her cell phone provider; but when it came in, it would prove that she had called the Kim household on May 24.

Because of charges in Yamhill, Benton, Multnomah, and now Washington counties in Oregon, one of Kim's lawyers, Joseph O'Leary, wrote a document in trying to combine all of the cases for a "release" of Kim. The Washington County charges were a new set of charges against Kim; they were comprised of eight counts, including "Encouraging Child Sexual Abuse in the First Degree." This stemmed from finding child pornography material on one of Kim's computers. Apparently, this had happened eight times between 2002 and 2004.

O'Leary's document contended that all of the charges should be lumped together so that Kim's attorneys could present just one "Release Hearing Motion." O'Leary noted once again that for the charges against Kim, the amount for bail was astronomical. It was now $4 million in Yamhill County, $1 million in Benton County, $1 million in Washington County, and $10 million in Multnomah County. This was a huge amount for allegations that Kim had only stolen women's undergarments. Obviously, what was fueling the high bail amounts was not what authorities knew he had done, but rather what they *thought* he might have done and was capable of doing.

The motion to consolidate the release motions into one noted that the SWAT raid at 3:00 A.M. on May 29 had supposedly been in the middle of the night because Sung Koo Kim possessed dangerous weapons. But O'Leary pointed out that no officers ever seized the weapons. In fact, it was Kim's father who later took the guns out of the house after the SWAT raid.

O'Leary wrote that if Kim was released, he would not have access to guns; he would constantly have to wear a tracking device; he could not leave his parents' house except for medical reasons, court appearances, or psychiatric sessions. This last part dealt with the fact that Kim was now meeting with Dr. Richard Wollert twice a week. One meeting was an individual session and the other was a group session; both of them took place in the county jail.

While all this was going on, television station KGW reported that they had learned that Sung Koo Kim had bought three 28-pound cinder blocks on the afternoon of May 24 at Parr Lumber in Newberg, about sixty miles from Corvallis. An employee there spoke with a reporter of KGW about this purchase. Asked about the fact that Kim was so far away from Corvallis on May 24, Lieutenant Noble said, "We're aware of that story. It's part of the investigation. But Sung Koo Kim is still a person of interest in Brooke Wilberger's abduction."

Benton County DDA John Haroldson went a lot further than that. He wrote a lengthy document as to why Sung Koo Kim should not have his bail reduced or be released from custody. And some of the points put forward were very damning. Haroldson wrote, *The evidence collected in this case uncovers a depraved individual with a perverse and diabolical obsession with the sexual torture, mutilation and murder of young women.*

Then Haroldson noted that the examination of Kim's computer revealed over forty thousand images of sexual torture, mutilation, and murders of women. Haroldson added, *The sheer volume of images and videos demonstrates that this is not a simple penchant for pornography, but rather an absolute obsession with brutal sexual torture, mutilation and murder.*

Haroldson acknowledged it was not a crime to collect such images, but he said that several women in the Corvallis area had been in the "crosshairs" of Kim's obsession. These young women included two Benton County female residents who were on the OSU swim team. Kim had gathered images of them, biographical information, address information, and maps of where they lived. Then Haroldson stated that Kim didn't have a job to which he was bound if released, but rather he had spent all of his time looking at violent porn and stealing women's undergarments. There was nothing in Haroldson's opinion that kept Kim from going on the run if released.

Haroldson went on to say that Kim kept name tags on some of the underwear he had stolen and collected women's names and the locations where he had stolen them. He also had bags of laundry lint that were tagged with names. And then Haroldson divulged something new: *The defendant took great pleasure in violating the personal living space of his victims, stealing their most intimate apparel and then sexually celebrating the violation by donning the fruits of his crime, as evidenced by images of the defendant striking poses in stolen underwear and photographing himself.*

Haroldson saw a "troubling coincidence" that Sung Koo Kim had stolen women's items from a laundry at the Oak Park Apartments in Corvallis. And one of his victims, Lynsey, had a strong resemblance to

Brooke Wilberger. Haroldson called Kim's alibi for May 24, "suspect at best."

Haroldson stated that the court should not define criminal activity too narrowly. On the surface stealing women's undergarments didn't seem to be that big a crime, but when coupled with the sheer volume of it, the stalking of specific females, and the violent images on his computer, Haroldson wrote, *Sung Koo Kim is a present danger of physical or sexual victimization to women. It is a simple concept of a depraved predator hunting prey, for a fate of such macabre proportions, that it would rival even the darkest nightmares of the human mind.*

Because of all the interest in Sung Koo Kim as a possible perpetrator of Brooke's disappearance, a crush of media showed up at the Benton County Courthouse on September 10, 2004, to watch a hearing in Kim's case. This concerned the defense's motion for a bail reduction. The whole proceeding was anticlimactic, however. After a few minutes Judge Janet Holcomb set a new date in the matter. DDA Haroldson told reporters after the brief hearing, "We were under the impression that we were going to argue our case today. All our deadlines were met for filing and responding to motions."

The only new developments going on in Brooke Wilberger's case that September were that three retired investigators from various sheriff's offices were volunteering their services. The trio were Jacqueline Meyer, of the Ventura County Sheriff's Office in California, and Bill Kennedy and Kurt Weist, of Oregon's Lane County Sheriff's Office. Another development was a large roadside billboard at the junction of Highway 20 and Highway 34 with Brooke's photo and a toll-free number to call with tips.

The CPD captain told reporters that the officers still working on the case were focused, but that it had taken its toll on them. And as far as Sung Koo Kim went, Captain Sassaman said that because Kim had "lawyered" up, they could no longer talk to him without his lawyers' consent. Sassaman added, "The courtroom drama puts law enforcement at a standstill."

In addressing how officers tried to stay upbeat on Brooke's case, Sassaman replied, "There have been peaks and valleys in the investigation."

Right around the corner, there were about to be some more peaks. And they were coming in areas that had not been foreseen by anyone.

CHAPTER 8

ABDUCTION CENTRAL

On September 29, 2004, around six-thirty, a twenty-one-year-old OSU student named Rachel was taking an early-morning walk near LaSells Stewart Center on campus, just blocks from where Brooke Wilberger had been abducted. Suddenly a man came charging out of the bushes and grabbed her around the shoulders. But because of all the media attention about Brooke, this young woman was ready. She managed to knock the attacker's hands away and then sprayed him with Mace, which she was carrying with her. As soon as he was sprayed with Mace, the man took off toward the bushes, and the young woman raced for help. As she did so, she screamed all the way down the sidewalk.

Rachel managed to call police within a very short time, and officers from OSU and the Corvallis PD were on the scene within minutes. A campus-wide search was soon implemented with a perimeter set up around Cauthorn, Poling, Buxton, and Hawley halls. The young woman was able to describe her attacker to the police as white, in his early twenties, wearing a black jacket with a hood and black pants. Every man in the area who remotely matched the description was detained and questioned by officers.

A tip came in that the man matching the description had been seen in the basement of Cauthorn Hall. This was checked out, but nothing turned up there. Despite a thorough search of the area, all of the residence halls were reopened by noon when no suspect was found in them. When reporters got wind of this latest attempted abduction, the police would not give them a description of the young woman who had been attacked or her full name. All they said was that she was an OSU student and not an Oregon native. Oregon State Police lieutenant Gregg Hastings did say, "She's very shaken, but she's assisting the investigation."

Lieutenant Ron Noble later chimed in as well, telling reporters that the CPD, Benton County Sheriff's Office, Oregon State Police, and even the FBI were looking into the matter. He added that at that point they didn't know whether this latest abduction attempt had anything to do with Brooke Wilberger or not. The only indication so far that it might be connected was the fact that it had happened within blocks of where Brooke had been taken. And Noble added that law enforcement acted very quickly on this latest case because of all the things they'd learned about investigating and cooperating in Brooke's case.

Lieutenant Phil Zerzan, OSP station commander, weighed in on the early-morning assault as well. He said, "One of the positive things is that educational efforts (about abductions) have had their effect. The young woman responded effectively and appropriately, and she was able to get away to a location where she could call police."

As far as all the attempted abductions that seemed to be occurring in the Corvallis area, making it seem like "abduction central," Noble said, "It's hard to say if there's actually an increase or if people are much more aware of suspicious persons and are willing to call police." Noble added that Greg Wilberger had contacted him and said that he was happy that the young woman was safe and had not been hurt.

All afternoon and into the night, plenty of behind-the-scenes investigation was ongoing. And then on the afternoon of September 30, twenty-one-year-old Aaron James Evans, of Albany, was suddenly arrested for the assault on Rachel, the OSU student. Evans's arrest came about in a peculiar way, which stretched clear back to August 20. On that date Evans had been arrested for public indecency by exposing himself in Albany. His arraignment was to have been in Linn County on September 29, but Evans called the court and said that his wife was at the hospital having a baby. It wasn't clear if he had shown up for his arraignment on September 29, but in the afternoon Evans did drive to Corvallis and approached a woman outside a Ross store, at the Timberland Shopping Center. He harassed her and stalked her, and the woman was so upset that she called the police department. Within a short time police detained Evans in the area, but apparently he talked his way out of what had occurred.

Evans's freedom was short-lived, however. The next morning an investigator went to Evans's residence and spoke with him once again. Because of certain evidence obtained overnight, and the answers that Evans was now giving, he was arrested.

The OSU vice provost for student affairs said that the swift arrest of Evans made students on campus happy, but that they still had to be on the alert, since so many kidnapping attempts seemed to be occurring. And the newest abduction attempt definitely made them jittery.

The big question now became: was Aaron Evans responsible for Brooke Wilberger's abduction?

Although he had not come up on any of law enforcement's list of possible suspects before, the fact that this latest attack had occurred within blocks of where Brooke was abducted raised a lot of red flags.

Lieutenant Noble told the media, "I guess you can say we added one more person of interest today. Now we're at six."

On October 5, 2004, Evans appeared in Benton County court via an unusual means. He stayed in jail, but his image was presented into a courtroom via a live television feed. The reason was that DDA Haroldson was keeping this preliminary hearing within a grand jury setting. That meant that the media and even Evans's defense attorney could not be present to have input into the matter. It was the grand jurors alone who would decide if there was enough evidence against Evans to hold him over for trial. And when they came back with their decision, Aaron Evans was charged with attempted kidnapping, attempted sexual abuse, menacing, and harassment.

In a vast understatement, the *Gazette-Times* reported, *Thursday, September 29th, was a seemingly busy day for Evans. He appeared in a Linn County Circuit*

Court that afternoon and was arraigned on a charge of public indecency stemming from an August 20th incident in which he allegedly fondled himself while talking to a woman in the parking lot of a Mervyns store in Albany. He also is a suspect in a September 4th incident in which he approached a seventeen-year-old girl in the parking lot of Albany's Heritage Mall and masturbated in front of her. He called the court on September 29th to say that his wife was in the hospital having a baby.

The police checked out this story of Evans's wife having a baby and found out that it was true. When she learned about all of Aaron's misdeeds, she promptly filed for domestic separation in a Linn County court. Fondling himself and masturbating in public were the least of Aaron's problems—if the police could prove he had something to do with Brooke Wilberger's disappearance.

Investigators on the Brooke Wilberger Task Force from the CPD, BCSO, and the FBI began looking at Evans's work records for May 2004. They noticed that he had been working for a roofing company in Albany that sometimes did roofing jobs in Corvallis. Evans had quit work for the roofing company by May 24, but he definitely knew the Corvallis area.

Portland television station KATU sent a reporter to speak with Evans's stepsister, Jessica Caywood. She told the reporter, "The possible connection of him to Brooke Wilberger gave me a sickening, sickening feeling. It actually made me throw up at one point." Caywood said that Aaron had a habit of disappearing for days on end and not saying where he had been. Then she related that around the time of Brooke's disappearance, she saw him looking battered and bruised.

Caywood related, "He had a blackened eye that was swollen completely shut. A bruised nose, bloody lips, scratches on his chest, neck, and hands. After I had heard about Brooke disappearing, I thought back and that was the nail in the coffin for me. I knew it then and there!"

Then in a statement that took everyone by surprise, Caywood added that she had a good hunch where Brooke was located. And by that, she didn't mean that Brooke was still alive, but rather dead and buried. Caywood said she planned to tell detectives what she believed in this regard.

In fact, Aaron Evans's name *had* come up in the flood of tips concerning Brooke Wilberger during the previous month. It did so after he exposed himself and was arrested in Albany. But at the time Evans's name was just one more in a list that numbered into the hundreds, and he was still a low priority at that point.

A press conference took place after Evans's arrest to address this latest revelation, and eight television news crews showed up, along with a legion of print reporters. Benton County undersheriff Diana Simpson read a statement to the press that began, "'The investigation of Mr. Evans is the same level of response that is given to all persons of interest. At this time there is no information directly linking Evans to Wilberger. The task force is very disappointed in the KATU story linking Evans to Wilberger without contacting local law enforcement to verify the information first. This affects the Wilberger family by putting them on an emotional roller coaster, which is very unfair to them.'"

Then Simpson related that the task force had

spoken with Jessica Caywood after KATU's story had aired. Detectives searched the North Albany home that Caywood and Evans had shared. Particular investigation was done in the basement area, where Caywood believed Evans might have buried Brooke. Nothing of evidentiary value was found, even when a cadaver dog was used, but Diana Simpson made one mistake in the press conference. She referred to the basement of the residence as having a dirt floor, when, in fact, it was cement. And soon a war of words went back and forth between KATU and the task force.

KATU's news director was not happy about his station being "lambasted" as he put it by Simpson at the news conference and he stuck by the story. He also pointed out to other news media that the basement in the house that was searched did not have a dirt floor. In fact, it had a cement floor, and one area of that cement had apparently been removed and then covered over with new cement. That was what had set off alarm bells in Jessica Caywood's head regarding Aaron Evans. She imagined that he had murdered Brooke Wilberger and had buried her body there.

Lieutenant Noble admitted to the media that the basement floor was cement, not dirt, and added, "It's definitely been cut up. It may be alarming, but it doesn't mean we can go in there and tear up the floor. There are other things we are doing to determine when changes were made to the floor and by whom." Noble stuck by Diana Simpson's statements and said that whether the basement floor was dirt or cement was not a big issue.

The *Gazette-Times* soon had an article about how Brooke's investigation was wearing on the task force, the media, and the public in general. The article spoke of the task force's own roller-coaster ride every time a new lead or person of interest popped up, only to have no connection to Brooke's abduction. It quoted Diana Simpson in the flap with KATU, about how the television news story made members of the task force stop the important work they were doing and go off on a wild-goose chase. Law enforcement knew about Jessica Caywood before the story even broke, and apparently she had canceled three meetings with them before she spoke with KATU. Diana Simpson said, "Every time an incident occurs similar to the story of Evans, it results in a tremendous workload for this task force. This then limits investigators from priorities established on the Wilberger investigation."

Whether there was a link between Aaron Evans and Brooke Wilberger remained to be seen, and the task force was looking very closely at it in their own way and at their own pace. What was certain was that Aaron Evans was back in the Benton County court on October 11 for the assault of the OSU student on September 29. And as if he didn't have enough troubles, his wife was in court as well, asking that the judge allow no visitation of their children, if Aaron was released on bail.

By this point more information about what had occurred on September 29 was revealed to the media as well. The charges noted on September 29, 2004, that Evans had attempted a *Kidnapping in the Second Degree, to interfere substantially with Rachel's personal liberty and to secretly confine Rachel in a place where she was unlikely to be found.* Another charge was *Attempted Sexual Abuse in the First Degree: Aaron Evans did unlawfully and intentionally attempt to subject Rachel, by means of forcible compulsion to sexual contact by touching sexual and intimate parts of Rachel.* There was also a misdemeanor charge of menacing *to place Rachel in fear of imminent serious and physical injury.*

In addition to the charges, there were revelations in court documents about what had occurred in relation to Aaron Evans during the investigation.

Benton County DA's Office investigator John Chilcote wrote about these developments in a document and noted that Rachel had been walking down a sidewalk on Western Boulevard, just east of Twenty-sixth Street, around six-thirty in the morning on September 29. She saw a young man in front of her on the sidewalk and hurried her footsteps to get past him. The area was *dark, deserted and next to some tall bushes.*

As soon as Rachel got past the man, he ran up and grabbed her from behind. But she was ready for him, already having placed a can of Mace in her hands. As soon as he grabbed her, she wheeled around and sprayed him in the face. He let go of her and took off running back toward the bushes. Rachel ran in the other direction, across the street and to a motel, where she told employees what had just occurred. It was from there that the police were contacted.

Chilcote noted, *Rachel was distraught, very nervous, scared and fearful. She was still highly affected eight hours after the incident occurred when I talked to her.* Chilcote also related that around 8:30 P.M. that same day, Corvallis PD responded to a Timberhill Shopping Center on Walnut Boulevard in North Corvallis. The report was about a white male adult harassing and stalking a female shopper. They learned that the individual wore a distinctive set of clothes, and they soon detained and spoke with Aaron J. Evans, born on March 27, 1983. He was five-six and weighed around 140 pounds. Taken in for questioning about this incident, the questions soon went over to matters concerning Rachel as well. Evans denied having anything to do with that; after several hours of questioning, he was released.

Overnight, however, officers learned that Evans's alibi about Rachel did not hold up. At 1:15 P.M., Chilcote went to Aaron Evans's residence in Albany. At first, Evans once again denied having anything to do with Rachel. But as time went on, he finally admitted that he'd had "contact" with her in Corvallis, and she had sprayed him with Mace.

Chilcote took a pair of Evans's black pants, and an FBI agent named Joseph "Joe" Boyer already had Evans's black jacket. Agent Boyer let Chilcote know that there was residue on the jacket consistent with Mace. Because of all this information, Chilcote arrested Evans and he was taken to the jail in Corvallis.

One incident seemed to follow another in rapid succession that autumn in the Willamette Valley. On October 10, a man in a Toyota Camry followed a group of young women to a 7-Eleven convenience store in Corvallis and watched them intently as he sat in his vehicle. He made them so uneasy, that they phoned the police from the 7-Eleven. By the time the officers arrived, the vehicle was gone; but forty-five minutes later, they spotted it and the driver, and pulled the car over. Once the vehicle was pulled over, a CPD officer discovered that the driver had placed masking tape over the license plates. The plates should have read 455BEX, but appeared as 455BLX, with the tape on the plates.

The driver, Aubrey Cutsforth, thirty-six, of Vancouver, Washington, was questioned about the altered license plates and the situation at the 7-Eleven. The CPD officer noted, "Mr. Cutsforth seemed very nervous as he spoke, sweating and talking very fast. He agreed to talk with detectives about the 7-Eleven incident and Brooke Wilberger."

A search of the vehicle turned up a second set of license plates from California, pornographic pictures, sexual lubricant, and masking tape. In the interview Cutsforth admitted that he sometimes got "urges." When that happened, he went somewhere in his vehicle, watched women, and "sexually gratified himself." But he denied having anything to do with Brooke Wilberger.

Cutsforth was cited for altering vehicle license plates and driving without insurance. He was also looked at closely to see if his alibi would hold up about Brooke. After investigating the matter, it was apparent that Cutsforth had not been involved with Brooke Wilberger's disappearance.

Eight days later, a more grim and potentially devastating event occurred.

A hunter in Tillamook County, thirty miles from Seaside, discovered human remains while he was out in the forest. The remains were found in a clear-cut area of timber, off a dirt logging road. The gender or age of the remains could not be determined until an OSP crime lab did forensic studies on them. OSP lieutenant Gregg Hastings told reporters, "They did look like they've been there for an extended period of time." Lieutenant Ron Noble, of the Corvallis PD, added, "We don't have any idea at this point if it is related to Brooke."

After forensic exams it was proven that the remains were not those of Brooke Wilberger's. It was just one more bump on the emotional roller-coaster ride that had become the Brooke Wilberger case.

Meanwhile, in the task force's eyes, Sung Koo Kim still looked to be the most promising suspect in Brooke's abduction. And by November 2004, Kim was on his third set of lawyers. Attorney Des Connall now represented Kim, and he sought a court order to make the Benton County DA's Office show him what law enforcement knew about Brooke's case and any ties Kim might have to that incident.

DDA Haroldson wrote his own document to the judge stating why Connall should not get any information gathered by law enforcement investigators concerning Brooke. Haroldson, in essence, said that it was still an open investigation, and there were no charges at this point against Kim on Wilberger's abduction. Haroldson noted, "The pending charges stand alone." Then he added, Connall would get all necessary discovery on Brooke *when* and *if* Kim was charged with that crime.

Despite all the charges against him in the thefts of literally thousands of pairs of women's underwear, Sung Koo Kim did have his supporters. Or to be more exact, he had people in the Korean community who thought Kim had been singled out and treated unfairly by law enforcement and the DA offices. These people noted that beside Aaron Evans, not one of the other "persons of interest" had their names and stories mentioned in the press to any great degree. More than anyone, Kim had been vilified, with one article after another about him in the newspapers and many reports on the televison news as well. He was often referred to derisively as the "Panty Thief" in the newspapers and on television.

In a petition to the court, members of the Korean community in Oregon and Washington, including a dozen pastors of Korean Christian churches, spelled out their concerns in the matter. The petition, in part, stated: *Sung Koo Kim should be treated in a manner that is unbiased, fair and not prejudicial or discriminatory. We should remember that people are innocent until proven guilty. Being different shouldn't subject a person to mistreatment and humiliation.*

Around this same time Aaron Evans entered into a plea negotiation with the Benton County DA's Office. Evans's lawyer, Brett Jaspers, told a judge that Evans waived his right to a speedy trial and was, instead, conferring with DDA Haroldson about a plea deal on the alleged OSU student assault and the harassment of the woman in the shopping center parking lot.

And so it went; as soon as news died down about Kim and Evans, a new abduction report popped up. On November 10, 2004, a woman was getting into her car in Corvallis about 6:30 P.M., after attending an ACES meeting. (ACES was a drug and alcohol treatment center.) It was dark, and as she climbed into her car, a man ran out from behind some Dumpsters and attacked her. He grabbed her and punched her in the face, but she fought back, kicking him several times, and managing to drive away. As soon as she got to a safer location, she contacted the Corvallis Police Department.

The woman who had been assaulted described her attacker as a thin white man, between the ages of twenty-five and thirty, about five-nine. At the time of the attack, he had been wearing a stocking cap, dark jacket, and dark-colored pants.

By now, it seemed almost like a mantra. There would be an attempted abduction, soon followed by a law enforcement statement addressing if they thought it was related to Brooke's case. This time CPD captain Jon Sassaman told reporters, "The signature of the incidents is very different. The person clearly did not bring his own car. He attempted to push the woman into her car."

As to why there were so many of these incidents lately, Lieutenant Ron Noble said, "I'm pretty sure there were incidents in the past that no one called us about." He related that since Brooke's abduction more women were willing to fight back and call the police later. Then Noble shook his head and added, "I've still seen young women running alone at night."

After all the recent abduction attempts in the area, that seemed like a recipe for disaster. And the abduction attempts were far from over.

CHAPTER 9
THE MAN IN THE SKI MASK

Even though one abduction attempt after another occurred in and around Corvallis, the search for Brooke Wilberger never ceased. Granted, it was now in a very scaled-back mode compared to the frenzied activity in May and June 2004, but law enforcement officers and volunteers were still working hard on the case. Lieutenant Ron Noble told reporters, "I had no idea I'd be here in five months still talking about Brooke and having nothing solid in this case. We still develop leads on a daily basis. This is not a cold case for us. We are doing work every day."

Noble related that by the five-month mark, detectives had received forty-five hundred tips and there had been 350 "possible sightings" of Brooke around the world. Five hundred people had been named as "suspicious" in the case, and fifty-four of them had been labeled "persons of interest." Citizen volunteers had spent over eight thousand hours searching four thousand acres in the area. Benton County

Search and Rescue had spent twenty-eight hundred hours searching sixty-six hundred miles of highways, roads, and dirt tracks. Noble still held out hope that Brooke was alive. He said, "We wanted it solved on the evening of May twenty-fourth. We're still looking for the one tip that will bring her home."

Greg Wilberger agreed and stated that many detectives still believed that Brooke was alive. Greg added, "That gives us a lot of strength. One of these days she'll show up. You kind of have to pace yourself. You spend an hour a day on her, and then you go on."

Greg and other family members thanked the community once again for all their support. The latest round of items to keep Brooke in the public consciousness were bracelets. The bracelets had a photo of Brooke and pertinent information on the case. They also listed how to contact the "Find Brooke" website on the Internet and a toll-free number to call. Twenty thousand bracelets were made, in large part due to donations that still came in from individuals and businesses. Volunteers continued to go out, in and around the area, taking down old battered posters and replacing them with new ones. Zak Hansen was amazed about how much people still cared about Brooke, and he told reporters, "We think very highly of people in this state."

But five months turned into six, the half-year anniversary of Brooke's kidnapping, and still there were no concrete clues as to where she might be either dead or alive. On that anniversary Noble noted that he still met with the Wilberger family on a regular basis, and he fielded questions from reporters at least once a week. Even at this late date, some detectives worked so persistently on the case that they were ordered to take vacations. Noble related, "One of the detectives said to me, 'How can I take a vacation? Brooke is still missing.'"

One question put to Noble by a reporter was if he thought Corvallis was more unsafe now than it had been in the past. Noble answered that he'd been in law enforcement for twenty years, and that there seemed always to be a cycle of these kinds of incidents that ebbed and waned. He thought that Corvallis wasn't any less safe now than in years past.

Asking about Elizabeth Smart's kidnapping— when she had been held for nine months and then was found alive—the reporter wanted to know if Noble thought Brooke was in a similar situation. Noble answered, "It was a different scenario and different circumstances. I know that the likelihood of this being a similar incident isn't great. But it's something they (the investigators and Wilberger family) have to hold on to. It's not outside the realm of possibilities."

As December 2004 arrived, the first order of business in the Benton County DA's Office was a plea deal with Aaron James Evans. Rather than face a trial, Evans agreed to make the plea deal wherein he had to give up his right to remain silent and give up his right to a trial by jury. Instead, he pled to attempted sexual abuse and menacing of OSU student Rachel in that abduction attempt. By making the deal he avoided being sentenced for harassment and the much more serious charge of attempted kidnapping, which would have brought him a long stint in prison.

Evans had no prior criminal record, and the judge sentenced him to sixty days in jail. And since Evans had already been in jail seventy days prior to trial, he walked out of court a free man. His freedom had many stipulations, however. If he broke any of the rules, he could find himself right back in jail once again. He had to register as a sexual offender, be on probation for several years in the future, attend sex-offender counseling, and take a polygraph test any time the court instructed.

There were also clauses that were going to be hard to enforce unless someone caught Evans in the act of disobeying them: *[Evans was not to] have direct contact or indirect contact with any person under the age of 18 without permission and consent of his supervising officer or the court. Nor frequent places primarily for the enjoyment of persons under the age of 18 or where children were likely to congregate, including but not limited to: playgrounds, arcades, child care agencies, amusement parks, zoos and circuses.*

[He was not to] possess or view images, magazines, motion pictures, video recordings, audio recordings, photographs, computer files or telephonic communication used for the purposes of sexual arousal. [He was not to] enter a business displaying live adult entertainment; strip bars, topless bars or peep shows.

At the end of a very long list of things he could not do, there was one thing that Aaron Evans had to do—he had to cooperate with law enforcement in the investigation of the disappearance of Brooke Wilberger.

Even with this relatively light sentence, which basically meant probation and not jail time, Evans still managed to violate the court order. His probation officer soon noted: *On December 21, 2004, Evans reported that he had been living with his wife and two minor children since being released from the Benton County jail.* Evans was not to have had any close contact with young children, even his own, and he was forced to move out of his house. He did so within days, and after that point he complied with the court instructions. But one more item was added to the list of places he could not be: *the offender shall not frequent any places of higher learning.* (This obviously stemmed from his assault on Rachel on the OSU campus.)

From that point on, Evans apparently lived up to the stipulations in the plea agreement and he began to recede from the headlines around Corvallis. He did so just in time for another man to have his name linked as the possible Brooke Wilberger abductor. And once again it would be a Portland television station that brought the man's name to public awareness.

Loren Krueger was forty-five years old in 2005, and he'd been in and out of trouble for years. In fact, in 1985, Krueger was convicted of attempted rape in Lincoln County, Oregon, and sentenced to five years' probation. Less than a year later, Krueger was again arrested—this time for kidnapping, attempted rape, and attempted murder in Benton County. This had occurred on Witham Hill Drive when a young woman returned to her apartment after jogging. During the attempted rape Krueger had pulled a gun on the young woman, struck her with it and with his fists, and savagely beaten her. Then he had tried pulling her into some brush. The woman managed to escape and was in luck. When she ran for help, there was an officer nearby who was checking out a dead raccoon on a nearby road.

Krueger had not been very secretive in his rape attempt. He'd left his vehicle nearby, with his wallet containing his ID inside it. Police went looking for Krueger and stopped by his parents' home. They found Krueger asleep in the basement. They also found a loaded handgun, several lengths of rope tied into loops, and rubber gloves. One of the ropes was tied into a noose and another had double loops, which the police report cited as *effective as wrist restraints.*

Loren Krueger pled guilty to charges and served eleven years in prison. Once Krueger was out, he was questioned again by police, when a young woman reported a man stalking her. Her description matched Loren Krueger and his vehicle. When he was detained by police, Krueger said that he was out in the area delivering newspapers.

Then in 2003, he was in trouble with the law again. He went to a neighbor's house and masturbated in full view of the residence. This was seen by an underage girl in the house. Krueger had also been stalking her for a period of time prior to this incident. Krueger was arrested, but he got a light sentence. He was barely through with that incident when he was arrested again, in Linn County. The arrest was for possession of marijuana, DUI, and improper use of a 911 call. Krueger had been found passed out in his pickup truck while it blocked a person's driveway.

And then in 2004, Krueger was in trouble once more. A resident in the small town of Blodgett, Oregon, about eighteen miles from Corvallis, reported to police that she saw a man in a black ski mask lurking in her backyard. The woman's husband saw the man leaving their area and followed him to the Blodgett Country Store. The man pulled off a ski mask, got into his pickup in the parking lot, and took off. The husband wrote down the license plate number of the pickup truck, and Benton County sheriff's officers soon tied it to Loren Krueger. He was arrested for attempted criminal trespassing.

Of course, this latest criminal activity by Krueger occurred all around the time that Brooke Wilberger was kidnapped. And it happened in and around Corvallis. None of this made its way as a possible link to Brooke Wilberger, until February 2005, when Portland television station KGW started looking into Loren Krueger's background and noted that he had once attempted to rape a young woman in Corvallis. KGW sent a reporter to talk to the Brooke Wilberger Task Force about Krueger, and Lieutenant Noble admitted that Krueger had gone onto the list of "persons of interest" one day after Brooke went missing. Noble said, "He's been on the radar since May twenty-fifth. He's a local guy we know about."

In one CPD police report, there was the line *Krueger is acting out like he did in the 1980's when he attacked two women.* Asked directly by the reporter if Krueger had been eliminated from the list of suspects in Brooke's case, Noble answered, "He has not. We're still doing work on the case involving him."

For Loren Krueger's court appearance in Benton County for the Blodgett incident, there was once again a crush of media there to witness the proceedings because of Krueger's possible links to Brooke.

And just as in Sung Koo Kim's case, Krueger's lawyer cried foul about all the media attention. Krueger's court-appointed attorney, John Rich, said, "My client is being intentionally persecuted for his status as a person of interest in the Brooke Wilberger investigation. That's the reason we have cameras here today."

Unlike Kim or Evans, who kept mum about their criminal activities, Krueger later spoke with a television reporter and claimed that he had nothing to do with Brooke's disappearance. He added that he was fully cooperating with investigators on that matter.

As time went on, the investigators seemed to agree that Krueger had not abducted Brooke Wilberger. At around the time of her disappearance, Krueger was caught on security videotape at a Corvallis car dealership. And even though he was fairly close to where Brooke had been abducted, he was not at the Oak Park Apartments complex in the time frame in which she disappeared.

Not that Krueger was out of the woods on other charges in the area. The Lebanon PD identified Krueger as a suspect in a June 2004 incident where a man entered a residence in that town through an open window. The man attempted to rape a fifteen-year-old girl inside the house and in the process he assaulted the girl's father, who came to her rescue. The suspect escaped at the time, and Krueger's link to the case only became apparent to police later. And if that wasn't enough, a girl came forward and told police that when she was fourteen years old, Krueger had sex with her. Now on top of the Lebanon attempted rape case, Krueger was charged with sex abuse and unlawful penetration of a minor in the Linn County case.

Once again a person who had looked so promising as the abductor of Brooke Wilberger was eliminated as a suspect. Which brought the investigators' gaze right back to the person on top of the list: Sung Koo Kim. Unlike all the others, Kim could be placed as doing criminal activity right inside the Oak Park Apartments complex. And Kim had a penchant for young female college students about Brooke's age.

CHAPTER 10
PSYCHIC VISIONS

Because Kim was being "painted with the brush" of being the possible abductor of Brooke Wilberger, especially in the eyes of the media, Kim's defense team demanded that all Wilberger police documents be handed over to them. And by now, Kim had a new defense team, which included Des Connall, Shannon Connall, and Laura Graser, of Portland. Like the other attorneys before them, they argued that the bail for Kim, which amounted to $15 million in four counties, was driven by the fact that he was perceived to be Brooke's kidnapper—even though he had never been charged with that crime. And because that was the case, they argued that they should be able to see the Wilberger investigative data so they could defend Kim against the allegation.

Sung Koo Kim's sister, Jung, also asked Judge Holcomb in Benton County to lower Sung's bail. During a break in the court proceedings one day, Jung spoke with a reporter. She asked why her brother was being "victimized" when video games and rap music often had themes of violence against women.

Jung said, "I'm really upset because not everybody who does this (views violent video games and rap music) commits a crime. And some people who don't do this, do commit a crime." Jung then described her brother as a "gentle, peaceful person."

Benton County DA Scott Heiser disagreed and said, "While we are confident the defendant would very much like to see what his exposure is in the Wilberger case, he has not been charged in that case, and he simply is not entitled to inspect or copy any records related to the Wilberger investigation." And on the issue of reducing bail, Heiser commented, "The defendant's threat of sexual victimization to the women he is hunting is well evidenced. There should be no bail reduction."

DDA John Haroldson, who was trying the actual case against Kim, went one step further. He asked Judge Holcomb to strike any references made earlier that may have connected Kim to Brooke Wilberger. Haroldson wasn't saying that Kim was no longer a suspect in Brooke's case—what he was saying was that nothing concerning Brooke should be in the present set of charges against Kim. That way, Kim's defense lawyers would have no right to look at any police documents connected to Brooke. The last thing anyone wanted in the DA's office or law enforcement was for details on their investigation to start leaking into the press.

Judge Holcomb eventually agreed with the prosecution on both counts. There would be no evidence on Brooke's case handed over to Kim's defense team, and bail was not going to be reduced.

On this last issue the defense was far from giving up. In fact, they had Kim's mother, Dong Kim, write a lengthy letter to the judges in all the counties where Sung Kim had charges against him. Perhaps the defense knew this would become a public document in court files, and it might make its way into the media, where the perception of Sung Kim as a "monster" might be altered for the better.

Dong started out by saying the Kim family had moved to the Portland region when Sung Koo Kim was four years old. He had gone to school in the area, and always done well there, even winning several awards. He had never been disruptive in class and didn't drink alcohol or use illegal drugs. Sung and his family regularly attended services and meetings at the Jehovah's Witness Kingdom Hall, and Sung often volunteered to help people in need.

After high school Sung went to Portland Community College, where he got an A.A. degree in electronics and computer engineering in 1994. Later he went to Clark College in Vancouver, Washington, where he continued his studies. After that, he attended Washington State University and obtained his B.A. in 2001. During the years prior to 2001, he also worked as a computer technician in Olympia, Washington, where he supervised a team of twelve employees. It was after Washington State University that Kim decided his real interest lay in cancer research. He quit his job in Olympia, and was living in Tigard, Oregon, with his parents and was self-employed in stock trading, when arrested.

As for the SWAT team arrest on May 29, 2004,

Dong related, *It was extremely traumatic.* She wrote that the front door had been blown open with an explosive device and an assault team rushed into the house at 3:00 A.M. A flash-bang device was thrown into her daughter's room, according to Dong, which terrified Jung. Her husband was struck with a rubber bullet, causing a major abrasion. She noted, *A member of the assault team said that my husband was one inch away from getting killed.*

Dong stated that the entire family had been handcuffed with plastic ties, and the handcuffs on her daughter were so tight that later they had to be removed by a knife blade rather than the usual use of scissors. Even now, Dong related, her daughter was so traumatized that she no longer worked, and she didn't have enough money for therapy.

In fact, several Korean-American leaders from the region went to meet with Multnomah County DA Mike Schrunk on February 3, 2005. They voiced their concerns about the way Sung Koo Kim was being treated and about the whole issue in general. They even pointed out correspondence they had come across from DA Brad Berry, of Washington County, to DA Mike Schrunk. In the note Berry had stated, *Kim may never be fully tied to the Wilberger abduction, but all of those involved agree that we need to do all we can to get as many burglaries on him as possible to get him off the streets. I'm happy to discuss this on the phone to let you know facts sufficient to make you comfortable that this isn't just a panty fetish, but much more.*

The Korean community pointed out that this was not the way American justice was supposed to operate. They said it was unfair to keep piling on charges until a bail amount was so high, no one could ever pay that amount to get out of jail before trial. To them it was imprisonment without due process.

Whether the meeting by the Korean leaders had its desired effect could be ascertained by what happened next. Within a few days Ron Noble held a press conference and stated, "We've exhausted all our leads involving Sung Koo Kim in the abduction of Brooke Wilberger. It appears right now that Mr. Kim, although he has some pretty strange behaviors and is alleged to have done some outlandish things, there's nothing we can find that we can connect him with the disappearance of Brooke."

With that information in mind Multnomah County reduced their bail amount from $10 million to $800,000, and Washington County reduced their bail amount from around $1 million to $480,000. Yamhill County reduced their bail down to $2.4 million from its previous higher total.

Judge Collins in that county added that if Kim somehow was able to make bail, he would have to wear an electronic device at all times, and a security camera would be placed across the street from his residence in Tigard. Collins added, "There are strong public and victim safety issues and risk of flight factors that require the court to take these precautions."

After such a long period of time with Sung Koo Kim seeming to be the top candidate on the abduction of Brooke Wilberger, everything went back to square one in the investigation. There were no new viable clues as to her whereabouts and no new individuals who rose to the status of "person of interest."

In fact, that list was now down to three, which included Aaron Evans, Loren Krueger, and one more individual whom authorities would not name. In fact, in regard to that matter, Lieutenant Noble said that they would not give out any names of people who had been on the list, unless those names somehow showed up in the media from the media's own investigation. Noble declared, "We need to be as responsible as we can be. We don't want to cause problems for innocent people by dragging their names in as suspects."

Noble added that the CPD, BCSO, OSP, and FBI still looked at the case on a weekly basis, and that it was not a cold case. He said, "We're looking for that one piece of information that will bring a solution to the case. More than likely what we're going to get is someone who *may not realize* that what they saw is of interest." Noble was going to be a lot more correct in this assessment than he may have realized at the time.

It was not only law enforcement investigators who were still searching for clues about Brooke; Benton County search-and-rescue teams were as well. They continued to act on new tips by doing "spot searches" in isolated areas. Benton County Emergency Services manager Mike Bamberger said they had done hundreds of such searches since May 24, 2004, and planned to do more as the tips came in.

Three days a week there was one more person in the county doing "spot searches"—Benton County Parole and Probation officer Kristina Bailey. She put on her hiking boots and headed out into overgrown areas where transient sex offenders had registered as their addresses. These locations were under bridges and in forested areas. Bailey told a reporter, "I'm confirming they're staying where they say they are staying."

Homeless sex offenders in Benton County had to go to the Benton County Parole and Probation Office every day and fill out a form of where they spent the previous night and where they planned to spend the coming night. Bailey would make unannounced trips to these locations to make sure the offenders were complying with their statements. Three of the individuals she checked on were listed as "predatory sex offenders." They got the designation because they had offended with children under twelve years of age and had been arrested and convicted.

DA Scott Heiser told the same reporter, "It takes a tremendous amount of oversight to ensure these people don't offend again." Then speaking about the county's sex offenders in general, and Brooke Wilberger in particular, Heiser said, "It would have been a godsend to have had ankle bracelets on every sex offender to know exactly where they were on May 24, 2004, and be able to interview them." The offenders had not had that technology placed on them on May 24. In some cases the investigators literally had beaten the bushes, tracking them down.

Even now, some volunteers still signed up to go out with an official search-and-rescue leader in the new year. On February 11, 2005, one group was heading for Linn County to check on a tip given by a person who lived near the town of Tangent. Another group was headed up to isolated logging roads near Marys Peak. These were old tips that never had been checked out because of the huge backlog of tips that had come in since May 24, 2004. The tip from the Marys Peak area concerned a man who had been up there in early June 2004. He had smelled something decaying and his dog had been particularly interested in that spot. The man didn't dig around to find out what was there. Bamberger noted of this site, "It was a remote area, where somebody can park in seclusion. It is a site common to abductor profiles."

Just how complex and thorough these searches could be was highlighted by the process that day as three searchers rappeled down into a steep ravine, which was used by poachers to get rid of deer carcasses and others to dump unwanted mattresses, carpet, and refuse. In the ravine the searchers found an old elk carcass and animal bones. Bamberger had advised them, "If you find something squishy, don't touch it. Use your poles to check it out." It was both physically and emotionally tiring work. The something "squishy" might turn out to be Brooke's remains, and that constantly weighed upon their nerves.

Meanwhile, four others hiked up the gravel logging road, searching the ditches on each side of the road. Anyplace that was overgrown with bushes and brambles was looked over more thoroughly. It could also be dangerous work. More than once, search crews had stumbled upon illegal marijuana-growing locations and meth labs. A searcher never knew if they were suddenly going to come upon a person with a gun protecting their illegal activities.

As for the searchers themselves, they were driven by many different reasons. Volunteer Christina Lodge worked for the Corvallis Chamber of Commerce. She told a reporter, "It was frustrating sitting back when everybody else was doing the work. I just wanted to get out and do my part."

Dan Kearl, who worked for Hewlett-Packard, said, "The people I've worked with on searches, they've probably created the strongest sense of community I've ever seen."

On February 28, 2005, there was a new wrinkle to developments as the Wilberger family and investigators asked anyone who had a FreshJive sweatshirt to bring it to authorities. The reason was, Zak Hansen knew that Brooke had been wearing an indigo-blue FreshJive sweatshirt when last seen polishing lampposts in the Oak Park Apartments complex. Captain Jon Sassaman said that a FreshJive sweatshirt was needed, just in case they found something in the future and a comparison needed to be made. Sassaman added, "It's just another tool that sooner or later we may need."

Law enforcement, professional search-and-rescue crews, and volunteers were obviously still working on Brooke's case. And so were psychics around the country. Many detectives hate working with psychics because they deem it to be wasted time and resources when time is of the essence. Law enforcement on Brooke's case, however, took in tips wherever they could find them—psychics included. Many of the psychic predictions were way off base; but as things would turn out, one, in particular, was a lot more accurate than anyone knew at the time.

Bonnie Wells, of Ohio, ran an Internet site, and part of it was dedicated to Brooke. What was interesting was a set of circumstances that occurred in February 2004, three months before Brooke's abduction. A person whom Bonnie had never met e-mailed her on February 14, 2004, Valentine's Day, because she awoke that morning to find a small silver ring lying in her bedroom. She had no idea who owned the ring or why it was there, but this person had worked with police before on several missing person cases. She wondered if it was some sort of sign.

The woman contacted Bonnie and asked about the strange occurrence. Bonnie replied that her feeling was that it concerned the abduction, rape, and murder of a young woman, but it had not occurred yet. For some reason the number 3 was going to be very prominent. Three months later, Brooke Wilberger disappeared. Despite all the disappearances and abductions of other young women in the United States between February and May 2004, Bonnie e-mailed the woman and told her, "This is it." As facts came out on the case, it was learned that Brooke had been wearing a silver ring, with the letters *CTR*, when she disappeared.

Since Bonnie knew virtually nothing about Central Oregon, she looked on a map of the area around Corvallis. For some reason her thoughts were pulled to the northwest of Corvallis in relation to Brooke. Even though the abductor could have taken Brooke in any number of directions, Bonnie felt that the man who took her already had a hidden campsite picked out before he grabbed the young woman. That campsite, in Bonnie's mind, was west of Corvallis.

A woman named Shawna, who lived in Oregon, read Bonnie's postings on the Internet and e-mailed her. Shawna had recently had her own vision that Brooke was being kept in a small building with lettering on the side of it. Shawna didn't know where or what type of building this was. On February 15, 2005, Bonnie told Shawna to drive out on Route 20, past the town of Philomath, on to Flynn and then to the small town of Noon. Something out there would catch Shawna's eye.

Shawna did as instructed and was absolutely flabbergasted by what she spied. Not far outside the town of Noon, Shawna spied a shed in a plowed field. Spray-painted on the side of the shed were the letters *CTR*. It already had been reported that Brooke's silver ring contained these letters. Not only that, the shed resembled the type of building that Shawna had seen in her vision.

Shawna was so astounded by this revelation that she told a local police officer about *CTR* being painted on the shed and that it should be checked out. The officer replied that it was private property and they couldn't just break in there on a whim. And besides, he added, "'CTR' is a common phrase in the Mormon religion, meaning 'Choose the Right.'" In other words, choose the right thing to do. It was akin to the letters *WWJD* in other Christian denominations—"What Would Jesus Do."

Shawna, who was a Mormon, said that in all her life she had never seen the letters *CTR* painted on any buildings, fences, or rocks. Nonetheless, the officer did not check out the shed.

When Shawna related all of this to Bonnie, Bonnie told her to go back to the area, which Shawna did a week later. She was stunned to see that someone had painted over the *CTR* lettering so that it could no longer be read. Just why someone would do that in the middle of February, an unlikely time to be painting, was anyone's guess.

In the end the shed was not checked out. Whether it had anything to do with Brooke's abduction may never be known.

But what was true was that Bonnie, living so many miles across country in Ohio, and no firsthand knowledge of Oregon, was going to be a lot closer in her estimate to where Brooke was than law enforcement could have imagined at the time.

CHAPTER 11
AN "AHA!" MOMENT

The big news in May 2005 was the one-year anniversary of Brooke's abduction. The Wilberger family held a press conference at the Hilton Garden Inn in Corvallis, which, of course, had played a prominent role during the first days of the search for Brooke. Now, at the conference, a dozen television stations had their camera crews in attendance, along with many print journalists as well.

Lieutenant Ron Noble started things off by telling the media that there had been numerous requests to the Wilberger family for interviews on the one-year anniversary, and they wanted to address everyone at one meeting. Then Noble added, "Are we any closer to solving the case today than we were on May 24, 2004? Only by the standpoint that we know what hasn't happened." Noble stated that by now they were sure that Brooke had not been abducted by a family member, her boyfriend, or anyone who knew her. Noble typified this case as a "stranger abduction."

Noble related that more than five thousand tips had come in since May 24, 2004, the previous year, and 250 of those had been about vehicles. Investigators in multiple agencies had spent thousands of hours sifting through the tips, and volunteer search teams had covered four thousand acres. Foster Lake had been searched by scuba divers using high-tech equipment, and even a satellite had been used to take photos from space. From all of this, Noble said, the areas that could be scratched off the list helped in the overall scheme. Then he declared, "Even though leads have dwindled, we're not done yet. Not a day goes by that some work doesn't get done on this case."

With a large poster of various photos of Brooke behind him, Greg Wilberger related, "It's been a hard year, as you can probably imagine. We keep hoping each week we might find something. Family beach trips aren't the same now. Brooke's absence has a dampening effect on what used to be joyous occasions. You continually miss her and don't have her and feel like we're kind of leaving her behind. You have to put your trust in God and move on. We keep hoping eventually it will be resolved."

Cammy related, "I take more than an hour each day to read, think, and pray before I walk out the door. Then I'm ready to face the day. We've tried hard to move on, but there's still one piece of life that's kind of stuck. Brooke was just an ordinary girl in the wrong place. I think people can identify with that. When people see that, they think it could be my child. You never as a parent ever give up. You always have that piece of hope, but you come to a realization that finding her alive is not as much of a percentage as it was in the beginning. We're still dealing with the unknown, and that's a piece we want to resolve. Coping mechanisms don't last forever."

Zak Hansen, Brooke's brother-in-law, said, "Oftentimes you find yourself wandering. You kind of find yourself in this haze. The coverage has been great, but sometimes it's overwhelming and you try to find a place where you can get away from it. I grew up in this community. It took me awhile to call law enforcement because I couldn't believe this could happen here. It hit me like a ton of bricks."

Brother-in-law Jared Cordon added that Brooke's abduction made all young women in the area be more aware of their surroundings, and that was a positive thing that had come out of the situation. Cordon said, "Brooke has become an icon. We've had a lot of people say, 'Keep doing what you're doing for all missing people.'"

Then Zak Hansen made a plea to Brooke's abductor. "Bring her back. You've had her for a year. It's time you bring her back to us."

A reporter for the *Gazette-Times* went around the area to gauge how the community had been affected by the girl's kidnapping at the one-year mark. Steve Isom, who had spent seventy-five hours as a volunteer searcher, said that there wasn't a day that went by that he didn't think of Brooke. Anne Merten related that her family had postponed a trip to Utah when the news first broke, and she spent many hours at the stake center in Corvallis. Anne recalled, "I was surprised at how emotional it was for me. I felt strangely connected to Brooke. I thought whatever we could do to help was worth it."

Loren Cochrun was actually shocked when he

realized it was now the one-year anniversary of the abduction. He said, "I still see posters of Brooke and Brooke bracelets everywhere, every day."

The reporter then spoke with Megan Zimmerman, who was wearing a Brooke bracelet. Megan related that it was a catalyst in striking up conversations with complete strangers. She said, "A girl disappears, and it's like our whole town got turned upside down."

Kevin Roddie, of Peak Sports, said that his shop had sold more than two thousand Brooke bracelets since May 2004. And a man named Josh remarked that the abduction had been a wake-up call for the region. "There [are] a few people who obviously are doing horrible things. But there are hundreds of people willing to give up what they are doing for someone they've never met. That was impressive to me."

One of those people was Emily Haymond, who went on several searches. She said, "It could be like the Elizabeth Smart thing or maybe she's buried somewhere. I feel like she was a friend I lost. It's something the whole community went through together."

In addition to the LDS wards, other churches kept Brooke's case alive as well. A large yellow sign on the First Presbyterian Church in Corvallis proclaimed: PRAY FOR THE SAFE RETURN OF BROOKE. The church's senior minister, John Dennis, stated that there were no plans to take the banner down. Reverend Dennis added, "We've prayed for her in a fairly consistent way each week. Part is for our respect for the Church of Jesus Christ of Latter-day Saints. Part is because she is a child of this community."

* * *

The other big story in Corvallis at the time was that of Sung Koo Kim's upcoming trial. He may not have been Brooke's abductor, but he'd had plenty of impact on the community and was looked at by the prosecution as a real and dangerous threat to young women.

Judge Holcomb, of Benton County, ruled that statements that Kim made to police during the May 13, 2004, search and seizure would be heard by jurors. It was during that interview that Kim told an officer that he considered the collection of women's underwear to be "a hobby." Kim said, "I mainly just store them away." And then he lied and said that he'd bought the undergarments on eBay, as well as from Dumpsters on college campuses.

During the interview Detective Baltzell told Kim about the declaration of some female students from colleges, that they'd seen him in the dormitories. Kim replied, "You have someone who actually saw me taking something, and I swear I did not. You're trying to pin something on me that I didn't take."

During the first search and seizure, Newberg PD officer David Brooks had been assigned to keep an eye on Kim, who sat nearby on a couch with handcuffs on his wrists. Kim wanted to see the search-and-seizure papers, and Brooks let him do so, by turning the pages for him. When Kim was done, he told Brooks, "You can't touch the computers." Apparently, they weren't on the list.

Kim may have wished he'd never spoken up about those computers. A new search warrant had allowed police to seize them, and it was then learned that Kim had thousands and thousands of images of women being tortured and raped. What many in law enforcement originally viewed as only a panty thief fetish turned into something much, much more ominous.

Des Connall, Kim's lawyer, sought to suppress a lot of the evidence from the May 13, 2004, search and seizure because of what he termed as "errors" in the warrants. This however was Connall's last hurrah for Kim. On May 24, 2005, one year to the day after Brooke Wilberger had been abducted, the Corvallis *Gazette-Times* reported that Connall was withdrawing as Kim's lawyer. In a document to the judges in four counties, Connall stated, *Because of very recent activities which have occurred between Mr. Kim and this law firm, we would move to withdraw representation in that matter in all four counties.*

When it was revealed why Connall and his law office was dropping Kim as a client, the news was dynamite. The Portland *Oregonian* got wind of the reason, and it was because Kim had just given a letter to Connall asking that Kim's father sneak a gun to him and help him escape. Kim wrote, *You have my rifles. They are better than anything the police have.* The plan was that Kim would somehow get a weapon while he was being transferred by two deputies, who were lightly armed. Then he would shoot his way out of the van.

Kim's parents or Des Connall must have alerted the authorities and Kim's violent escape plan was averted. Kim's mother soon told a reporter, "This proves just how delusional my son is." Because of this episode Kim's bail amount was doubled.

By June 2005, Kim was on another lawyer. This time it was Charles Wiseman, of Hillsboro. Wiseman told the various judges in the four counties that he was nowhere near ready to go to trial. In one statement he wrote, *I have about 5,000 pages of documents I haven't even looked at yet.*

And Kim's family was fighting back on another front. They obtained a different lawyer, David Park, to represent them and filed a lawsuit in federal court. The Kim family claimed that on May 29, 2004, during the SWAT team "invasion" of their home, they experienced, "shock, fear, anxiety, humiliation, mental and emotional trauma." They were seeking $11 million in damages against the Newberg Police Department, Oregon State Police, the Tigard Police Department, and Benton County. They specifically named Newberg detectives Eric Ronning, Todd Baltzell, and Mark Cooke, as well as OSP trooper Timothy Gallagher. There were also "thirty-five John Does" who worked for various agencies.

Despite all the hoopla surrounding Sung Koo Kim, it was something else that happened around that time that had a tremendous impact on Brooke's case, and this "something" went back to the Reser parking lot on the OSU campus. It had all started clear back on December 1, 2004, when members of the task force started looking once again at the possible link of a green minivan near Brooke's abduction site on May 24, 2004. At the time the green minivan was just one more possible lead in a mountain of tips that had come in.

Lieutenant John Keefer, of the CPD, went to the OSU police headquarters and spoke with Lieutenant Phil Zerzan. Zerzan recalled of the events of May 2004, "We (the OSU police force) recognized this abduction would have a significant impact on the campus community. Even though it was off campus, we often responded to that area as well. It was very near the parking lot for Reser Stadium. My involvement was to ensure we provided whatever resources were necessary to the Corvallis Police Department. And to act as a liaison to those aspects of the investigation that involved the campus and campus community."

On December 1, 2004, Keefer spoke with Zerzan and said that he wanted his help in locating a few people who had an association with the campus. (He was probably talking about Diane Mason, Jade Bateman, and Bob Clifford.) These people had left tips on the tip line about a man in a green minivan acting strangely on the morning of May 24, 2004. Zerzan took Keefer out to the Reser Stadium parking lot, where a couple of the people who'd called in—Jade Bateman and Bob Clifford—had reported the green minivan at the time.

As the two officers were standing there, Lieutenant Keefer told Lieutenant Zerzan that his report indicated that the green minivan had come from the northwest corner of the parking lot and traveled in a southeasterly direction. Zerzan recalled, "As we stood there, just kind of looking over the scene, you could see the roof of the Oak Park Apartments. It was a direct line of sight. It was kind of an 'aha!' moment for me. This was where the van was, and a short distance away is where the crime occurred."

Keefer also had that "aha!" moment. Out of all the thousands and thousands of tips, this one seemed to have some teeth to it. Because of that, both Keefer and Zerzan contacted Bob Clifford, the man who worked as an athletic assistant and had been so worried about Jade Bateman being alone in the parking lot, talking with a man in a green minivan, that Clifford had driven over to investigate what was going on. Now on December 1, 2004, Lieutenant Zerzan noted, "Mr. Clifford remembered a green van in the parking lot. The driver was speaking with a student named Jade there. It had Minnesota license plates. Mr. Clifford had seen the occupant of the van."

Later, Jade Bateman filled in the officers all about what had occurred to her on the morning of May 24, 2004, in the Reser Stadium parking lot. And Diane Mason spoke to investigators about her recollections of a man in a green van asking for directions. His actions had made her so uncomfortable that she made up an excuse as to why she had to leave.

Zerzan noted, "From Diane's location to Jade's location to the parking lot of the Oak Park Apartments was a distance of about eight hundred yards."

Things on the Brooke Wilberger case were about to take an unexpected and dramatic turn. And it all came about because of excellent police work being done at the Albuquerque Police Department. Already having information about the man who had kidnapped a young woman off the street near the University of New Mexico, APD sent out memos to other police departments around the nation to see if they had experienced similar situations. APD particularly keyed in on Oregon, since it was learned that the man who called himself "Joel" had recently been living in Oregon.

On getting this information from APD, the Brooke Wilberger Task Force was indeed interested about this guy Joel in relation to Natalie Kirov. They alerted APD that they'd had a similar incident near the Oregon State University campus. APD detectives John Romero and Jinx Jones decided that this Corvallis, Oregon, case sounded an awful lot like their Natalie Kirov case. Joel hadn't been driving a green minivan in Albuquerque, but he had abducted a petite blond college student just blocks from campus shortly after 6:00 P.M. on November 29, 2004. This wasn't an abduction in the dead of night or in some isolated location. It had happened on the sidewalk of a city street.

The New Mexico detectives got in touch with Keefer, who passed the information on to Detective Shawn Houck, of the Corvallis Police Department. Houck had been working on Brooke's case since day one. Interested in what the New Mexico detectives had to say, Houck phoned Detective Romero back and learned that a white adult male named Joel was in custody for abducting a female college student at knifepoint just blocks from campus. Romero gave Houck all the details and then added that Joel was "willing to take a huge risk by abducting a victim off the street, in plain view, and place her into his vehicle, all in the hope of not being seen. This was done at about six P.M., and even though it was dark outside, there was both vehicular and pedestrian traffic in the area." Romero said that Joel was so bold in this that

Romero suspected he had done this before. And the "before" could have very possibly been with Brooke Wilberger.

Romero added one more thing—he believed that if Natalie Kirov had not escaped, Joel was going to take her to an isolated area, rape her some more, then kill her when he was tired of her and worried about being caught. Romero saw a lot of similarities between this and what had happened to Brooke Wilberger.

From the thousands upon thousands of tips and supposed sightings of Brooke since May 24, 2004, it was this "aha!" moment that was the key that was about to unlock the door of who had abducted Brooke more than a year previously. This clue was so viable that the task force released a short statement to the media. They wanted anyone who may have seen a green 1997 Dodge minivan around Brooke's abduction area on May 24 to contact them.

Very closemouthed about information concerning Brooke up until this point, the task force was now seeking the public's help on a very specific matter. The Corvallis *Gazette-Times* headline for June 1, 2005, was VAN MAY BE CLUE IN DISAPPEARANCE. The article stated that investigators were seeking information about a 1997 green Dodge Caravan in connection with the Brooke Wilberger abduction. And there were three photos of either the van in question or one that looked similar. They were photos of the van front, side, and rear. It was noted that the van had tinted dark windows in the rear passenger area.

Lieutenant Noble also let it be known that the task force wanted to contact a man named Brian. On the morning of May 24, 2005, this Brian had phoned a 911 dispatch center about a green van speeding away from the area where Brooke had disappeared. In Brian's words the van had been "speeding and recklessly driven."

Noble said now, "There are certain things that we've left out on purpose because we need to be able to validate the information. That is not to say that anyone should hesitate to call the task force. Especially if they had seen one around that time being driven erratically, on an old logging road, parked in a farmer's field or if its driver was acting suspiciously. We assume that whoever took Brooke would be acting in such a manner."

The authorities particulary wanted to hear from Brian. Noble released one more bit of information. "There are potentially hundreds of green minivans in the mid-Willamette Valley. But investigators know exactly what they're looking for." Then he added that there were some other witnesses besides Brian whom they had already spoken with about the van.

A short time later, Ron Noble told the media, "At this time we're not looking for a green van. What we want to do is find out whether the van we know about was in a certain area. We want to know whether or not our guy, with a green van, was possibly related to Brooke. We want to know if anyone saw a green van in the area when Brooke was abducted."

Noble said that they did have a person of interest

in connection with the van. Noble wouldn't say what the name was of the person in question. Noble did add that this "person of interest" was not in a position to harm anyone at the present time, which indicated that the person was already in jail somewhere.

As of June 6, 2005, the task force was still hoping to hear from Brian. In fact, they even had *America's Most Wanted* television program air a segment about Brooke and put out a request that Brian call the 800 number listed on screen if he watched the program. Several Brians did call in, but it wasn't the task force's Brian.

One thing the *America's Most Wanted* program did was cause a flurry of supposed sightings of the green minivan, especially down in Arizona. Noble responded to this by saying that they knew exactly where the van was, and it wasn't in Arizona. What the task force wanted was information from people who may have seen it in the Corvallis area on May 24, 2004, and not where the van was today.

Out of view of the public, Brooke's task force was now connecting the dots between a green 1997 Dodge minivan and a man named Joel who had abducted Natalie Kirov in Albuquerque, New Mexico. A man named Joel who had phoned the Newport court that he wouldn't make it there for a hearing on May 24, 2004, and a man in a green van in the Oak Park Apartments complex area between ten and eleven that morning. When the lines began coming together between the dots, they pointed toward one man:

thirty-nine-year-old Joel Patrick Courtney. The same Joel Courtney who had abducted and raped Natalie Kirov in Albuquerque on November 29, 2004. The same Joel Courtney who was now sitting in jail in Albuquerque, New Mexico.

CHAPTER 12
AN ARREST AT LAST

The whole green van scenario had been a topic of discussion for some time with the task force, and it was the reports of three people connected to it that made it seem so valid. Jade Bateman, independently of Bob Clifford, had phoned in a tip about the van back in May 2004. Eventually CPD detective Karen Stauder interviewed her, and Bateman said that she had been approached by a man driving a "dark green, boxy, older-model minivan." The man appeared to be in his early thirties with "short, thinning hair and a pointy nose." She said the driver asked her for directions to the OSU athletic office, and she directed him to Gill Coliseum, at which point the man drove away. A few minutes later she saw the van drive out of the lot with a second person in the passenger seat. (Bateman was almost certainly wrong about this.) She believed the second passenger was also a male.

Detective Houck noted, "This encounter, as with

Bob Clifford's observation, occurred within blocks of the Oak Park Apartments and within an hour of when Brooke Wilberger was abducted." And then Houck added that a third tip about a green van came in from Diane Mason.

Mason was interviewed by FBI agent Joe Boyer and Benton County DA investigator John Chilcote. Diane told them that she saw a "newer, clean, dark green minivan" at the intersection of Thirtieth and Western at around 9:30 A.M. on May 24, 2004. She described the minivan as having a round body with gray interior and tinted windows. She described the driver as having blue eyes, short blond/gray hair, a goatee, and two earrings in his left ear. Diane told about the driver having a road map of Idaho in his lap, and that he wanted her to point out on a Corvallis map, which he said was in the interior, about the locale of a fraternity house he was looking for. Boyer noted, "Diane Mason became suspicious and concerned, so she started backing away from the van. She then told the driver she was late for class and began walking toward Southwest Thirtieth Street and north toward the OSU campus. She saw the driver get back into the driver's seat and drive away."

At the time these three tips about a green minivan and a description of the driver were good, but they still did not give enough information as to who the driver was. And amongst the hundreds of tips flowing in at that time, they didn't seem to be any more legitimate than any of the others. And that sense of legitimacy may never have happened if the Albuquerque Police Department detectives hadn't been so conscientious about seeking other information on Joel

Courtney after Courtney's arrest on the abduction of Natalie Kirov.

APD detective Romero sent on information about their suspect in Natalie Kirov's case, even though that man was driving a red Honda at the time of the incident. The man was Joel Patrick Courtney, born on June 2, 1966. And when Romero sent out that information, he was basically looking to see if Courtney had done anything of a similar nature to the Kirov case, especially in Oregon, since Courtney still listed his address as being at his brother-in-law's residence in Portland.

Once APD's query on Joel Courtney reached the Brooke Wilberger Task Force, CPD detective Houck went online and looked up information on the National Crime Information Center (NCIC) and the Law Enforcement Data Systems (LEDS). What he found was that Courtney had been arrested seven times in Oregon, one time in California, and one time in New Mexico. One of these arrests occurred in Oregon in 1985 for first-degree attempted rape. He was also arrested on a separate incident for second-degree escape, probation violation three times, and driving under the influence. It was this last arrest that really caught Houck's eye. The DUI arrest had occurred on January 20, 2004, by the Oregon State Police in Lincoln County. Joel's arraignment was scheduled for May 24, 2004, the day that Brooke disappeared. Records showed that Courtney had not shown up for his arraignment.

There was also information describing Joel Patrick Courtney. He was listed as being five-eleven, weighing 185 pounds, having blue eyes, and two ear piercings in each ear. A photo from his 2004 arrest showed him having a peppery brown moustache, goatee, and closely cropped hair.

Because Joel Courtney was scheduled to appear in Lincoln County court in Newport, about fifty miles away from Corvallis, on May 24, 2004, Detective Houck contacted Nancy Jo Katner, who had been Nancy Jo Mitchell before getting married. Nancy Jo was a clerk for Judge Littlefield, in whose court Courtney was supposed to have appeared on May 24, 2004, but didn't. Katner related, "On Monday morning it can be quite chaotic. A lot of motions on those days. May 24, 2004, was a Monday, and the first thing I would do when I came to the office was to get the computer up and running. Then I'd check all my voice mails and e-mails before I went into court, which was usually at eight-thirty A.M.

"I usually had a number of voice mails about cases that were going to be dealt with that day. And one of the voice mails was from Joel Courtney. I had written about it on my notebook, 'Courtney and Montana.' The voice mail said the person was Joel Courtney and he was not going to make it to court on time for his arraignment because he was driving in from Montana."

Nancy Jo played a portion of a tape from court proceedings on May 24, 2004, for the investigators. On the tape Judge Littlefield's voice could be heard as he said, "Joel Courtney. Is Mr. Courtney here?" There was no answer. So the judge said, "Okay, let's move on."

Later, on what was called a ForTheRecord (FTR) log, Judge Littlefield's voice could be heard again. He said on the tape, "There is a matter of Joel Courtney, who is on his way from Montana." Even later, on the

FTR log, one of the attorneys in court asked the judge if Joel Courtney ever showed up, and Judge Little-field facetiously answered, "No, I think he took a boat with the Lewis and Clark expedition (of 1803). He probably won't get here until 2005." Then the judge related that Courtney had phoned the court a couple of times and said he was going to be late. The real clincher for Detective Houck was that in one of the calls Courtney said that he was now in Corvallis and was going to be late to the court in Newport. Court-ney made that call on the morning of May 24, 2004, in Corvallis, shortly before Brooke Wilberger was abducted.

Because of the revelation that Joel Courtney, by his own admission, stated that he was in Corvallis on May 24, 2004, Detective Houck began looking into Courtney's work history. Houck discovered that Courtney was working in May 2004 for the Creative Building Maintenance (CBM) company and was as-signed to a territory in Washington, Idaho, and Montana. CBM had its employees do janitorial work at retail stores, malls, and work sites in various states. Joel Courtney worked alone, traveling in a dark green minivan with Minnesota license plates. The same kind of license plates that Bob Clifford re-called. During the month of May, Courtney was living with in-laws Jesus and Susanna Ordaz in Port-land, Oregon. Joel's wife and kids appeared to have been there, too.

Houck started running numbers of distance and time for May 24, from Portland to Newport, where Courtney was scheduled for his arraignment. Houck noted, "To drive from Portland to Newport, the common and most direct route would be to drive through Corvallis. The phone call Joel Courtney made on May 24, 2004, was received at the Lincoln County court sometime between eight A.M. and nine-seventeen A.M. I spoke with Dodi Turnbull about Courtney and this court date. She told me that Courtney didn't appear on May 24, 2004, and the arraignment was postponed to May 25, 2004, at one-fifteen P.M. When Joel Courtney did not appear on the twenty-fifth, a warrant was issued for his arrest."

Because of all this information, Lieutenant Keefer met with Bob Clifford to present him with a photo lineup. Lke most in the law enforcement of the area, Keefer referred to a photo lineup as a "throw down." He met Clifford at Clifford's office on the OSU campus and placed six photos of men on a table. One of the photos was of Joel Courtney, and the other five were of men who looked similar in appearance to Courtney. Clifford looked at the photos and had a hard time picking one, and told Keefer the reason why. The man he saw in the green minivan in the stadium parking lot had been wearing a red baseball cap. To compensate for this, Keefer covered up the top portion of all the men's heads on the photos. Once he had done this, Clifford immediately picked photo Number 3. Photo Number 3 was a photo of Joel Courtney.

Keefer asked Clifford how sure he was of his choice. Clifford answered that he was sure that photos 1, 2, 4, and 6 were not the man he had seen, and he was pretty sure that photo 3 was. Clifford said, "He has the right look." And then later on a form, Clifford wrote down, *Number 3.*

FBI agent Boyer went to talk with Jesus and Susanna Ordaz. Jesus said that both he and Joel worked for CBM and that on May 24, 2004, Joel had packed a gray duffel bag and left, supposedly going to take care of his court appearance in Newport, Oregon. Joel did not reappear at the house until after 10:00 P.M. on May 25. During that time he did not phone them or even his employer, although he was supposed to be working on May 24 and 25. Jesus said that Joel had been driving a dark green Dodge minivan with Minnesota plates. He also said that Joel often wore a red baseball cap and dark glasses. This description matched the man whom Bob Clifford had seen at the Reser Stadium parking lot on the morning of May 24, 2004. Jesus added that when Joel came home, all he would tell his in-laws was "I slept in the van."

According to Houck, the Ordazes also added that when Joel came home, he began telling two different stories of where he had been. In one story Joel said that he'd been at some kind of party that got out of hand. Sometime near the end of the party, Joel said he had been kidnapped for a while. Houck wrote in a report, *Talking with Dr. John Cochran, a forensic psychologist who has worked on the Green River Killer Task Force and with the FBI Behavioral Science Unit, that many times violent offenders will tell a parallel story that tracks with his criminal conduct as a cover story.*

Joel stuck around Portland, Oregon, for the next two and a half weeks after May 25, and then he suddenly took off without telling his in-laws the reason why. He took off in the green minivan owned by CBM; then he gave them no reason why he was leaving the area. A few days later, Joel suddenly showed up back at the home he shared with Rosy, his wife, and the kids in Rio Rancho, New Mexico. He drove the green minivan there. Houck was able to discover that Joel Courtney took virtually all his possessions to New Mexico with him, without telling his employer he had quit working for them.

Joel was not long at that Rio Rancho home before he got into an altercation with his wife, Rosy, who was there now as well. She called the police and Joel was arrested. When he got out of jail, he did not move back into her house, nor did he go back to take anything from there. After he moved to Albuquerque, it wasn't long before he was in trouble again. Joel, of course, abducted and sexually molested Natalie Kirov in November 2004 and was arrested. And what he had done in New Mexico and Oregon was just coming to light to the authorities.

Detective Houck, in the meantime, sought a search warrant, wherein New Mexico law enforcement agents would go into Rosy Courtney's house to see exactly what Joel had taken with him when he left Oregon without even telling his in-laws where he was going. In the warrant Houck asked for the search and seizure of many items including *an Oregon Coast Aquarium postcard addressed to Joel Courtney and dated 1997, a composition notebook labeled Joel Courtney, an Idaho Official Highway map, receipts and documents evidencing travel expenditures of Joel Courtney, clothing belonging to Joel Courtney, weapons, binding materials, objects related to Brooke Wilberger which could be viewed as a memento, body fluids, blood, semen, saliva, sweat, latent fingerprints, hairs and fibers, bones, bullets, cartridge casings and fabric.*

Albuquerque police were going after their own search warrant as well, to help out Corvallis with their interest in Joel Courtney. Detective Michael Hughes, who had been a law enforcement officer for eighteen years by 2005, spoke in person with Detective Houck, who had flown out to New Mexico. Houck brought along a copy of the search warrant he had filled out. Detective Hughes let Houck know that he'd already gone out to Rosy Courtney's house on Apple Court in Rio Rancho, along with FBI agents.

The official Albuquerque PD search warrant, in part, asked for *a nighttime search on the property which is a tan stucco dwelling. The items to be searched for and seized included a gray T-shirt with the words BYU soccer, an indigo sweatshirt with the words FreshJive, a woman's pair of size 4-6 blue jeans, a bra, a pair of small to medium panties, a silver-colored ring engraved with the letters CTR, earrings, a stained extra large T-shirt.*

During that search Rosy had given a key to the house to Special Agent Tim Suttles "without incident." While the FBI agents were in the house, Detective Hughes went around the neighborhood, talking to the Courtneys' neighbors. He apparently didn't get very much information, since few neighbors knew Joel very well.

After talking to the neighbors, Hughes went into the Courtney home and helped with the search-and-seizure process. At the time they were basically looking for things connected to the Natalie Kirov case. Hughes noted that they seized one black string and several green pieces of string from a toolbox in the garage. They also seized a white string and duct tape from above the dryer in the garage, and three black shoestrings from the garage. The agents collected a white piece of rope and a gray duffel bag from underneath the bed in the master bedroom. A hair tie containing a blond and brownish hair was located inside the bag. Hughes noted, "The bag is consistent with what Susanna Ordaz described Joel as having in Oregon."

And then the agents found and seized one very important item: a floorboard mat containing blond hair fibers. At the time they didn't know who the blond hair belonged to. The fibers could have come from Natalie Kirov, Brooke Wilberger, or some other person.

Detective Hughes spoke with Rosy Courtney about a case that was being investigated in Corvallis, Oregon, although apparently he didn't mention the name "Brooke Wilberger" at that point. Rosy said she would cooperate with Hughes. Hughes asked Rosy about the gray travel bag, and Rosy said that only Joel used that duffel bag. Hughes asked Rosy about the day Joel was supposedly going to Newport, Oregon, for a DUI court appearance. Rosy recalled that he left and returned a couple of nights later, which would have been in the night hours of May 25, 2004. When Joel returned, he told her he wasn't feeling very good.

Hughes passed on one more bit of interesting information to Detective Houck. Hughes had been at an interview with Natalie Kirov in December 2004. Joel Courtney had asked her how old she was when he had abducted her. Before she could answer, he said, "You must be eighteen or nineteen years old." Then Joel asked if she was a virgin. Hughes noted that all indications were that Brooke Wilberger was a virgin when she was abducted. And she was nineteen years old. Whether Joel had gotten that information out of Brooke Wilberger at some point was still not known by investigators.

Both Detectives Hughes and Houck knew that the FBI had already seized the green Dodge minivan that Joel Courtney had been using in May 2004 when Brooke Wilberger disappeared. Even as the new search warrant was being implemented at the Courtney home in New Mexico, unidentified hairs, fluids, and stains discovered in the Dodge minivan were being analyzed at the FBI Crime Laboratory in Quantico, Virginia.

This lab analysis took a long period of time, as always happened at the crime lab, because so many police agencies around the country were also seeking the lab's help in their major cases.

And then indisputable evidence came back from the FBI Laboratory. A blond hair that had been found within the green Dodge Caravan had belonged to Brooke Wilberger. There was a lot of circumstantial evidence that Joel Courtney had abducted Brooke on May 24, 2004. And now this one hair could prove that she had been inside his van. Joel Courtney was going to have a very hard time explaining what a missing nineteen-year-old girl had been doing inside the van he had driven.

At long last, after looking at "persons of interest" such as Sung Koo Kim, Aaron Evans, and Loren Krueger, the Brooke Wilberger Task Force now had a person who had moved up to the category of full-fledged "suspect." After all of the false leads, dead ends, and disappointments of the preceding year, they were finally zeroing in on what had happened to Brooke, and who had been responsible for her kidnapping.

PART II

Even at the age of 18, Joel Courtney was in trouble with the law. In 1985, he pled guilty to first-degree sex abuse in an Oregon case. *(Mug shot)*

In 1991, Courtney was arrested again on similar charges. *(Mug shot)*

Brooke Wilberger was a beautiful young woman. She attended Brigham Young University in 2004 and was good at academics and sports.
(Yearbook photo)

Brooke grew up in the pastoral Willamette Valley of Central Oregon.
(Author photo)

On May 24, 2004, Joel Courtney tried to abduct Diane Mason, a student at Oregon State University, on this corner of 30th Street in Corvallis, Oregon. *(Author photo)*

When the kidnapping attempt on Diane failed, Courtney spotted another young woman, Jade Bateman, in the parking lot of OSU near the Reser Football Stadium. *(Author photo)*

On his third abduction attempt on May 24, Courtney spotted Brooke Wilberger, who was on vacation from college, in the parking lot of the Oak Park Apartments complex in Corvallis. *(Author photo)*

Brooke was cleaning lampposts for her sister and brother-in-law, who managed the Oak Park Apartments complex. *(Author photo)*

When Courtney blocked Brooke's escape route near these garbage cans, she had nowhere to run. He may have used a knife to force her into his minivan. *(Author photo)*

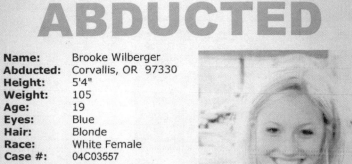

ABDUCTED

Name: Brooke Wilberger
Abducted: Corvallis, OR 97330
Height: 5'4"
Weight: 105
Age: 19
Eyes: Blue
Hair: Blonde
Race: White Female
Case #: 04C03557

Identifying Marks: Scar on right forearm, extending from wrist to elbow.

Last Seen Wearing: Gray BYU Soccer T-Shirt, Blue "Fresh Jive" Sweatshirt Ring Engraved with "CTR"

Word soon spread all over the region about the missing girl. Thousands of posters and flyers went up in an ever-widening area around Corvallis.

(Missing person police photo)

Hundreds of volunteer searchers scoured the fields and forests around Corvallis for traces of Brooke throughout the summer of 2004. *(Author photo)*

Volunteers searched creeks, riverbanks, and even underneath covered bridges for Brooke. *(Author photo)*

Law enforcement checked out hundreds of leads about potential abductors, including Richard Wilson, who had gone on a crime spree in the Northwest that spanned four states, including kidnapping, rape and murder. He was known to have been in the Willamette Valley around the time of Brooke's kidnapping. *(Mug shot)*

Aaron Evans became a suspect in Brooke's case when he harassed a woman in Corvallis and then attempted to abduct an OSU student on September 29, 2004. She sprayed him with Mace and escaped. Evans was soon tracked down and arrested. *(Mug shot)*

Sung Koo Kim became a "person of interest" in Brooke's disappearance when law enforcement discovered he had stolen over a thousand women's undergarments—some of them from OSU and even from the Oak Park Apartments. *(Mug shot)*

To spread the message about Brooke, her parents, Greg and Cammy Wilberger, handed out flyers at OSU's popular Da Vinci Days Parade. Many of the people attending the parade were from out of the area. *(Author photo)*

No concrete leads to Brooke or her abductor surfaced throughout much of 2004. Then, on November 29, 2004, Joel Courtney struck again. This time he kidnapped a woman near the University of New Mexico in Albuquerque. *(Author photo)*

Foreign exchange student Natalie Kirov was walking home from campus when she was abducted at knifepoint near this corner in Albuquerque. *(Author photo)*

After being sexually assaulted, Natalie managed to escape and gave a detailed description about her attacker and his vehicle. Her description led Albuquerque police to apprehend Joel Courtney, who now lived in the area. *(Mug shot)*

Courtney was arrested on multiple charges, including criminal sexual penetration and kidnapping. His court hearings took place at the Second District Court in Albuquerque. *(Author photo)*

Because of the Albuquerque Police Department's good work, a link was established to a green van that witnesses had seen in the Corvallis area where Brooke had been kidnapped. Joel Courtney drove a green minivan on May 24, 2004. *(Photo courtesy of Albuquerque Police Department)*

After Courtney was arrested for Brooke Wilberger's kidnapping, he became a suspect in the disappearance and murder of other young women and girls in the area, including Leah Freeman, 15, of Coquille, Oregon. *(Yearbook photo)*

Twenty-two year old Katheryn Eggleston of Portland, Oregon, disappeared under mysterious circumstances on August 2, 1993. Like Brooke and Natalie Kirov, Katheryn was blond, pretty and petite.
(Yearbook photo)

Another area girl, Stephanie Condon, went missing from Myrtle Creek, Oregon, in October 1998. Detectives looked very closely at Joel Courtney to see if he had been Stephanie's abductor.
(Yearbook photo)

Farther away than any others was Kristin Smart, who disappeared near a college campus in San Luis Obispo, California. Kristin was also a pretty blonde. *(Yearbook photo)*

A billboard was put up in the area concerning Kristin's disappearance.
(Author photo)

Joel Courtney was extradited from New Mexico to Oregon in a death penalty case for the kidnapping and murder of Brooke Wilberger, even though her body had not been found. Once again, he changed his looks. *(Mug shot)*

Benton County Sheriff Diana Simpson spoke at a news conference concerning Joel Courtney's extradition. *(Photo courtesy of Benton County Sheriff's Office)*

Pretrial court hearings for Courtney took place in the ornate Benton County Courthouse in Corvallis. *(Author photo)*

Benton County District Attorney John Haroldson worked tirelessly to bring Joel Courtney to justice in the Brooke Wilberger case. *(Photo courtesy of John Haroldson)*

Defense lawyer Steven Gorham took his job seriously and fought hard for Courtney. *(Author photo)*

In a plea deal to spare his life, Courtney pleaded guilty to the kidnapping and murder of Brooke Wilberger. He then told authorities where her remains could be found. Hundreds of people attended Brooke's memorial service at this building on the OSU campus. *(Author photo)*

In September 2009, Brooke Wilberger's remains were recovered in the Oregon Coast Range near the small community of Blodgett. *(Author photo)*

CHAPTER 13

BREAKING NEWS

The media around Corvallis, Oregon, knew that something big was in the works on August 2, 2005. They had just received a notice from the Brooke Wilberger Task Force that on the next day there would be a press conference about "significant developments in the case." In fact, the task force was having the media gather at the LaSells Stewart Center on the OSU campus, which was a large auditorium. The *Gazette-Times* reported, *Lt. Noble did not give any indication what the break in the case might be.* Nonetheless, there was a great deal of anticipation about what might be revealed.

The next day at the LaSells Stewart Center, in front of a throng of reporters, Benton County DA Scott Heiser announced what so many in the area had been waiting to hear for so long. There was an arrest in Brooke's case. Not another person of interest, or even a possible suspect, but an actual arrest of an individual. And it was a name that had not been reported on before anywhere in connection to Brooke Wilberger.

DA Heiser announced that the man was thirty-nine-year-old Joel Patrick Courtney, and he was presently sitting in a jail cell in Metropolitan Detention Center in Albuquerque, New Mexico. Courtney was awaiting trial there for having kidnapped and sexually assaulted a female student in that city. Heiser said of the young woman in that case, "The credit goes to her because she didn't give up. She didn't give up on the moments and opportunities to take action."

DA Scott Heiser went on to say that a Benton County grand jury had just indicted Joel Courtney on fourteen counts of aggravated murder, two counts of aggravated kidnapping, and one count each of rape, sex abuse, and sodomy. All of these counts came in despite the fact that Brooke Wilberger's body had not been found, and Joel Courtney had not confessed to anything concerning her. Heiser told the assembled members of the press, "Under Oregon law the maximum possible penalty for aggravated murder is death."

Heiser went on to say that the break came in the case back in December 2004 when police in Albuquerque, New Mexico, conducted a background check on Courtney. It was Courtney's prior convictions in Oregon that prompted detectives of the Albuquerque Police Department to contact law enforcement in Oregon to see if they had any outstanding cases that might match Courtney's MO on Natalie Kirov's case. And, of course, the one case that popped up immediately was that of Brooke Wilberger—a blond, petite girl, about Natalie's age, abducted near a college campus during daylight hours.

Heiser noted, "The huge difference between the New Mexico case and our case is that the victim in their case managed to escape and make a report to the police." Because of Natalie's description of her assailant, Courtney was arrested and Oregon detectives tried connecting him to a green minivan. The authorities were able to talk to Courtney's in-laws, and Heiser said of them, "They've been nothing but cooperative, helpful, and forthcoming." And it was Joel Courtney's brother-in-law who placed Courtney directly with a green minivan that he drove in May 2004 in connection with his job with CBM.

Heiser didn't say much more, even though he was subjected to a barrage of questions from the gathered media. In response to the questions, Heiser replied, "I know you guys are dying to hear all the pieces of the puzzle and the entire story. But it's just not appropriate to answer at this time. As the prosecutor I play by the rules, and adhere to the Oregon State Bar rules of professional conduct. I play those rules very close to my chest."

Cammy Wilberger also made a short statement to the press. She said, "This is not over yet. To come this far, a lot of prayers have been answered. Our main goal remains the same. To find Brooke and to see that justice is served."

Scott Heiser and the other authorities may have been very tight-lipped about Joel Courtney, but already the Oregon media was ferreting out whatever it could about him. And the New Mexico media helped them in this regard. The *Albuquerque Journal* reported that Captain Henry Perea, a Bernalillo

County Metropolitan Detention Center spokesman, said that FBI agents from Oregon had shown up at the detention center and served Courtney with paperwork about the charges against him in the Brooke Wilberger case. Perea added, "A fugitive hold has been placed on Joel Courtney. Once his case is done here, he will be extradited back to Oregon."

The *Albuquerque Journal* also gave details about Natalie Kirov's kidnapping and assault. This was the first time that the Oregon media knew any details about this case and its relationship to Brooke's case. In fact, the Salem *Statesman Journal* quoted an Albuquerque PD spokeswoman who said, *"This guy was a bad dude! We found out he had prior sex offenses in other states."*

That set off a new round of Oregon media trying to find out exactly what those sex offenses had been and how many of them had been in Oregon. The Oregon media also went around the area talking to ordinary people about their thoughts on the latest developments and about the "bad dude" who was the suspected kidnapper sitting in jail in New Mexico.

Jan Mattson, of Lebanon, told a reporter, "If this man proves to be involved, I hope they can finally find Brooke and put to rest all of the concerns and heartaches that surround this." Jan's wife, Kathy, who had been out on several searches, said, "I really didn't think she was alive [when I did the searches]. But the family needs closure. I'm glad they've charged someone. It's about time."

Sue Doolen, of Corvallis, had also been on searches, and had worked with Brooke's brother at

Linus Pauling Middle School. Sue stated, "I hope they have all of the evidence they need to tie him to this." She expressed a concern that was on many people's minds, after the fact that at one time Loren Krueger, Aaron Evans, and especially Sung Koo Kim had looked good for the crime.

People in restaurants, coffee shops, and bars all over the area sat glued to the television screens inside the establishments as the news came out about Joel Courtney. Even the waiters and waitresses stopped what they were doing to watch the televisions. Waitress Katie Peterson at Squirrel's Tavern told a reporter, "This is the first I've heard they found anybody. When it first happened, I was afraid to walk around alone." Squirrel's owner Greg Little related, "I'm sure the family is glad for some type of closure." And then Greg added one fact that no one had picked up on before. He said, "Corvallis is not immune to this sort of thing. It happened back in the 1970s. Ted Bundy was here." In fact, on May 6, 1974, Ted Bundy abducted OSU student Roberta Parks and later killed her.

At a different establishment, Clodfelter's Public House, employee Grant Stocks said that he'd noticed less signs and talk about Brooke as the months after May 2004 went on. Grant said, "I don't think it was because people lost hope. It was more because you have to move on." Then he added in relation to how long the legal process with Courtney would probably take, "It's kind of disappointing when they talk about how it's going to be years before this is resolved. It's too bad we have to wait that long for everything to finally be over."

A journalist for the *Statesman Journal* asked people

around the Benton County Courthouse what the mood was like there. Employee Rod Jarvis said, "The two biggest things I've observed on this case is the unbelievable dedication that law enforcement officers had for finding this guy. And the second thing is the tremendous relief that it's over."

Even Joel Courtney's sister read a short statement in her hometown of Portland. Within the statement Dina McBride said how sorry she felt for the Wilberger family. And she added, "Because of what we know of God, we believe that justice must be served." Law enforcement authorities let it be known that Dina had been very cooperative with them about Joel.

Some of the people most affected, of course, had been female students who lived on campus at OSU, not far from where Brooke had been taken. One of these was Liz Miller, who went to school at OSU and then actually moved into the Oak Park Apartments complex during the summer of 2004. Liz said, "I had a night class and had to walk all the way across campus. You see some random guy and it's always in the back of your head. I want this (Courtney's arrest) to be an end to it all. It's scary to know, just that knot in your stomach, thinking 'what if?'"

On that theme of safety, another OSU student, Jordana Price, commented, "I know it happens a lot, especially on college campuses. You've got to be smart about it." Jordana walked with others whenever possible on campus.

Also addressing the safety issue was Melissa Moser, of the Old Mill Center for Children and Families. She said, "Parents or family members should really listen to their children and find out what their concerns are." Something like Brooke's abduction and apparent murder could be very scary for younger children. Moser related that it was okay for children to express their fears, but also to let them know that their parents or older siblings were watching out for their safety. And for teens it was important to stress that they always needed to be aware of their surroundings, especially at night. Even with those commonsense tips, Moser admitted, "Brooke's situation just didn't follow any of the rules. This was a young woman, during the morning, just out doing her job in a relatively safe neighborhood."

Liz Miller, the OSU student, with whom a reporter had spoken earlier, asked a question that was on a lot of people's minds. "How do you convict someone of murder without a body?" And then she made a statement that also was on a lot of people's minds. Of all the suspects and persons of interest who had been mentioned in the previous months, Joel Courtney's name had not been mentioned once. She wondered how long the authorities in Oregon had known about this person before they let the public know about their findings.

To that effect, law enforcement authorities, not unlike DA Heiser, were playing things close to the vest. Lieutenant Mark Cotter, of the Oregon State Police, would only say, "Since Brooke's abduction we've had our eyes open to anything that might relate to her disappearance." And Peggy Pierson, emergency services coordinator for Benton County, added, "Of course, we are disappointed that there is a charge of murder because we would have liked to have seen her returned. What we are seeing is the apparent reality that she's not coming home."

Then Pierson let it be known that the news of Brooke probably being dead came in so quickly, and unexpectedly, from law enforcement that it caught even professional search teams off guard. Pierson said she would be contacting Corvallis Mountain Rescue Unit (CMRU), Marys Peak Search and Rescue, and the Benton County Sheriff's Mounted Posse to let them know about the latest developments. Some of them were still out in the field and had not yet heard the news.

And Mike Bamberger, Benton County Emergency Services manager, let it be known that some search teams were still going to go on with their work despite the latest news. He said, "We will continue to search all credible tips that the detective task force will give us. All my team members are anxious and ready to go. We haven't been able to bring her home yet." The unspoken word was that they would probably be bringing Brooke's body or skeletal remains back home, and not a live Brooke.

Churches around the area had been very supportive of the Wilberger family, right from the beginning. At the Corvallis First Presbyterian Church, the banner about Brooke was still hanging on a wall: PRAY FOR THE SAFE RETURN OF BROOKE. Reverend John Dennis told a reporter, "I always hoped Brooke would emerge alive from this. If I'm going to be pulling those stakes up [which held the banner], it will be really personal for me."

At the Corvallis Church of the Nazarene, Reverend Russ Stiverson said that even before the news about Brooke and her abductor broke, his sermon for the upcoming Sunday was titled, "Why Is This Happening to Me?" Stiverson said he would be preaching about Joseph, whose brothers sold him into slavery. And this sermon fit in with Brooke Wilberger's parents' statement that good would come from evil. Stiverson quoted from Genesis 50:20— "As for you, you meant evil against me, but God meant it for good in order to bring about this present result."

None more than the Latter-day Saints in the area had been touched by the news. Dr. Wade Haslam, president of the Corvallis Stake, said that the acts of wicked men and women could not alter a righteous individual's quest for eternal life. Haslam related, "Based on the way Brooke conducted her life, I am confident that her course remains unaltered by her tragic abduction and apparent murder." And he reiterated Mormon belief that though a person's physical body might die, the spirit lived on and eventually the body and spirit would be reunited in heaven, where the spirit was born in the first place. Families were forever, and Brooke would be reunited with her family when they passed away.

Even reporters, who had seen many terrible things in their time, had been profoundly touched by Brooke's abduction. One of these was Theresa Hogue, who wrote for the Corvallis *Gazette-Times*. In an article she related about how angry she was after the news about Joel Courtney broke. She slipped off the pink "Find Brooke" bracelet she had been wearing for over a year, and put it away. Hogue wrote, *I got angry because it finally hit me that those secret hopes I held about Brooke had been dashed.* She also wrote about being angry because, *For every Brooke, there are hundreds of other girls and women who have disappeared, or been killed by their boyfriends, husbands, fathers or uncles.*

We can ask, "Why Brooke?" But we know, deep down, it could have been any girl, any one of us.

Perhaps in one place the capture of Brooke's suspected abductor left profound relief. That was in Sung Koo Kim's family. At last they could put to rest the idea that Kim had abducted and murdered Brooke Wilberger. Kim's mother told a reporter, "I heard the news that they caught the man. I'm very happy, but at the same time I'm sorry for the Wilberger parents. As a parent my heart goes out to the Wilberger family."

Almost as a side note, the article mentioned that Sung Koo Kim was now on his fifth attorney—the fourth one having dropped off the case. Kim's new lawyer was Clayton Lance, of Portland.

For journalists and ordinary people alike, the question was "Who is Joel Courtney?" Until now, his name had never been mentioned once in newspapers or on television in connection with Brooke Wilberger. Bit by bit, information about Courtney's past came to light, and the spokeswoman for the Albuquerque PD hit the nail on the head when she said, "He is a bad dude."

CHAPTER 14
A BAD DUDE

Joel Patrick Courtney was born in Panorama City, California, which is in the southern part of the state, not far from Los Angeles. Before long, however, the family moved to Beaverton, Oregon.

Beaverton, Oregon, named for the abundance of beaver dams in the area, was initially settled as a shipping point on the Oregon Central Railroad. By the time Joel was growing up, Beaverton was fast becoming a suburb of Portland, with a wide array of light industry, electronics companies, and research centers.

Joel was a slow learner and didn't like school. Whether it is true or not, Joel would later state that he dropped out of school by the time he was fourteen years old, in 1980. This may not have been the case, since other individuals would speak of being a classmate of Joel in high school.

Joel's sister, Dina, said that at age eleven Joel started using illegal drugs. Because of his taste for drugs and an unrestrained temper, Joel ended up in juvenile hall at age fifteen. According to Dina, Joel developed an interest in Satanism around this time as well. He definitely liked rock music that had a dark, sinister side to it.

Dina later told authorities that when Joel was fourteen years old, she awoke one night in bed to find Joel on top of her. He had his hand around her neck and he was partially undressed. He had an erection and was trying to undress her. Dina struck him on the side of the head with a clock to make him stop, preventing herself from being raped.

Corvallis PD detective Shawn Houck later spoke with one of Joel's female cousins, who was younger than Joel. Detective Houck discovered that this cousin said that Joel had sexually abused her on four different occasions when she was between the ages of twelve and seventeen. The first incident occurred when she spent the night at the Courtney home. She was twelve years old, and awoke to find Joel, then age fourteen, completely naked and straddling her body. She was wearing overalls at the time, which somehow kept him from undressing her. He might have persisted, but a family member walked down the hallway at that moment. It frightened Joel into ceasing his attack on her. Joel told her not to say anything to anyone about the incident, or "life will be bad for you!"

Joel left the bedroom and went downstairs; she soon followed. When she did, Joel told her to go back upstairs and get into bed. She wouldn't do it. She was afraid that once she did, he would follow her and complete what he had started.

A later incident probably occurred in 1983, when

Joel was seventeen years old. The cousin and several relatives were staying at their grandparents' home in Burbank, California. On at least two occasions, she woke up with Joel lying next to her. On both occasions he had an arm around her and was touching her breasts. She didn't recall him touching between her legs on those occasions. Joel once again told her, "If you tell anyone, things won't go well for you!"

The next set of incidents occurred either in 1987 or 1988, when the cousin was a junior or senior in high school. She was visiting Joel's sister, Dina, at Dina's residence. The cousin didn't know that Joel was going to be in town. She was taking a nap in one of the bedrooms, only to be awakened by Joel. He was unbuttoning her blouse, but he stopped when she woke up. After she awoke, Joel just left the room without saying a word. She didn't tell anyone because she was concerned for her safety if she did so. The cousin related one more important thing to authorities later. She said at the time she was five-three and weighed about 108 pounds. This was relatively the same height and weight as Brooke Wilberger and Natalie Kirov.

In 1985, Joel pled guilty to a first-degree sex abuse case in Washington County court, admitting that he had snorted cocaine, had drunk beer, and had forcible sexual contact with his teenaged victim. All of this would come out later in court. For something so serious, Joel got a very light sentence—ninety days of jail time and probation. But even with this light sentence, he was soon in trouble again. Joel violated probation by not checking in with his supervisor, failed to pay fines, and failed to return to a low-level work-release detention center. Eventually he was caught again with marijuana on him and was sentenced to ninety more days of jail time, and his probation period was upped to five years. Within a year Joel broke the law again, by being a minor in possession of alcohol.

Joel Courtney would just not play by the rules. In 1987 a judge issued a bench warrant for his arrest, since Joel had failed to meet with his probation officer and had engaged in employment without permission. And once again he was found to have a "controlled substance" on him. This time, however, Joel didn't serve any more jail time, but he did have his probation period extended for another three years.

One of the very few people who kept tabs on Joel Courtney during the late 1980s and 1990s was Washington County probation officer Bob Severe. Severe was able to piece together that Courtney absconded from supervision sometime in 1987 and went up to Alaska to work on a fishing boat. Courtney worked the fishing season there, and then spent the off-season in Mexico. This pattern went on for several years. Just what Joel was up to in the realm of criminal activity in these years, not even Severe knew. There would be a lot of speculation on law enforcement's part in the years to come.

Joel Courtney might have kept flying under the radar if he hadn't returned to Washington County in 1991. As Severe recalled, "Someone who knew he was supposed to be on probation called the department." Joel was arrested once again and went before a judge. Yet, once again, Joel didn't receive any more jail time. Severe related, "In those days the judge would oftentimes put them back on probation

if they didn't get into trouble while they were gone."
If Joel had been in trouble, either in Alaska or in
Mexico, there was no documentation concerning
that. Courtney received three more years of probation from the judge.

Severe noted, "We didn't have any problems with
him after he came back." By 1994, Courtney had
done his three years of probation time without any
further problems, and he was now free and clear. In
that era he didn't have to register as a sex offender.
And then he really fell off the radar, as far as the authorities were concerned.

Joel eventually seemed to settle down a bit. He
married a young woman named Rosy, and they had
three children. Even then, he had a restless streak,
and was often on the move to various jobs, especially
to Florida. It's not apparent now if Joel always took
his family with him. What is known is that Joel and
his family eventually moved to a nice neighborhood
of Rio Rancho in New Mexico. It was an area of well-
kept middle-class homes northwest of Albuquerque,
across the Rio Grande River. The Sandia Mountains
rose majestically to the east, and the high desert to
the west was a series of mesas and valleys, all the way
to the fabled "lost city" of Chaco Canyon.

The Courtneys' neighbors liked Rosy, and noted
how she kept the house and yard looking neat. Patsy
Atkin later told a reporter for the *Oregonian,* "Rosy is
a good person. She works hard and the kids are
really nice. Very mannerly. My granddaughter plays
with the little girl." No one had anything good to say
about Joel, however. In fact, they had almost nothing to say about him at all. He never seemed to be
out in the yard helping Rosy in the yard work. He

didn't interact with other neighbors. He was like a ghost in his own neighborhood.

It's not quite clear why Joel, Rosy, and the kids moved in with Rosy's sister Susanna and brother-in-law Jesus Ordaz's residence back in the Portland area in the spring of 2004. Perhaps it was because Joel was out of work and needed a job. Jesus Ordaz was a hard worker and was well liked at CBM. It was on Ordaz's recommendation that Joel was hired for CBM. And it was the hiring of Joel—and his use of a green Dodge minivan—that set in motion all of the troubles of May 2004.

Once Joel was arrested for a DUI in Lincoln County, Oregon, it would set him on the path for a journey directly through Corvallis on the morning of May 24, 2004, and a fateful meeting with Brooke Wilberger.

CHAPTER 15

MAY MADNESS

In April 2004, Joel, Rosy, and the kids were living with Susanna and Jesus Ordaz. Joel went on a job to Montana and Idaho, and that seemed to work out okay. But in early May, Joel was speeding in La Grande, Oregon, and got a ticket. Sometime after that, he angered his supervisor by not phoning in as required and missed several appointments where he was supposed to work. Some of those businesses complained to Joel's supervisor.

On Sunday, May 23, 2004, a friend of Jesus Ordaz invited him and his family to a First Communion party after church. Jesus, his wife and kids, Rosy and her children, went to the party, but Joel was on a job when the party first started. Joel eventually showed up there at around 6:00 P.M. As Jesus recalled later, "We stayed there at the party pretty late. There was food and drinks. Me and Joel drank beer and tequila. And if you know a Mexican party, well, there is quite a bit of drinking going on. People started going back and forth to a certain room. I think maybe drugs were being used in there. Like cocaine. I saw Joel go in there more than once.

"I don't know how many drinks I had or Joel did. Around eleven, my wife and Joel's wife wanted to leave. My wife asked if I wanted to stay, and I said yes. And Joel wanted to stay, too. So we stayed on after my family and Joel's wife left. The drinking continued after they left.

"Joel and I didn't leave the party until six o'clock the next morning. We got home and Joel was pretty drunk at the time. When we got to the house, my wife was kind of mad, because we had stayed so long. When we got home, Joel told me he had to be in Lincoln County at court that morning, so he asked if he could use the phone to say he was going to be late. And he did use the phone."

Joel called Lincoln County court several times that morning of May 24, using Jesus Ordaz's phone. Joel called at seven-nineteen and again at seven twenty-one. Then he called at seven twenty-two and at seven twenty-seven. It's not apparent why all the phone calls, unless other people were calling into the court as well, and Joel was only able to leave his message on the machine at 7:27 A.M. But later phone records would prove he had called Lincoln County court four times.

Jesus Ordaz recalled, "Joel left the house right after the phone calls. He was driving the green van and it was clean on the outside at the time. He was wearing the same clothes he had worn at the party and a baseball cap. And he usually wore dark sunglasses when he drove, if it was sunny.

"Joel didn't come back to the house all of May

twenty-fourth. He didn't come back when I was home on May twenty-fifth. I worked from five-thirty P.M. until two A.M. then. But I remember my wife called me about eight P.M. at work, and told me that Joel had just come home.

"When I got home at two A.M. on May twenty-sixth, the van Joel had driven was outside. It was very dirty all over. Like when you drive a van up into the mountains. It was muddy. I saw the van and I knew the supervisors didn't like seeing it like that. So I took it to work the next day, where there was good water pressure, and washed it there.

"Joel just stayed in his room when he got back. He didn't come out for some time. I didn't see Joel at all on May twenty-sixth. Sometime later, maybe May twenty-seventh, my wife called and said Joel had to go and see a doctor."

This whole doctor scenario was very interesting, in light of what was later learned about Joel Courtney and Brooke Wilberger. Dina McBride recalled in more detail about her brother's visit to the doctor. Dina said, "I was living at my grandmother's house with my husband and children. I remember the date because I was coordinating a large children's event at church. On that date Joel came over [to] my grandmother's house a little before noon. I was so concerned about the way that Joel was acting that I actually e-mailed my husband (who was at work). I asked my husband to pray for Joel.

"The house was pretty quiet that day, and I had just finished getting Grandma lunch. She hadn't been feeling very well, and she lay down. When Joel came in at about eleven forty-five A.M., he wasn't exactly agitated, but he was on edge. He walked through the door and said, 'You won't believe where I've been for the last three days.' His conversation was very animated.

"I said, 'Oh, what went on?' And he said, 'I was kidnapped for three days and there were some guys with guns and knives. There was a kind of party at first, and people were there, and then they weren't. I was hiding in the bushes, and it rained for part of the time, and I was naked part of the time. I was freezing and hungry, and I haven't had anything to eat.'

"It was a lot of information coming in a fairly disjointed manner. He mentioned there was a girl there with him, but there wasn't a lot of description about her. She was just in the proximity of where he said he was located. He didn't give any specifics about if she was short or tall, fat or thin. There was a mention that she was blond. Then Joel mentioned about guns and knives being there. Someone had an automatic firearm, and it was frightening. And he said, 'There was blood on the girl, and she died.'"

Dina didn't know what to make of this wild story. She knew that Joel often exaggerated about things, and she had no idea how much of this story was true.

According to Carol Courtney, Joel's mother, he was stressed out about something that had just occurred. He had to seek medical attention for this on May 26, 2004, and went to the emergency room of the Oregon Health and Science University hospital in Portland, complaining of chest pains. He had extremely high blood pressure. An EKG was taken and a chest X-ray as well. It was determined that Joel had stroke-level blood pressure. Joel was given some medication for his problems and told to get some rest.

In light of the fact that Joel was only thirty-nine years old then, Detective Houck later asked Dr. John Cochran, a forensic psychologist with the FBI Behavioral Science Unit (BSU), about this. Dr. Cochran told him that it was a highly relevant event. Houck noted, "Dr. Cochran specifically said that even stone-cold rapists experience some guilt about what they've done. When Courtney had an acute bout of high blood pressure after being gone for two days, his need for medical assistance is consistent with his need to deal with the guilt he was feeling as a result of his involvement with Brooke Wilberger's disappearance."

In early June 2004, days after Brooke Wilberger went missing, Jesus Ordaz went on vacation to California and had Joel take him to the airport. Ordaz had no idea that there was any connection between Joel and a missing teenager in Corvallis. Ordaz related, "When I came back on June fifth, I found out that Rosy and the kids had gone back to New Mexico, and now Joel was gone. He was supposed to have been at work when I was in California. They kept calling him and calling him, and he didn't answer. He just disappeared. And then one day he called me from New Mexico. He had taken the green van there. So it was me who went out to New Mexico to get it and bring it back to the company. I flew out to New Mexico and went to Rosy's house. The green van was there, but I didn't even see Joel. I got the van and drove it back to Portland." Ordaz had no idea that the 1997 Dodge minivan had been part of an abduction and crime scene, and neither did CBM. Ordaz kept on using that van for months to come.

Once he was back in New Mexico, Joel may have wanted to lay low, and the home in the small town of Rio Rancho seemed like a good place to do so. Once again he was drinking too much and may have been using crack cocaine. Instead of laying low, Joel was soon in trouble with the law in New Mexico. On June 18, 2004, Joel got into a heated altercation with Rosy.

Rosy wasn't taking it this time. She filed a "Petition for Order of Protection from Domestic Abuse" for herself and her three children, aged twelve, six, and four. In the portion of the form entitled "Physical Abuse," Rosy wrote, *He pushed me and spoke to my face very close like he was going to harm me. He was very aggressive. At another time he intended to kill me by choking me very hard and my eldest son was present.*

On a portion entitled, "Threats which caused fear that you or any household member would be injured," Rosy wrote, *Today he said he is going to kill me and that he will go to my sisters' houses to kill them too.*

As far as other abuse went, Rosy related, *He used my credit cards and got me into debt for over eighty thousand dollars.*

On the portion "Were weapons used during the abuse?" she wrote no. But for the section "Has there been prior domestic abuse?" she wrote yes. Rosy asked that the request order state that *the respondent (Joel) not contact me, not abuse me and that the respondent stay away from my residence.* She also checked the box "That I be given temporary custody of the children listed in this petition, but that the respondent shall have contact with the children with supervision."

Rosy also checked the portion "Relief is necessary to resolve this domestic abuse problem with child care."

Rosy noted that Joel was in jail at the time she wrote out the document and she checked the portion "I have not told respondent that I am filing a petition to ask the court for an order of protection because I believe irreparable harm would result if I told respondent before coming to court."

Because of the restraining order, Joel could not write, phone, or talk to Rosy. He could not go within one hundred yards of Rosy's home or workplace; and if at a public place, such as a store, he could not go within one hundred yards of Rosy there, either. He was not to cause any physical damage to her property; and for the time being, he could not be around his children as well. A document noted: *If the respondent violates any part of this order, the respondent may be charged with a crime, arrested and held in contempt of court. A law enforcement officer shall use any lawful means to enforce this order.*

On June 25, 2004, both Joel and Rosy had to show up at the Thirteenth Judicial District Court. Interestingly, Joel wrote down an address in Beaverton, Oregon, as his home mailing address, even though he was now living in New Mexico. The judge ordered Joel to attend counseling in the area about his anger issues. There was also a stipulation that he had to "address his problems with drugs and alcohol." Rosy must have mentioned these things in court. All of the elements of the restraining order were to be in effect until Christmas Day, 2004. Joel could not even go to his home in Rio Rancho to get his personal items. A deputy sheriff would do that for him. Joel could only have contact with his children at a supervised monthly meeting at a Family Services center.

It was also noted that when Joel obtained a valid New Mexico driver's license, he would be able to use the family's 1997 Honda Civic. A Honda Civic that just happened to be red in color with a gray interior and a stuffed-animal monkey adhered to one window. A red Honda Civic that would play such a vital role only five months later with Natalie Kirov.

Ten days after the restraining order, Rosy Courtney apparently had a change of heart. She filled out an "Application to Modify or Terminate" the "Domestic Abuse Protection Order." Like many women who have been abused, Rosy was swayed by the words of the abuser that he would change his behavior. On this document dated June 28, 2004, Rosy checked the box to terminate the protection order because "My husband promised that he is going to try to control his anger." Apparently on the same day, both Joel and Rosy signed a document that was an "Order of Dismissal." It was noted that the petitioner Rosy appeared at a hearing in the Thirteenth Judicial District Court in Sandoval County, New Mexico, and asked that the original protection order be dismissed. It was done so, and the *cause of the action was dismissed without prejudice.*

So Joel Courtney had been able to talk his way out of another damaging situation. Just how long he stayed with Rosy and the children at the home in Rio Rancho didn't come out in later documents. What is certain is that sometime between June 28, 2004, and November 29, 2004, Joel was living outside the home once again. His residence seemed to have been not far from where Natalie Kirov was abducted off the corner of Harvard and Garfield in Albuquerque, south of the University of New Mexico. And, of course, by that time, Joel was heavily into smoking crack cocaine.

Everything was like a snowball heading down a very steep hill from June 2004 onward. Joel, who could not control his behavior, was on a crash course with Natalie Kirov, who would be the one person who would set a chain of events in motion that would lead directly back to the abduction and murder of Brooke Wilberger in Oregon. Joel didn't know it yet, but he was on a one-way track to the worst problem in his life. In fact, his actions were about to put his very life at risk of a death penalty as all the facts came out into the open.

Chapter 16
Serious Charges

When Officer Taylor detained a man named "Joel" in front of a red Honda Civic in Albuquerque, New Mexico, on the evening of November 29, 2004, he had no idea how far all of this was going to lead. Because this detained individual's weight and height matched the description given by Natalie Kirov, and the Honda certainly matched the description she had given, Joel was taken down to the police substation by Officer Taylor.

Natalie Kirov had been transported to a hospital and attended to, after she came into contact with police. After that was finished, Natalie was driven to the substation, where Joel was being detained. While Joel sat in a room, being interviewed, Natalie looked in through a one-way glass window. As soon as she did, she told the officer standing next to her, "That's the man who attacked me!"

Joel Courtney was arrested at the substation and was soon on his way to the Metropolitan Detention

Center in Albuquerque. He had his mug shot taken and was listed as living on Apple Court in Rio Rancho. He was noted as being thirty-nine years old, hair shaved almost bald by that point, a goatee, blue eyes, and weighing 185 pounds. Joel's place of birth was listed as Panorama City, California. Interestingly, in case of emergency, Joel gave Rosy's phone number.

His long road through various jails was just now beginning. And so was the paperwork on Joel Patrick Courtney. Instead of going the usual route of a preliminary hearing on the case, the Bernalillo County district attorney sought a grand jury indictment against Joel. This, in essence, meant that all of the proceedings would be behind closed doors, with no press being allowed in the courtroom. It also meant that Joel's defense attorney could not question witnesses.

Of course, the main witness before the grand jurors was Natalie Kirov herself. In a shaky voice, and often in tears, she recounted her November 29, 2004, evening of terror. DDA David Waymire asked her very pointed questions; and in exacting detail Natalie recounted her harrowing experience after being kidnapped at knifepoint. Waymire agreed with Natalie that she was lucky to be alive.

Also testifying was Detective John Romero. He recounted APD's involvement with the incident, and the arrest of Joel Courtney, a man whose description and vehicle matched that of what Natalie Kirov had seen. Natalie's detailed description of the vehicle was particularly potent—she spoke of its interior and exterior color and the stuffed animal inside the vehicle.

After listening to these witnesses, the grand jurors

agreed with the district attorney that Joel Courtney should stand trial. He was specifically charged with "Count One—Criminal Sexual Penetration—Personal Injury." *That on or about the 29th day of November 2004, in Bernalillo County, New Mexico, the above-named defendant caused Natalie Kirov to engage in fellatio, by the use of force or coercion, resulting in personal injury to Natalie Kirov.* There was also an alternative to Count One, which was much the same, except it added the word "kidnapping" in the text. Another alternative to Count One added the word "knife" in its text.

Count Two dealt with the *insertion of Joel Courtney's finger into Natalie Kirov's vagina.* There were two alternatives to this text, and Count Three dealt with *Joel Courtney inserting his finger into the anus of Natalie Kirov.*

Count Four stated: *That on or about the 29th day of November, 2004, in Bernalillo County, New Mexico, the above-named defendant took and/or restrained and/or confined and/or transported Natalie Kirov by force, intimidation or deception, intending to inflict death, physical injury or commit a sexual offense against Natalie Kirov.*

The news, at least on Natalie Kirov's abduction and rape, started making its way into newspapers and on television in Albuquerque, New Mexico. And APD took one crucial step beyond what many police departments will do. They noted that Joel Courtney had an arrest record in Oregon, and APD asked various law enforcement departments in Oregon if they had had a similar situation to that of Natalie Kirov's abduction and rape. Of course, Corvallis, Oregon, had in the case of Brooke Wilberger. Brooke's task force was very interested in what APD had to say about Joel Courtney.

The news media had no idea what was transpiring in early December 2004 between Oregon law enforcement and New Mexico law enforcement. But already agencies were starting to construct a scenario of what might have happened in the Corvallis area in May 2004. And the trail led right through Joel Courtney's failure to appear in court at Lincoln County on the morning of May 24, 2004. It was noted that Corvallis was right on the way of the most usual route taken by someone going from the Portland area to Newport, Oregon. In time the media was going to have in exacting detail what was occurring between the various law enforcement agencies on Brooke's case.

As serious as the charges were against Joel in New Mexico, they were nothing compared to what was now brewing back in Oregon. Soon FBI agent Joseph Boyer filled out a fugitive complaint against Courtney. In part it stated that the state of Oregon sought to extradite Joel from New Mexico to Oregon for *aggravated murder, kidnapping and rape.* This was a very aggressive stance in light of the fact that Brooke Wilberger's body had never been found. FBI agent Boyer noted on the form: *The reason I believe that the defendant is the person identified in the fugitive warrant is: the physical description of the defendant, a copy of an NCIC message is attached.* This dealt with all the possible links between Joel and Brooke Wilberger in Corvallis, Oregon.

* * *

It wasn't going to be an easy road from New Mexico to Oregon, however. In a document of August 4, 2005, Metropolitan Court Division judge Sharon Walton in New Mexico let it be known, *The Court finds that the defendant will not waive extradition and orders this case transferred to District Court for further proceedings.* Through his lawyer, James "Jim" Loonam, Joel Courtney was going to fight extradition, every step of the way.

In fact, Joel took this intransigence to extremes. Bernalillo County DDA Melanie Harper let it be known, "Yesterday, Courtney was contesting identity, saying that it wasn't really him. He was refusing to leave his cell." This was only the beginning of a pattern of disruption and outlandish behavior that would mark Joel's relationship with the court system, especially when it came to Brooke's case.

And there was still the whole matter of Natalie Kirov's case in New Mexico before Joel would ever set foot in an Oregon courtroom. Bernalillo County DDA Theresa Whatley told reporters that it would take a couple of months of discovery before they even got to pretrial hearings on Natalie's case.

Extradition of a person from one state to another goes clear back to the early days of the federal government and laws in the United States. In some ways it is almost a "gentleman's agreement" between one governor to another. In September 2005, Governor Ted Kulongoski, of Oregon, sent an extradition warrant to Governor Bill Richardson, of New Mexico, asking that Joel Courtney be brought back to Oregon to stand trial for the kidnapping, rape, and murder of Brooke Wilberger. Benton County DA Scott Heiser noted that Courtney was being held on charges in New Mexico, and it was unlikely that Governor Richardson would sign the extradition order until after the Natalie Kirov trial. That wasn't expected to take place until the spring of 2006.

Through his lawyer, Joel Courtney was compiling a witness list for the defense on the Natalie Kirov case. Despite Kirov, obviously, being an eyewitness to the attack by the nature of her being the surviving victim, Joel was nonetheless going to try and beat the charges against him.

Just how far Joel Courtney was willing to go in fighting the charges can be seen by a document he presented to the court from jail. In essence, it stated he was not being allowed to help in his own case. Joel wrote, *I have had one opportunity to visit the law library. I believe this to be a violation of my 5th Amendment Right to due process. I feel as though I have purposely been deprived of the chance to assist in my own defense, educate myself in the legal aspects of my case, and reserve my right and option to defend myself pro-se.*

The last sentence indicated that Joel was thinking about being his own defense lawyer, with the assistance of counsel. And Joel was asking for daily access to the law library at the jail. If he did decide to be his own lawyer, it was going to be a very bumpy road ahead at court. There's a reason attorneys attend law school. The admission of evidence and testimony at trial have a very exact and procedural dynamic, and it is the most difficult thing for non-attorneys to grasp and be able to do themselves.

CHAPTER 17
THE OTHER GIRLS

If the Corvallis Police Department and Benton County District Attorney's Office weren't giving the media much new information about Joel Courtney, the news reporters had elsewhere to turn. And one of their most intriguing in this regard was the FBI's Violent Criminal Apprehension Program (ViCAP) website. A description was given about Joel Courtney and right up front the FBI admitted that they were conducting an extensive investigation on Courtney. The FBI stated:

> It is believed that he is a serial sex offender and killer. The FBI has identified three additional victims that Courtney may have sexually assaulted and killed within Oregon. He is inclined to abduct white females, fifteen to 25 years of age, with blonde hair and blue eyes, in an outside setting.

The FBI noted that Joel Courtney had grown up

in the Portland area, and had moved around the country throughout his adult life:

> There is a high possibility that he has assaulted other victims in other areas—Albuquerque, New Mexico (7/1994–8/1994, 8/1997, and 11/2000). Anchorage, Alaska (1989–1992), Beaverton, Oregon (1986–1992), Bernallilo, New Mexico (5/1995–8/1997). Cape Canaveral, Florida (5/2001–3/2003), Cocoa Beach, Florida (5/2001–9/2002), Grants, New Mexico (9/1995), Pensacola, Florida (5/2001), Portland, Oregon (1980–1989, 1993 and 2004), and Rio Rancho, New Mexico (6/1996–2004).

It was also noted that Courtney had traveled through Mexico via Arizona.

There was an alert to law enforcement agencies across America from the FBI in which they stated:

> Law enforcement agencies should bring this information to the attention of all homicide, sex offender and cold case units. Anyone having cases similar to the described modus operandi with the suspect's DNA evidence should contact Crime Analyst Vicki McRoberts, Corvallis Oregon.

Even though the FBI didn't post what other murders of young women might have been committed by Joel Courtney in Oregon, the news media soon had leads of their own on who those victims might be. And the first one on the list was Katheryn Scott Eggleston, of Portland, Oregon. She had been born on May 4, 1971, and by 1993, Katheryn was a five-four, 125-pound, blue-eyed blonde. She was relatively petite and pretty—just like Brooke Wilberger.

Katheryn went by the nickname of Katie and was the daughter of Paul and Heather Eggleston. Paul was a former Seattle high-school teacher and later a superintendent of schools in Central Oregon. And Heather, just like Brooke Wilberger's mom, was a teacher of young children. They all lived a quiet, comfortable life on the edge of Redmond in Central Oregon. Katie was very athletic and was on the high-school swim team.

In college Katie was popular and a good student. Her roommate, Treasure Lewis, later said of Katie, "She was very outgoing, very friendly, someone that people were drawn to. She was always joking and wanting to go do things." Katie let her parents know that she was careful about her surroundings and took self-defense classes. She stayed out of bad areas and always carried a whistle with her when she was alone.

Katie was an OSU graduate, and was temporarily staying with her sister in Gresham near Portland. In early August 1993, Katie returned from a trip to Central Oregon, where she had visited her boyfriend for the weekend. On August 2, 1993, Katie left her office at Allnet Communication Services in Lake Oswego, Oregon, where she sold long-distance services. She made her way to Portland, where it was her first day on the job alone. Even though it was a warm day, she wore a purple blazer, white blouse, black skirt, and heels.

That morning she attended a business meeting about making sales calls and then went to businesses on NE Whitaker Way in Portland. She stopped at a bank, at a gasoline station, and then at a Burger King restaurant, near the Lloyd Center in Portland.

That afternoon Katie made calls at the Port of Portland Building on Multnomah Street. Witnesses later said Katie had a worried look on her face while she was there. At 2:15 P.M., a man to whom Katie had just made a sale, saw her get off the building's elevator with a man who wore a blue blazer. The witness recalled the man as having dark hair and a dark complexion. And from that moment forward, no one ever saw Katie Eggleston again.

Around 5:00 P.M., Katie's silver/gray Volkswagen Golf was spotted in the Port of Portland parking lot by a person who would later be a witness. At some point the car was driven away. Katie had been scheduled to meet with her supervisor at 5:00 P.M. at the Lake Oswego office. She never made it to that appointment.

When Katie didn't show up back at her sister Janet's residence, Janet was initially irritated, then alarmed. All through Monday, there was no word from Katie. By Tuesday, August 3, Janet called her father about the situation, and he and a friend started on their way from Redmond, in Central Oregon, to the Portland area.

Meanwhile, a security guard at a parking lot in an industrial complex on Northeast Airport Way in Portland discovered Katie's Volkswagen Golf, which had been parked there into the early hours of the morning. This was about nine miles from the Port of Portland Building. Katie's car had its windows rolled down; the doors were unlocked and the keys were still in the ignition. Her purse and its contents were on the front seat and her workout clothes on the backseat. Katie's Allnet binder was missing, however.

Almost from day one, Paul Eggleston kept a log on what was transpiring. On August 5, he noted that he and his wife were worried that Katie might be held hostage in one of the numerous warehouses in the area. Adding to Paul's worries was the fact that Katie's boyfriend joined them in the search, and he displayed "exceptionally strange behavior," according to Paul. Paul already knew that Katie planned to break up with her boyfriend, and apparently she had told him so over the past weekend. The boyfriend related that he had "wigged out" when he got the news of the breakup. Paul noted in his log, *This made him suspect number one.*

The boyfriend as suspect lasted only one day. Portland police detectives checked him out and discovered that the boyfriend had been in Central Oregon all day on August 2. Not helping matters, the lead detective on Katie's case, Joe Goodale, told Paul that his bureau was "desperately overworked" right then. They'd had a homicide come in on August 4, August 5, and August 7.

By August 7, scent-trained dogs were being used to try and pick up a trail of Katie from her car to the surrounding area. The dogs could find no trace of Katie being dragged away from her car or just walking away. It appeared more likely that she had gotten into or been forced into another vehicle and driven away.

Then on August 12, the case started going off track, as far as the Egglestons were concerned. Detective Wagner, one of the investigators, asked Paul why he hadn't told them everything about the family's dynamics. Paul asked what she was talking about, and she said that they'd discovered that daughter Janet's ex-husband was facing trial on tax evasion. Paul was floored and said that had nothing to do with Katie's present circumstances. In return, Detective Wagner told him, "You mean to tell me you don't see the connection between a trial for a felony and a key witness disappearing!" And then Detective Wagner implied that the Egglestons were hiding Katie somewhere so that she could not testify. Wagner point-blank asked Paul, "Do you know where Katie is?"

"No!" he replied.

"Would you be willing to take a lie detector test?"

"Yes!" he responded with anger.

Almost immediately Paul sent two letters to Detective Wagner. In the first he told her how distressing it was to think that somehow his former son-in-law was the reason that Katie had disappeared. There was a federal tax case that involved that son-in-law and Janet for failing to report $190,000 in business income, and Paul admitted that Katie was to be a witness in the case. But her contribution was going to be minimal, at best. And then Paul related that Katie was barely thinking about the impending trial at all, but was excited about her new job with Allnet.

In the second letter Paul's anger showed even more as he blasted Wagner for thinking that for some reason he and his wife would hide Katie and ruin their reputation for a son-in-law they had not seen or spoken with in years. A few days later, Paul passed the polygraph test, exonerating him of having any knowledge of Katie's disappearance.

After the test Paul still had to deal with Detective

Wagner. He asked her if she had contacted John
Davis, the man who had seen Katie's car on Multnomah Street around 5:00 P.M. She said she didn't
recognize the name. Paul theorized that Katie would
not have driven her car there when she had a five
o'clock appointment with her supervisor in Lake
Oswego. He mused that someone else must have
driven Katie's car to the place where it was abandoned, for whatever reason.

And then Detective Wagner told Paul that there
were no leads on the case, and that the main theory
now was that Katie had disappeared of her own will.
Fed up with the Portland detectives, the Egglestons
used money they had been receiving in donations to
hire a retired OSP detective. This detective did develop a lead about a security guard who had keys to
the Port of Portland Building. There was also an
anonymous phone call that came in from a man who
said that he had killed Katie two weeks after abducting her.

Then on October 12, 1993, the same day that
Janet was sentenced to home detention and probation on the tax case, Detective Wagner told the
media that they still believed that Katie's disappearance was of her own volition so as not to testify in the
case. They noted no signs of struggle near or in her
car, as well as Katie's missing passport. The Egglestons were outraged, and Paul told the media that
not once had the detectives ever searched Katie's
room. If they had done so, they would have discovered that her clothes, makeup, prescriptions, and
suitcases were all still there.

As far as the passport was concerned, Katie's mom
recalled that Katie had asked for a passport on July

18, 1993, as proof of citizenship for her new job at Allnet. Heather Eggleston surmised that the passport might have ended up in Katie's Allnet binder, which was not found in her car. And there was also proof that Katie's passport had not been used to get her out of the country in 1993 or 1994.

The case lay fairly dormant until May 4, 2001, on Katie's thirtieth birthday. The Egglestons had recently run an ad in the *Oregonian* with a short synopsis of the case and a phone number to call. They also wrote, *Katie, your family and friends are waiting to hear from someone who can tell them what happened to you on August 2, 1993.*

Then suddenly Joel Courtney appeared on the radar because of his abduction of Natalie Kirov, and alleged abduction and murder of Brooke Wilberger. There had been some inner demon that made Joel talk to his sister about being kidnapped himself and the death of a blond girl. It made some in law enforcement wonder if Joel had been the anonymous phone caller to the Egglestons. Joel obviously had high stress levels after the abduction of Brooke Wilberger, and a certain amount of guilt in concocting the story of his own abduction.

An FBI agent contacted the Egglestons and actually drove all the way out to Redmond from Portland to talk to them about Joel Courtney. Paul later said, "I was surprised he drove all the way out here to do that." The agent told them that Katie was of the same general type of young woman that Joel liked. He also said that Joel was in the Portland area at the time of Katie's disappearance.

Paul gave the agent seven loose-leaf binders that he had been keeping as a log on the case since it had started. The FBI agent also took samples of Paul and Heather's DNA. A short time later, Portland PD sergeant Wayne Svilar, who was head of the Cold Case Unit, also contacted the Egglestons. Svilar told them that Courtney's possible connection to their daughter was under review by his unit. This was the first time in several years that anything tangible had surfaced about the disappearance of Katie Eggleston. And to the Egglestons' relief, the matter was being looked at as if Katie had met with foul play, and had not just vanished on her own accord.

The second case that caught law enforcement's attention about Joel Courtney and a blond young woman in Oregon was that of Stephanie Elizabeth Condon. Stephanie was fourteen years old in 1998 and lived in Myrtle Creek, Oregon, about 120 miles south of Corvallis on I-5. She was five-two, weighed 120 pounds, and had blue eyes and blond hair.

On October 30, 1998, Stephanie was babysitting a relative's child in Myrtle Creek. She was in the residence and then just disappeared. There were no signs of struggle or forced entry into the residence. None of the children whom Stephanie was babysitting were harmed or turned up missing. Stephanie was last seen wearing two-piece Winnie the Pooh pajamas.

When Stephanie's cousin came home at 1:30 A.M., she found the door locked, the children asleep, and the house undisturbed. Stephanie's shoes and backpack were still in the mobile home.

All of this left many unanswered questions: Had she answered the doorbell and been kidnapped? Had she simply walked away for some reason? But then why leave without shoes in the middle of the night? And why leave her backpack in the mobile home?

Investigator Joe Perkins told reporters, "We're interested in a blanket, described as a comforter." The implication was that it was now missing from the mobile home. Many wondered if Stephanie had been rolled up or draped in the comforter while being spirited out of the residence. She had obviously not been seen by anyone after going into the residence on her babysitting job.

The FBI offered a $10,000 reward for information about Stephanie, and tips and leads came in from all directions. Not only that, but just as in Brooke Wilberger's case, psychics and self-styled psychics were soon weighing in on the disappearance of Stephanie Condon. Out on the island of Hawaii, an organization called the Hawaii Remote Viewers' Guild did what they called a "remote view" of the incident. They noted that it was done in double blind conditions, wherein the viewers, monitor, and analyst did not know who the target was. (The target was Stephanie Condon.) In fact, the target was only given code letters to them as CGAN-NSBV. None of the viewers had ever been to, or even heard of, Myrtle Creek, Oregon.

A person identified as "Rose" analyzed what the viewers "saw" and made a report that the target was deceased and was probably killed by a bearded man. Her body was buried in a remote location, with heavy vegetation, in the Northwest United States. All of this was fairly accurate, given the fact that the "viewers" had no idea who or where their target was. The target could have just as well been a person in other regions of the United States or even in Europe or in Asia.

Other psychics from around America jumped in on the disappearance of Stephanie Condon. One person said that Stephanie had been murdered on the night of her abduction and that she was buried approximately two thousand meters from the FM radio station transmitter in Tri City, Oregon.

And just as things had often taken a twisting and erratic course with Brooke Wilberger, such as with Sung Koo Kim, they now did so with Stephanie Condon. Television station KOIN reported in 2003 that there were "new investigators on the scene of an old crime, looking for evidence they hope will solve the case of missing fourteen-year-old Stephanie Condon." KOIN noted there was a team from the United Kingdom that was highly trained in finding missing people. Pam Frank, of the Douglas County Sheriff's Office (DCSO), stated, "These people from the UK—this is their job. They have great success. They do searches—not once in awhile when a child comes up missing, but it is something they do every day."

The organization was known as the National Crime and Operations Faculty. To help defray the costs of bringing the UK team over to Oregon, the Ford Family Foundation had picked up part of the cost, and the Mercy Foundation also helped. The local Seven Feathers Hotel and Casino in Canyonville provided free hotel accommodations for the UK team members.

KOIN also reported that a Black Hawk helicopter would be flying overhead in the area to be searched, and the FBI, Douglas County Sheriff's Office, Air

National Guard, and University of Oregon would be involved in the search.

The Black Hawk helicopter did fly over an area near the small town of Riddle as the searchers fanned out in the area. Douglas County detective Joe Perkins said, "I had Mrs. Condon down here. She was able to see what was going on and meet with the National Center for Missing and Exploited Children. So for her, I think it's reassurance that this case is ongoing and we haven't quit."

The UK crew also showed the media just how they went about searching an area. On a patch of ground near Lawson Bar Road in Myrtle Creek, work crew inmates cleared weeds and brambles from a patch of ground near the South Umpqua River. Lead investigator Detective Perkins said, "We needed to take the brush back five years."

Once the brush had been cleared, a ground-penetrating radar device was used, which gave a rough picture of what was underground. The team was looking for soil disturbance and depressions in the ground, where a body might be buried. Anomalies in the soil were noted and stored on a computer so that forensic experts could return later to excavate the most promising locations.

The searchers went to a "hot spot" they had developed near Riddle, Oregon, not far from where Stephanie had disappeared. Brush was cleared from the area so that ground-penetrating radar could be used there. British officer Mark Harrison related, "The speed at which the beam bounces back will actually tell us whether there are human remains there, or whether it's just a rock." Harrison also related that they used special scent-trained dogs in trying to find remains. The oldest case they had ever cracked had gone unsolved for twenty-three years until the team was able to solve it.

And then, as had happened so often in the Brooke Wilberger case, the Stephanie Condon case took a very strange turn. An article on a UK website Bedford Today announced on June 27, 2003, BODY FOUND: STEPHANIE CONDON. The article reported that a Bedfordshire resident, Mark Harrison, had found the remains of Stephanie. The article related that Sergeant Mark Harrison had found the missing girl's remains wrapped in a bedcover. It even reported Harrison as saying, "I am delighted I was able to help in this case, in particular for Stephanie's family, so they can come to terms with what happened to their daughter."

The article went on to relate that the suspect was believed to have been looking for someone else, but instead found Stephanie, and abducted her in a drunken rage. Then he took Stephanie to his residence at gunpoint, raped her there, shot her, and dumped her body in the woods. Harrison went on to say, "We were met with open arms (in Oregon) and people are eager to learn the new techniques. We had everything we could possibly ask for to do a job [that] until then had seemed impossible."

All of this was great news, except for one thing— it wasn't true. In fact, it was all an elaborate hoax. Even KOIN television had been fooled by the posting on the Bedford Today website, and ran a story that Stephanie Condon's body had been found.

Within a short period of time, however, the DCSO said that Stephanie Condon's body had not been found; there was no suspect in custody; the case was not solved. The DCSO detectives weren't even sure where the story on the website had originated, or why someone would want to pull off such a prank.

Two more years went by; then suddenly Joel Courtney's name came to light in relation to Natalie Kirov, Brooke Wilberger, and Katie Eggleston. Now the FBI was taking a hard look at Courtney in connection with the disappearance of Stephanie Condon.

A third disappearance of an Oregon girl happened in one more area that Joel Courtney had been known to travel. It occurred in Coos County on the Oregon coast. Fifteen-year-old blond Leah Freeman was dropped off at a friend's house in the small town of Coquille by her boyfriend on the afternoon of June 28, 2000. He was to pick her up at around nine o'clock; but for some unknown reason, Leah started for home on foot earlier than that time. Then she simply disappeared.

Leah's mother, Cory, awoke around three in the morning to check if her daughter ever made it home. Not finding the girl there, Cory called the police. A search went on throughout the area; a few weeks later, Leah's shoes were found near a local road. Then on August 3, 2000, Leah's body was discovered twelve miles away, near Fairview, in a section of woods.

Just as in Stephanie Condon's case and Katie Eggleston's case, forensic and police work came up empty-handed as to who the killer was. The murder of Leah took a terrible toll on the family. Leah's father suffered a heart attack, and Cory was often distraught. All she had was the official report about her daughter, which mentioned "homicidal violence" and "pending investigation." Even the term "homicidal violence" was just a catchall phrase about how Leah had died. Not even Leah's mother knew by what means she had died.

Like the parents of Brooke Wilberger, Stephanie Condon and Katie Eggleston, Cory had to deal with the loss of her daughter. Cory joined an organization called Parents of Murdered Children. It is a group that no parent wants to join, but circumstances beyond their control often send them into that doleful and select group. At one meeting Cory met with Jenie Shilling, whose daughter Heather Anderson had been strangled to death by her roommate in The Dalles, Oregon.

Also in the group was the mother of Emily Krevi, who had been given a ride home by a man from a grocery store. Once they got to her apartment, he demanded sex, which she refused. The man returned with a steel pipe filled with cement. The man then hit her so hard that he bashed in part of her skull, raped her, and robbed her apartment. Emily died from that attack. As if that wasn't enough for Phoebe Krevi, her husband committed suicide after their daughter's murder.

Phoebe later told a reporter for the Eugene *Register-Guard* that when she met Heather's mom on the Oregon coast, they went out to the beach and talked. "We looked out at the ocean. We cried a lot. It was invaluable to connect with somebody who's been through the exact same thing." Soon Leah Freeman's mom joined their small group.

On the National Day of Remembrance for Murder Victims, they tied red and black balloons to their

THE LAST TIME WE SAW HER

cars—red to mark the blood that had been spilled, black for violence. They went to a small park in Coquille to remember their daughters. Cory read a short statement: "'Oh, Leah! I don't know why, why it had to end this way, but it did. I know you're with Grandma and Grandpa now. Give them hugs. I'll never forget you, ever.'" Then Cory let a helium balloon sail into the sky.

Phoebe Krevi and Jenie Shilling promised to help Cory in her fight for more information about Leah's case. For years it had been stalled with only a death certificate of "pending investigation, homicidal violence."

Cory said, "I don't even know whether she was shot, stabbed, or strangled." Cory was fighting for the case to be transferred to another police agency and have the state attorney general's office look into the matter. It was an uphill battle, but Jenie Shilling noted, "We're a small, tiny group. But it's a start, isn't it?"

And then as time went on, Joel Courtney's name popped up in relation to Leah Freeman, just as it had done with Katie Eggleston and Stephanie Condon.

CHAPTER 18

THE BLOND GIRL WITH BROWN EYES

In some ways the crime that most matched those of Brooke Wilberger and Natalie Kirov didn't happen in Oregon at all. It occurred on May 25, 1996, in the college town of San Luis Obispo, on the central coast of California. Nineteen-year-old, blond, brown-eyed Kristin Denise Smart was a student at the California Polytechnic State University, where she majored in architecture. She was at an off-campus fraternity party until around 1:30 or 2:00 A.M. on May 25. At the party it was noted that Kristin seemed to be intoxicated or under the influence of drugs. She had trouble walking, and only later would it be wondered if a date rape drug had been slipped into one of her drinks.

Kristin left the party in the company of another student, Cheryl Anderson, to return to their dorm rooms on campus. A fellow student, nineteen-year-old Paul Flores, offered to walk with them to their dorms. When the trio got to the intersection of Perimeter Road and Grand Avenue, on the edge of the college campus, Cheryl went her own way. Flores told Cheryl that he would make sure that Kristin made it safely to her dorm. She never got there.

Later on May 25, Paul was seen with a black eye. When police finally were called into the situation, because Kristin had not made it back to her dormitory, Muir Hall, Paul told them that he had last seen her on Grand Avenue. But it was very suspicious that his story kept changing about the black eye. At first, he told the police that he'd received it while playing basketball. Later he told them he got it while working on his truck at his father's home. Even later he admitted to a friend that "I just woke up with it. I don't know how I got it. But it would have been pretty stupid to tell the police that."

The police noted that Kristin's clothing, toiletries, cosmetics, medicine, and identification were all left in her room. Even though it was obvious that she had not disappeared on her own, a missing person report was not created immediately, because it was Memorial Day weekend. The police knew that students often took impromptu vacations at that time.

Later, Kristin's parents were very upset about this delay, and even the police department admitted that the four days between the time she was gone and when they started searching hampered the investigation. When the police finally did contact Kristin's parents, her father, Stan Smart, said, "I was first frustrated that she might have done something embarrassing." It was only as the days passed, and there was no word from or about Kristin, that her parents began to think something more sinister than just "embarrassing" had occurred.

Posters began going up around San Luis Obispo about Kristin Denise Smart, the way posters would later go up around Corvallis about Brooke Wilberger. Kristin was known to go by the nicknames of "Roxy" and "Scritter" at times. She was last seen wearing a light gray cropped T-shirt, black nylon running shorts, and red-and-white Puma athletic shoes. Her case was termed: "Endangered/Missing."

In the beginning Paul Flores cooperated with the police. However, after talking with them twice, he refused a third time. To make matters even more suspicious, Paul dropped out of Cal Poly shortly after Kristin disappeared. He had been making poor grades and was in danger of failing his courses. He had also been arrested for driving while intoxicated and lost his driver's license. Prior to a search of his dorm room in Santa Lucia Hall, Paul removed his belongings. Eventually the San Luis Obispo Sheriff's Office (SLOSO) used three scent dogs in his dorm room. One of the dogs led the handler to Paul Flores's mattress in connection to Kristin Smart, but no other evidence of any kind was found in the room.

Because Paul Flores was the last person to be seen with Kristin, and his story kept changing about how he got a black eye, Paul became the main suspect in Kristin's disappearance. After the third attempt at questioning him by police, Paul Flores invoked his Fifth Amendment right to remain silent. Even when offered a plea deal, where he could plead guilty to involuntary manslaughter in exchange for showing authorities where Kristin's body was located, Paul refused to cooperate. SLOSO sergeant Bill Wammock stated, "Because of inconsistencies in Mr. Flores's activities, or claimed activities during that period, we believe he has further knowledge about what happened, and he is a suspect in her disappearance."

And then everything about Paul Flores stalled. Even though investigators looked at him from every angle, they were never confident enough that he was the perpetrator to make an arrest. He had looked very good for the crime, but so had Sung Koo Kim for the abduction of Brooke Wilberger, as well as Aaron Evans and Loren Krueger. As the FBI had told the Brooke Wilberger Task Force, it is not always prudent to become focused on one individual. In fact, had Kim or the others been arrested on the Brooke Wilberger case, it would have made the defense for Joel Courtney much easier in that case. All the defense would have to do is tell a jury that another man had been arrested in her disappearance, but now the police were saying their client had done it. If they had been wrong once, then why not twice?

The same thing could have occurred in Kristin Smart's case. Even though Flores looked good for the crime, the very fact that Joel Courtney had done things so similar had to be taken into account. Natalie Kirov, Brooke Wilberger, and Kristin Smart were all college girls of about the same age. They had all been abducted or disappeared very close to a college campus. What often seemed so crystal clear—as in Sung Koo Kim's case and Paul Flores's as well, only got murkier over time with lots of unanswered questions.

Eventually in February 2006, the FBI eliminated Joel Courtney from two Oregon cases. The FBI wouldn't say which two cases, but the consensus was by journalists that it must have been the Leah Freeman and Stephanie Condon cases. The reasoning was that Paul Eggleston still spoke of the FBI's involvement with his daughter Katie Eggleston's case. And, in fact, Leah Freeman's boyfriend was later arrested for her murder.

FBI spokesperson Beth Anne Steele told reporters that Joel Courtney was being looked at "as a normal part of the process." She emphasized that he was still a "high possibility in cases involving victims in Alaska, Florida, New Mexico and Oregon." Just which cases in Alaska and Florida remained a mystery.

And it was noted once again that Courtney tended to "abduct white females, fifteen to twenty-five years of age, with blond hair, in an outside setting." This, of course, met some of the parameters into which San Luis Obispo's Kristin Smart fell. The inclusion of her being near a college campus when she disappeared only added to circumstances akin to those of Brooke Wilberger and Natalie Kirov. And the fact that Joel Courtney had mentioned to Diane Mason that he was looking for a fraternity in Corvallis only added one more element to that scenario. Kristin had last been seen leaving a party at a frat house in San Luis Obispo. It was exactly the kind of area that Joel Courtney liked when he wanted to abduct a young woman. Even DA John Haroldson had spoken of Courtney going to "target-rich environments," such as the OSU campus.

Despite all the rumors swirling around Joel Courtney in 2006, there were now concrete circumstances that he and his lawyer had to contend with. The first of these was for the abduction and rape of Natalie Kirov. And as 2006 progressed, it became apparent that Joel Courtney was not going to be cooperative with anyone, even his lawyers. Joel would argue with them and be intransigent on the Kirov case, and even more so when it came to anything concerning his eventual extradition to Oregon on the Brooke Wilberger case.

Despite Joel's combative and often irrational nature, there were the beginnings of a plan within the Benton County DA's Office to make some kind of plea deal arrangement with Joel Courtney. If he would confess to *all* of the kidnappings, rapes, and murders he had committed, the death penalty would be taken off the table. In their minds, Courtney had done a lot more than just the kidnapping and rape of Natalie Kirov, and allegedly the kidnapping and murder of Brooke Wilberger. Joel Courtney might not have been involved in all of the cases that law enforcement thought he was capable of doing, but there was a very good chance that he had been responsible for some of them. It was going to boil down to how much of a gambler Joel Courtney was.

Would he proclaim his innocence on all of these cases, including Kirov and Wilberger? Or would he buckle under the pressure and start telling exactly what he had done—and to whom?

CHAPTER 19

"I WOULD SPIT IN YOUR FACE . . ."

As far back as the summer of 2005, it became clear that there wasn't going to be a speedy road to justice concerning Joel Courtney. This was even true in the Natalie Kirov case, much less the Brooke Wilberger case. As early as December 2004, the prosecutor in the Second Judicial District of New Mexico was putting together a witness list in the Kirov case. And hearings went on, month after month, throughout 2005. These included a "Notice Regarding Evidence" on April 13, 2005, to an extension hearing on May 24, 2005, to a "Motion to Review Conditions of Release" on June 22, 2005.

The defense wrote that *the present conditions of release are more strict than necessary to reasonably assure the defendant's appearance.* In essence, they were saying that Joel Courtney should be out on bail, and that he would make his court appearances when scheduled.

But Judge Michael Kavanaugh wasn't buying that argument, and Courtney stayed right where he was in the Bernalillo County Metropolitan Detention Center. Had he been released on bail, there would have been a firestorm of protests from Oregon.

About all of this interstate interest in Courtney, Benton County district attorney Scott Heiser said, "[Governor] Richardson will serve the warrant on Courtney when he deems appropriate. A Bernalillo County case is pending against Courtney, and he is not likely to be extradited to Oregon until that case is resolved."

And then the Corvallis *Gazette-Times* added a very interesting bit of new information. It noted, "The trial date (in New Mexico) has already been delayed because Courtney's attorney was reportedly arrested on a charge of driving under the influence of intoxicants and was fired." Courtney now had a new attorney named Liane Kerr.

Joel Courtney was not content merely to address the court through his lawyer. Irritable as usual, he addressed the judge on his own behalf in a statement he wrote that his rights were being violated. Calling himself the "petitioner," Courtney stated: *Petitioner is not provided sufficient access to law library* in the detention center. He went on to relate, *I have had one opportunity to visit the law library in the seven plus months since being incarcerated. I believe this to be a violation of my 5th Amendment Right to Due Process and New Mexico Constitution Right, Section 2, Article 18.*

Hearing after hearing followed: a "Petition to Extend Time," a "Petition for Writ of Habeas Corpus," and then a judge recusal filing on August 24, 2005. This concerned Judge Michael Kavanaugh, who briefly stated in a court document: *I, J. Michael Kavanaugh, do hereby recuse myself as District Court Judge assigned to the above case.*

Judge Mark Macaron was assigned the Courtney case on August 26, 2005, but that lasted less than a week. For whatever reason, Judge Macaron was replaced by the Honorable Kenneth Martinez, and he would see things through for the rest of the court proceedings into the years ahead on Joel Courtney.

Judge Martinez soon had his hands full. A sealed document came before him about Joel Courtney's competency to stand trial. So did an emergency motion from Liane Kerr to reinstate Joel's medication. Kerr said that Joel had been taking eight hundred milligrams of Motrin twice a day, twenty milligrams of Baclofen twice a day, two milligrams of Phenergan twice a day, and two milligrams of Synthroid once a day before his arrest. Since being confined, he'd been off medication, and Kerr stated that Joel had been supervised for suicide attempts, and that "his deprivation of medications clearly does not help." Kerr wanted Joel's medications to start again at once. Within a few days, Kerr not only said that Joel needed his medication, but that he was "bipolar and suffers from depression."

By November 2005, Judge Martinez ordered a psychiatric evaluation of Joel Courtney to deem if he was competent enough to assist his attorney at trial. By this time Courtney was not only hostile to the prosecution, but there was a great amount of friction with his defense as well. On April 6, 2006, there was a filing motion by Liane Kerr to withdraw as Courtney's lawyer. In fact, it was Joel Courtney who let

Judge Martinez know that he no longer wanted his female attorney, Liane Kerr.

Judge Martinez finally agreed with Courtney and put the whole process on hold while an available male attorney could be selected for Joel. John McCall was on the list, and he became Courtney's attorney. It only added to the time consumed as McCall had to read through thousands of pages of documents to get himself up to speed on the case. But speed was the last thing Joel Courtney wanted in New Mexico. With every day of delay, there was one more day he put off being returned to Oregon on a death penalty case.

Things even got more convoluted when Liane Kerr let Judge Martinez know that a Dr. Westfried had contacted her about a mental evaluation he was to perform on Joel Courtney. Kerr related, "Dr. Westfried indicated to me that he believed Mr. Courtney to be disturbed. But without an evaluation he could not provide a report of any kind." Unfortunately for Dr. Westfried, Kerr was no longer Courtney's attorney. So there things stood, until the whole mess could become untangled.

By the end of May 2006, McCall put in a request for a "Speedy Trial and Request for Discovery." McCall stated that United States Constitution Amendments V, VI, XIV, and an article in the New Mexico Constitution, protected Courtney's rights to due process and a speedy trial. But this rush to justice was short-lived. Less than a month later, McCall put a "Notice of Unavailability" before Judge Martinez. In it McCall stated that he would be completing a complex murder appeal in *State* v. *Manzanares*, working on a series of cases between June 28 and July 10, and also remodeling his office.

It was apparent there was going to be no trial coming soon for Joel Courtney on the Natalie Kirov case. This became even more evident when Judge Martinez ordered that Joel be sent to the Forensic Treatment Unit at Las Vegas, New Mexico, for a mental evaluation to see if he was competent to stand trial. Judge Martinez wrote: *The Bernalillo County Sheriff shall forthwith transport the defendant to the forensic treatment unit for no more than 72 hours, then return him to the Bernalillo County Detention Center. The Las Vegas Medical Center is to provide assessment and treatment to address defendant's possible dangerousness and his competency to proceed in his criminal case. Defendant shall be provided with treatment available to persons involuntarily committed pursuant to the Mental Health Development Disabilities Code.*

Speaking about this, the Benton County DA told reporters, "If Courtney is found to be competent, the case could be put back in the trial queue. If he is found to be mentally ill, it could take months before the trial could resume."

That may have been the initial plan to have short evaluations of Joel Courtney at the Las Vegas facility. But before long, Joel Courtney was bouncing back and forth between the Metropolitan Detention Center and the Forensic Treatment Center, more than one hundred miles away. Courtney was sent to the facility in Las Vegas on July 1, 2006, and October 3, 2006, as well, for psychological evaluation. There was only one problem with all of this: Joel Courtney was not cooperating with anyone.

Almost beside himself with frustration, Judge

Martinez let both the prosecution and the defense know: *Given defendant's current refusal to participate in an evaluation of his competency, the Court cannot make a determination of competency at this time. Therefore, the defendant shall be committed to the care and custody of the Department of Health of the State of New Mexico in Las Vegas, New Mexico, for evaluation of the Defendant's present competency. If the Defendant is found incompetent, the Defendant shall be treated for competency to stand trial for a period of not to exceed nine months.*

Judge Martinez was going to do everything he could to make sure that Joel Courtney was able to assist at his defense when a trial occurred. And it was Joel's mission to put that off as long as possible. If he acted and seemed incompetent now, there was no way he was going to Oregon anytime soon, and that suited Courtney just fine.

With that mission in mind, Joel dug in his heels, refusing to cooperate in mental evaluations and being as unruly as possible. He griped and swore and acted out at the facility in Las Vegas, New Mexico. Sometimes it was hard to tell if he was "just acting crazy" or if he really was "crazy."

All throughout the autumn of 2006, the prosecution and defense held competency hearings in front of Judge Martinez. But without the cooperation of the main character in the drama, it was like trying to walk up a muddy, slippery slope on a steep hill. No one could get any traction.

Finally by February 2007, Judge Martinez had had enough. He sent out a document, "Order Ending Competency Stay." Martinez related in it that the Department of Health in Las Vegas, New Mexico, had information to say that Joel Courtney was competent to stand trial. And then Martinez noted: *The defendant's lack of communication with Defense Counsel is not the result of the Defendant being incompetent.*

Joel Courtney might have tried fooling everyone into thinking he was incompetent to stand trial, but he wasn't fooling Judge Martinez. Martinez saw the misbehavior as a ploy by Courtney to put off trial until the end of time.

Commenting on this latest event in the Joel Courtney saga, Benton County, Oregon, DA Scott Heiser said, "We're glad it's finally going to trial in New Mexico. At last there's some progress in that case."

And Greg Wilberger added, "We're glad it's (the Kirov case) finally going to trial."

Progress, however, still meant pretrial hearings on witnesses and evidence in the Natalie Kirov case. These went on through January, February, and March 2007. The prosecution's witness list included the likes of Dara Finks, Zoraida Oviedo, and, of course, Natalie Kirov. The list also included APD personnel, such as Detective John Romero, Officer F. Aragon, Officer E. Taylor, Officer R. Sanchez, and Sergeant Gallindo. As far as crime scene techs went, there were personnel from the Metropolitan Forensic Science Center, which included Laura Galbraith, Cathy Pfefferle, Catherine Dickey, and Donna Monogne.

John McCall, Joel's defense attorney, was also constructing his own list of witnesses, which included David King, of the APD, Tanya Hicks, a private investigator, one unlisted African-American male, who was present when Joel was arrested, and one Hispanic female, who was present when Joel was arrested. Interestingly, McCall had Zoraida Oviedo on his witness list, and she was also a prosecution witness. A short time later, McCall added psychologist R. Edward Geiselman to the list. Geiselman was a professor of psychology at the University of Southern California.

Judge Martinez no longer wanted this case just to drift, as it seemed to have done for so long a period of time. Martinez set in writing an exact scheduling order for the months leading up to trial: *Discovery must be completed by April 6, 2007, motions must be filed by April 13, 2007. The parties shall submit their proposed jury instructions to the court by May 3, 2007.*

Even with these marching orders, the actual trial date was not set until September 2007. And before that time Joel Courtney had another matter to take care of. His wife, Rosy, finally had had enough of Joel and his errant and destructive ways. She filed for divorce and a petition for support to the New Mexico Human Services Department. Named as the defendant in this case was Joel Courtney. He was ordered to pay monthly child support, as well as medical and dental care for the children. Just how Joel was supposed to do so while in jail was not addressed.

Spring turned into summer, and still pretrial hearings dragged on. It wasn't until September 2007 that jury selection began and twelve jurors were empaneled. And by now, even the New Mexico television stations were more interested in the case than they had been, because of the impending Brooke Wilberger case in Oregon. Station KOB sent out a reporter, who learned that the prosecution in Natalie Kirov's case had offered Joel Courtney a plea deal, but Joel wouldn't say one way or another if he would take the deal. What was being offered was eighteen years in prison on the Kirov case if Joel pled guilty.

Joel's attorneys told KOB that Courtney was acting in his usual erratic manner. One of those attorneys said that Courtney did not want to talk about the case. All he would do was talk about unrelated things and about the medication he was taking. It was almost as if Joel didn't think about the case, it would all go away.

On September 17, 2007, the Natalie Kirov trial was set to begin. Print and television journalists filled the gallery, as did curious onlookers. So did investigators from Oregon and even a news crew from a Portland, Oregon, news station. And then they waited, and waited, with no defense attorneys, prosecutors, judge, or Joel Courtney appearing.

Finally it was announced the reason for the long wait. At the very last instant, just before the jurors were to be brought in, Joel Courtney accepted the prosecution's plea deal. The *Albuquerque Journal* noted: *After nearly a year of barely communicating with his attorney and sitting trance-like through much of jury selection, Courtney entered a guilty plea to two of four charges before Bernalillo County District Judge Kenneth Martinez.*

DDA Theresa Whatley told reporters, "This was always my hope. It always is better if the victim doesn't have to testify in a trial."

In the plea bargain Courtney admitted to the forcible abduction and sexual assault of Natalie Kirov. Joel Courtney, who had refused to change into civilian clothes that his lawyers had provided for him throughout much of the hearings, wore a charcoal gray suit on the day of his plea bargain.

After the hearing John McCall told reporters that

Joel finally explained his strange trancelike behavior that he'd adopted throughout most court hearings. McCall said that Courtney related that he'd adopted Zen Buddhist practices. Just where and when Joel had picked these up was anyone's guess.

One thing the trances had done was to make it extremely hard for any attorney to work with Joel Courtney on his case. McCall said, "He just sat and stared. It was a very difficult case for a defense."

Even though Joel Courtney was quiet and behaved himself on the day of his plea deal, that manner didn't last long. On December 11, 2007, the date of his formal sentencing on the Natalie Kirov case, Joel pretended to be ill and tried to fire his attorney and renege on the plea deal.

Judge Martinez wasn't having any of this and proceeded toward sentencing. When asked if he had anything to say, Joel Courtney replied to Judge Martinez, "I have no respect for this court. You are the rudest person I have ever met. I would spit in your face if I was close enough."

Those were probably not the best words to say to a judge just before being sentenced. Judge Martinez frowned at Courtney's outburst; then he quietly sentenced the defendant to the maximum of eighteen years in prison.

CHAPTER 20
ENDINGS AND BEGINNINGS

There may have been an extradition order in place for Joel Courtney to be sent from New Mexico to Oregon, but that did not mean that Courtney wasn't going to fight it every step of the way. The order was ER Number 05-00081, and it stated: *The State of New Mexico notifies the Court that the Governor of New Mexico has issued a Governor's Warrant authorizing the return of the fugitive to the state of Oregon.*

There were other battles being waged before Courtney was returned to Oregon as well. Hungry for any scrap of news about Courtney and Brooke Wilberger, Oregon media outlets were up in arms against the Corvallis Police Department and Benton County DA's Office and their complete blackout on any new information concerning Brooke's kidnapping. The Associated Press, KGW-TV, and the *Oregonian* newspaper all filed suit against those offices, citing that a free press had the right to documents and files. A lawyer representing the three news outlets claimed, "Disclosure of public records before trial in Oregon courts is standard practice." Basically, the news outlets were asking for the original affidavit in the arrest of Joel Courtney in the Brooke Wilberger case. This kind of document is almost always public record that anyone could look at by merely going to a court clerk's office and viewing the information.

This time, however, both DA Scott Heiser and CPD chief Gary Boldizsar said that releasing information from the affidavit and other "public" documents would compromise their case. They cited in particular the fact that there was no body in the case. A death penalty case without a body was always tricky business.

Heiser went on to say, "If this was a case that involved the questionable dealings of a public agency, the corruption of a public official, or some other issue that strikes the underpinnings of our democracy, then the balance might very well tip the other way for disclosure. However, that is not the situation in this case."

Before long, the Oregon State Attorney General's Office was involved in this matter as well. The spokesman for that office, David Leith, urged the court to keep the documents sealed. Leith said, "The court should exercise caution to avoid impeding an important criminal investigation and to avoid prejudicing an important criminal prosecution."

And then as a bit of a tease to the news media, Leith also let it be known, "The state anticipates that the continuing grand jury investigation will result in at least one additional indictment against Joel Courtney." This left a lot of possibilities in the air. Had

Joel done another kidnapping? Had he committed another murder in Oregon? Leith was closemouthed on the matter.

Finally Judge Locke Williams came down with a ruling as to whether the media outlets were going to view the affidavit and other documents. Williams ruled that the affidavit and documents should remain sealed because of "the risk of interfering with the state's ongoing investigation of this and other crimes that may have been committed by Mr. Courtney."

This only added fuel to the fire in the media: What other crimes? Were there other victims? Were they still alive? Or just like Brooke Wilberger, had they disappeared?

If the answers to the media questions couldn't be put to rest, there were a couple of other matters that could be. The matter of Sung Koo Kim, who had looked so "good" as the abductor of Brooke Wilberger, finally came to a conclusion. At the height of the furor, Kim's bail amount had exceeded $16 million in four counties. Even when he was no longer a suspect in Brooke's case, DDA Haroldson stated, "The evidence in this case alone justifies it being taken very, very seriously. We're not relying on the Wilberger stuff. We consider him to be a very dangerous person."

It was such a tangled web by now—involving Benton, Multnomah, Yamhill, and Washington counties—Kim's fifth lawyer, Clayton Lance, attempted to get all of the prosecutors at one table to discuss plea negotiations. Even Circuit Court Judge Janet Holcomb urged the prosecutors and defense to work toward some kind of plea deal.

Finally when the plea deals came, involving Sung Koo Kim, they came in a scattergun fashion. Kim pled guilty in Yamhill County to burglary and panty theft charges and was sentenced to four years of state prison and eighteen months of county jail time. He also had to read a statement in court.

Sung Koo Kim, in part, read, "'I would like to sincerely apologize with all my heart to all the girls affected by my shortsighted, selfish, abnormal behavior. It was never my intention to scare or instill a sense of insecurity in them. I want to reassure them that I pose absolutely no threat or danger to them or the community.'"

Soon Kim was pleading to porn charges in Washington County. For that crime he was to receive four years of prison time, which would begin after he had served prison time for the Yamhill County charges. And quickly following the Washington County sentencing, Kim made a plea deal with Benton County. Judge Janet Holcomb gave Kim thirty-one months in prison on one count of first-degree burglary and thirteen months for second-degree burglary.

Speaking about his son, Joo Kim said that Sung Kim was mentally ill and had a hard time in prison. Joo added that Sung Kim spent most of his time in his cell with another inmate who was also mentally ill. Dr. Paul Leung, Sung's psychiatrist, said that Sung suffered from a schizoaffective disorder.

Around that same time Aaron Evans, who had also once looked "good" for the kidnapping of Brooke Wilberger, was having his own new set of problems. Albany PD officer Chad Barr was dispatched to a home on SE Denver Street in Albany concerning a domestic dispute. When he got there, Michelle Evans told Officer Barr that she'd gone to her residence to see if "everything was all right." Michelle and Aaron were now separated, and Michelle lived with a new boyfriend across town. Michelle added that she allowed Aaron to stay there "as long as he didn't have tweakers over there with him." (Tweakers meant people who used meth.)

Officer Barr noticed that Michelle Evans had a cut on her lower lip and bruising on her face, and she told Barr that Aaron had "beaten her up." Asked to be more specific, Aaron's ex said that she had arrived at her residence to find that Aaron had people there whom she suspected of using meth. An argument ensued, which turned to shoving back and forth on Michelle and Aaron's part. Then according to Michelle he balled his hand into a fist and struck her in the face.

Officer Barr said to her, "On a scale of zero to ten, can you rate the pain? Zero being no pain and ten the worst pain you ever felt."

Michelle replied that the injury on her lip was an eight, and she also had pain in her back, because he had pushed her to the floor at one point. She said that pain was also an eight.

Officer Barr asked Michelle more questions about her relationship with Aaron, and learned that Aaron was a convicted sex offender. Asked where Aaron was now, Michelle Evans said that he had fled on foot in a northerly direction. Officer Timothy Sousa directed Officer Fandrem, of the APD, to search for Aaron, and Fandrem soon located Aaron on a street. But as soon as Aaron spotted a police vehicle, he took off running and evaded capture. In fact, he was not going to make it easy for the Albany Police Department. One officer's report noted: *Suspect fled down the railroad tracks, wearing a green backpack, hooded sweatshirt, jeans. Running past Salvation Army store. Out on foot near railroad tracks going towards Geary Street. Suspect fled from me west down the tracks then south across them then north again. He had something on his head.*

Michelle's interview took place around seven in the evening. Later that night, around eleven-thirty, an APD officer got a call about a prowler in the Third Avenue area. A resident there said that a young man wearing a baseball cap and red jacket was trying to break into a blue sports utility vehicle. Officer Timothy Sousa drove to the area and noticed a male wearing a red jacket walking south on Baker Street. Sousa pulled over and detained the suspect, making him sit down on the curb. And then Sousa noted: *I recognized the suspect as being Aaron Evans. I had dealt with Evans a few times in the past.*

Officer Sousa read Evans his Miranda rights and noted: *Aaron was very nervous. Based on training and experience, I believed Aaron to have been under the influence of a controlled substance. Aaron could not sit still and he continually moved his hands and feet. I thought Aaron might take off running. I placed Aaron in handcuffs and already knew that Officer Barr had probable cause for an arrest.*

Asked about prowling around cars and trying to break into them, Aaron said that he might have walked past some cars and looked at them, but he didn't try to break into any of them. Asked if Aaron knew any reason why he might be the subject of being arrested for a domestic dispute, Aaron replied,

"Yeah, probably." Then a short time later, he stated, "Of course, I'm the man."

Once in the interview room, Aaron had a story that was different from Michelle's. Aaron said, "She attacked me! I have a witness that pulled her off of me. All I wanted to do was leave, when she attacked me."

Officer Sousa read the report that Officer Barr had taken from what Michelle told him about the incident.

Aaron's response was "It didn't happen that way! I did not pull the phone from her hands. I never hit her and she was never calling the cops." Asked why Michelle had a swollen lip, Aaron said that he didn't know.

Despite what Aaron claimed now, he was booked into the Linn County Jail on the charges of an "Assault IV" and "Interference with Making a Police Report." The latest charges against Aaron were the least of his problems. What made it so damaging for him was his new interviews by his parole officer. The officer contacted Aaron at the Linn County Jail and, at first, Aaron denied using any illegal drugs. After a while, however, Aaron admitted to smoking marijuana. Asked if he used any meth, Aaron at first denied this as well, before admitting, "I smoked a couple of bowls of meth."

A few days later the parole officer wrote: *This is Mr. Evans' fourth known time that he has violated his condition of supervision. He has been sanctioned to two days of work crew for failing to report as directed and from alcohol and drug treatment non-compliance. He has been sanctioned to six days jail time for committing the crime of Theft II and failing to cooperate with a polygraph examination. Mr. Evans was sanctioned to twenty-two days jail time for committing the crime of Failure to Register as a Sex Offender.*

With new charges on top of all of that, the parole officer wrote in another report: *It is recommended that Mr. Evans appear before the Benton County Circuit Court to show cause why his probation should not be revoked. It is further recommended if Mr. Evans is found in violation, that his probation be revoked and he be placed on Post Prison Supervision.*

While all of this was going on with Sung Koo Kim and Aaron Evans, and Joel Courtney fighting his extradition in New Mexico, Brooke Wilberger's parents were fighting a new battle of their own. They decided to sue Creative Building Maintenance, the company that Courtney had been working for when he allegedly kidnapped Brooke. According to KATU television, the Wilbergers sought at least $75,000 in a federal case against the maintenance company for hiring someone with a violent felony past without doing a thorough background check. In the lawsuit the Wilbergers claimed that the company provided Joel with a vehicle, which allowed him the opportunity to commit crimes no matter where he was assigned. Not only that, much of the time Joel was not even supervised as he went into neighborhoods all around the West.

The $75,000 amount was the absolute low side in the lawsuit. Before long the Wilbergers were seeking $26.5 million from CBM. The Wilbergers' lawyer in the federal lawsuit told reporters, "We're not going to get there. We're limited to the amount covered by the insurance carrier for CBM."

There was one big problem with this lawsuit, however. Eleven days before the new amount was posted, Creative Building Maintenance filed for bankruptcy after it lost several large accounts. CBM was a Canadian company, with a United States subsidiary, and Joel Courtney had worked for that entity. And just how convoluted this all was, by now, could be ascertained by a comment made by the Wilbergers' lawyer. Gerald Doblie related, "There are a lot of things we haven't found out about the workings of the company. They say they have the files in about one thousand banker boxes in Canada."

Even while this financial nightmare was making its way through the courts, friends of Greg and Cammy Wilberger set up a scholarship in Brooke's name. The scholarship grants would go to high-school students who shared Brooke's ideals about community service.

This idea came about when one of Brooke's friends, Jessica Marks, was at Whitman College in Walla Walla, Washington. Jessica sent out letters to hundreds of potential donors, writing: *Brooke blessed the world with her selfless kindness. She shared her time and energy unquestioningly. Each day that passes without her is a little darker, lacking the care that Brooke so readily gave. The life stolen from my friend will never be returned—but we can carry her spirit through us.*

The scholarship fund was to be administered by the Oregon Community Foundation (OCF). When it reached $50,000, the minimum for a permanently endowed fund, it would generate $2,250 annually to help in sending a high-school student to college. OCF's Sara Brandt noted, "This fund is different than many we manage. The unique part is it will be created by multiple donors—some who never knew her."

Cammy Wilberger, for her part, called the fund "a wonderful idea." And Cammy was on her own crusade to have her daughter's memory stay in the public arena. At an annual women's conference at the Philomath Ward of the Church of Jesus Christ of Latter-day Saints, Cammy spoke of Brooke's funny and reflective sides.

Cammy told the audience, "I'm so happy to talk to you, sister to sister. I've never really had the opportunity to thank you. You did everything for us."

The conference theme that year was "My Heart Delighteth in Righteousness," and Cammy told the gathering, "Delight in the good around us." Cammy said that her hour of prayer each morning helped her cope with the loss of her daughter. "Some days are so hard, and yet there's always tomorrow."

Then Cammy related, "I know that I will see Brooke again. I'm not worried about that. I know where she is. If they find her body, that's great. But I can live without that. I know where she is." Cammy was sure her family would be reunited in heaven.

Then on September 13, 2006, it appeared that Brooke's remains might have indeed been found. Loggers who were clear-cutting at a site near Lincoln City on the Oregon coast discovered a human skull and some bones. The bones were found in a heavily wooded area about a quarter mile from the nearest road. The only way to get into the spot was by walking.

It was recalled by many that Joel Courtney had been scheduled to attend a hearing at court in Newport on May 24, 2004. What if he had kidnapped Brooke in Corvallis on that day and then took off for this isolated spot? A spot he very well may have known. Even Sergeant Ralph Turre, of the Lincoln County Sheriff's Office, agreed that the debris covering the bones probably placed the time of death in the two-year range or more.

A forensic anthropologist was called in to help the local medical examiner (ME). Statistics on Brooke Wilberger were looked at once again. She was noted to have been five-four and weighed between 105 and 110 pounds. She had been wearing hoop earrings and an engraved ring with the letters *CTR* at the time of her abduction. She also had a metal plate in her right forearm because of a gymnastics accident.

Newsmen were clamoring for information about the remains in Lincoln County and speculating if they really were those of Brooke Wilberger's. On September 26, 2006, they got their answer. The bones and skull were those of a young man. An examination by deputy state ME Larry Lewman, as well as items found at the scene, pointed to a young man who had committed suicide by hanging himself. No foul play was suspected. One more "possible sighting" of Brooke had once again come up empty.

There was one thing that was for certain by the late autumn of 2006, however. Whoever the district attorney was in Benton County who would prosecute Joel Courtney—it wouldn't be Scott Heiser. Six months into his third term as DA, Heiser resigned, stating that he could no longer work with Circuit Court Judge Janet Holcomb.

As an example, Heiser recounted Holcomb's actions in a recently completed trial concerning

Shawn Field. In that trial Heiser said that Holcomb's rulings were "arbitrary and capricious." Members of the victim's family were particularly upset by Holcomb's actions during pretrial hearings. They told Heiser that Holcomb often rolled her eyes or sighed when listening to arguments put forth by the assistant district attorney (ADA). The family went so far as to tell Heiser that they thought the judge personally disliked them and didn't seriously take into account the brutal murder of a three-year-old child.

In fact, before resigning, Heiser filed motions to disqualify Judge Holcomb in nine important future cases, including the case concerning Brooke Wilberger. A district attorney in Oregon could do this in relation to a particular judge before a trial had begun. Once a trial was occurring, such as the Field trial had been, the district attorney's hands were tied.

It wasn't the first time Heiser had been at loggerheads with Judge Holcomb. Heiser told a reporter, "Several years ago I was in a similar situation with this same judge." In fact, it didn't take much in Oregon to disqualify a judge from presiding over certain cases. An attorney could submit a motion to disqualify a judge simply by asserting that he believed he couldn't get a fair trial before that judge. In 2006, attorneys had asked for disqualification of judges 187 times in Benton County. Most of the time the disqualification motions came from defense attorneys. That was until the blowup between Scott Heiser and Judge Holcomb. After the blowup, DA Heiser attempted to have no major cases in Janet Holcomb's courtroom. Once again Heiser stated that he believed Holcomb had a pronounced bias against the Benton County DA's Office.

Before he left his office, Heiser made a recommendation who should succeed him as DA of Benton County. The person he picked was John Haroldson, the man who was scheduled to prosecute Joel Courtney, once Courtney was extradited from New Mexico.

Haroldson had begun his career in law as an ADA in Linn County, starting in 1990. During that time he had prosecuted everything from traffic cases to aggravated murder. In 2002, Haroldson joined the Benton County DA's Office. He had his share of important cases before the various judges there. Once the Brooke Wilberger case came across his desk, however, the glare of media attention and public awareness was intense. Every step he would now take, every motion he filed and document he signed, came under the spotlight of analysis. For the newspapers and television stations in Oregon, the Brooke Wilberger case was *the case*.

And yet, as 2007 rolled along, there were two more crimes for which Joel Courtney was just about to be charged. Details on these crimes had not yet made their way into the local newspapers, but all that was about to change.

PART III

CHAPTER 21
AS IF BY MAGIC

Ever since Joel Courtney had been arrested concerning the Brooke Wilberger case, the investigators had been looking into what other crimes he may have committed. In May 2007, there was strong evidence against Courtney, and John Haroldson indicted Joel on two more serious charges. The charges were that on the day Courtney abducted Brooke, he also "attempted to kidnap and murder two other women." It was important that the charges included the word "murder," because it was now assumed by the prosecution that he had done *just that* to Brooke Wilberger.

Haroldson told reporters about these latest charges, "These are two victims approached by Courtney very shortly before he abducted and murdered Brooke Wilberger. The evidence will show Courtney attempted to abduct them with the same method, but because of the way they reacted, they got away. They are very important witnesses in identifying Courtney and the van he was driving."

Even though the two women were not named, they were obviously Diane Mason and Jade Bateman. Haroldson went on to tell reporters, "I consider it to be a very significant piece of evidence. It shows exactly what Courtney was doing—coming to our community to prey on young females."

The next step for Haroldson was to extradite Joel Courtney from New Mexico, and Courtney was still fighting that every step of the way. Once Joel was sentenced by Judge Martinez on the Natalie Kirov case, that eventuality was much closer than it had ever been. On December 12, 2007, Haroldson submitted a formal request for a governor's warrant to Oregon governor Ted Kulongoski. Governor Kulongoski then would send on his request to New Mexico's governor Bill Richardson. The swift extradition of Joel Courtney from New Mexico to Oregon, however, was not a foregone conclusion.

As always, Courtney himself caused as many legal disruptions as possible. He refused to cooperate with his attorney in the New Mexico case, and in frustration that attorney filed a motion with Judge Martinez not only to reverse Courtney's plea deal, but to resign from being Joel's attorney. Both motions were denied.

Haroldson knew that things would probably not go smoothly with the extradition, and he told reporters, "The Wilbergers and the state of Oregon have waited a long time for Courtney to face these charges. The main challenge I'd anticipate would be on the governor's warrant, where Courtney could challenge and fight it all the way. Provisions in the statute can create issues, with regard to prosecution in death penalty cases. And in this case I will be seeking the death penalty."

At least in one regard, Haroldson got exactly what he was looking for. In an e-mail statement about Joel Courtney, New Mexico governor Bill Richardson wrote, *Now that justice has been served here, the State of New Mexico will do everything in its power to see that justice is served in Oregon. We will process this extradition as quickly as possible to help bring peace to the Wilberger family.*

The phrase "as quickly as possible" was appropriate in light of Joel Courtney's determination to fight the extradition to Oregon. In February 2008, Courtney was in a courtroom in Santa Fe facing a different prosecutor because he had been moved to a penitentiary in Santa Fe County after having pled guilty in the Natalie Kirov case. By now, Joel Courtney's court-appointed attorney was Stephen Aarons, a lawyer with a lot of experience handling difficult cases.

On Courtney's behalf, Aarons noted that an original attempt had been made in 2006 to extradite Joel to Oregon, and it had been quashed. Aarons now looked into whether a second extradition attempt violated Courtney's legal rights. Another challenge by Aarons was about the green van that police had seized, stating that Courtney did not own that van, and another person could have used it to kidnap Brooke Wilberger.

One person not surprised at all by Joel Courtney's intransigence in being brought back to Oregon was Benton County DA John Haroldson. He told reporters, "These events certainly do not signal any change in Courtney's approach we've seen to this point. I will support the process of getting him back up here as soon as possible, even if that means going down there for any reason whatsoever."

Finally in April 2008, John Haroldson and Oregon got the news they had been waiting for, for so long. After looking into possible legal avenues of staying the extradition, Stephen Aarons apparently didn't find any, and he did not challenge it. Haroldson said of this watershed event, "We will be in the process of arranging to bring Joel Courtney back to Oregon in the most secure and expedient manner. I anticipate that just as soon as he gets here, he will be scheduled for his court appearance."

New Mexico had a month to extradite Courtney to Oregon. So it almost seemed to be a conjurer's trick, when less than a week later it was learned that Joel was in Corvallis, Oregon. As if by magic he was suddenly in a jail cell in Benton County, Oregon. Speaking of the dramatic turn of events, Benton County sheriff Diana Simpson told reporters that seven Benton County deputy sheriffs and one FBI agent escorted Courtney back to Oregon. Asked why it took so many law enforcement officers, she replied that it was because of the high-profile nature of the case.

Simpson added that the officers had picked up Joel Courtney from the Central New Mexico Correctional Facility in Los Lunas, a town eighteen miles southwest of Albuquerque. Sheriff Simpson would not go into details about the mode of transportation in which Courtney had been brought to Oregon, except to say that federal law banned such prisoners from commercial flights. One thing Simpson did say was that the transference had taken from Sunday through Tuesday afternoon, which appeared to many to be an indication that Courtney might have been driven the one thousand miles from New Mexico to Corvallis, Oregon.

With such big news about the extradition, both Sheriff Simpson and DA Haroldson held a news conference. Haroldson noted that at 11:30 A.M. on April 9, Courtney was scheduled to hear charges formally read against him. The interesting thing was, Courtney would not even be in a courtroom. Just as had happened to Aaron Evans earlier, Joel would listen to the charges as he sat in a jail cell, linked by audio and video to the courtroom. As to what kind of cell he was in, Sheriff Simpson would only state that Courtney was in a single-inmate cell in the Benton County Jail for his safety, and for the safety of others.

Without Joel Courtney present at his arraignment, not even his court-appointed lawyers Steven Krasik and Steven Gorham entered a plea in his arraignment, so Judge Locke Williams entered a plea of "not guilty" for him. It was no surprise when DA Haroldson asked that Courtney be held without bail, and Judge Williams granted that request. Attending the short court hearing were five members of the Wilberger family.

There was a whole host of charges against Joel Courtney in the Brooke Wilberger case—nineteen in all. They included aggravated murder, first-degree rape, and first-degree sexual abuse. The aggravated murder charge was, of course, the most serious. The document let it be known that the district attorney's office was seeking the death penalty on that charge.

Haroldson later explained to a *Gazette-Times* reporter about why there was a multiplicity of charges against Courtney. "You have various forms of homicide under Oregon law. Murder is defined as intentionally causing the death of another human being. Aggravated murder is murder plus other factors. You could have a murder committed in the course of a particular crime, murder to cover up evidence of a crime or to conceal that evidence in a place not likely to be found. You couldn't just plead one count and have all these things included."

As far as Joel Courtney's lawyers went, Steven Krasik had a long history of handling tough cases in Oregon, including death penalty cases. One of Krasik's cases had been a death penalty case against Christian Longo, a man who was charged with killing his wife and three children, and dumping their bodies into the ocean near Waldport, Oregon.

DA John Haroldson still wanted to keep much of the evidence against Joel Courtney secret, but his nemesis in this regard once again turned out to be KGW-TV. Right from the start, KGW had wrangled with the Benton County DA's Office about the public's right to know. Not getting any information about Courtney from Benton County, KGW turned to the recently released information on Courtney from the New Mexico court system. Once this was out, Haroldson decided to step forward and release a great deal of information in public records in Benton County. For the first time the press and public learned why Joel Courtney had become a suspect and about the path to his arrest in the kidnapping and murder of Brooke Wilberger.

One new piece of information was that a blood-hound, handled by a U.S. Marshal, had tracked Brooke's scent to the southwest corner of Twenty-sixth Street, then south to Southwest Philomath Boulevard, and east on Southwest Philomath Boulevard to the overpass, seven-tenths of a mile from the apartment complex. The bloodhound then lost track of the scent. This was all remarkable, since Brooke had probably been in the back of a van during all that distance.

The public now learned as well that Joel had not returned to his in-laws' residence in Portland until 10:00 P.M. on May 25, and he seemed to be stressed out. In fact, within a short period of time, he went to the hospital complaining of chest pains. He also told his sister-in-law a very strange story about being kidnapped and that he thought one of the kidnappers had killed a young blond woman.

Two or three weeks after these incidents, Joel suddenly left the Portland area with the green minivan. He later gave his brother-in-law and sister-in-law two different explanations about why he had suddenly left. In one version Joel said that he'd been the victim of a kidnapping and was afraid the kidnappers might find him again. In the second version he said the police were after him, although he gave no reason why they were after him.

The public learned that when a search warrant was executed on the van that Joel had been driving in May 2004, it contained DNA evidence that Brooke Wilberger had been inside that van. Blond hairs, white rope with one end tied like a noose, a gray duffel bag and floorboard mats containing blond hair—all contained trace evidence belonging to Brooke Wilberger.

As to why DA Haroldson was now releasing all of this information that he had so stringently guarded up to that point, he said, "I had requested that the affidavit for a search warrant remain sealed until we were able to have a meaningful conversation with the defense. Once those documents were given to the media by the New Mexico court, they became public record, and I am bound by law to release them."

Commenting on all of this, Courtney's defense lawyer Steven Krasik commented, "Haroldson has been absolutely straightforward and absolutely within the spirit of the legal requirements. But I'm concerned, as is Mr. Haroldson, about unverified information being related that may or may not be admissible in a trial. It can do nothing but taint the jury pool and might prevent a fair trial for Mr. Courtney or for the state."

Defense lawyers often speak of the right of their client to be tried in a court of law and not in the press and on televison. But in this case Krasik was correct in his assessment that the more people who read accounts about Joel Courtney or watched news reports about him on television, the harder it was going to be to empanel a jury once the case went to trial. There were sure to be plenty of people who did not want to serve on a death penalty case. As the pool of potential jurors grew smaller and smaller, the job for the defense and prosecution would become harder.

* * *

Not that the news about Joel Courtney and Brooke Wilberger was going away anytime soon. The *Gazette-Times* wanted to know how hard it was going to be for the prosecution to get a death penalty conviction against Joel Courtney without Brooke Wilberger's body. For that purpose they sent out reporter Bennett Hall to ask this question of prosecution and defense attorneys.

Susan Rozelle, of the University of Oregon School of Law, told Hall, "It's certainly harder if you don't have a body, but not as hard as you might think." There were murder cases all of the time in Oregon that were successfully prosecuted without a body being found. "All you need are enough facts that look suspicious enough that the jury is convinced beyond a reasonable doubt. There are a lot of definitions of reasonable doubt, but one thing they all agree on is that it doesn't mean the foreclosure of any doubt at all."

In other words, a juror might have some doubt about certain "facts" the prosecution was giving them via testimony. However, if the juror believed the preponderance of the "facts," then they could vote guilty.

Prosecutor Josh Marquis had no body, nor even any physical evidence to work with, on a 1993 Deschutes County murder case he prosecuted. Marquis had a missing person, Carolann Payne, and a suspect, Joel Abbott. Marquis related, "We had suspected Abbott for some time. We wired up a friend of his with a body wire, and Mr. Abbott made some fairly incriminating statements."

In that case Marquis convinced the jury that Payne must be dead, because there was no evidence that she was still alive. There were no contacts by Payne to her friends or family, no financial transactions, and no sightings of her anywhere. Marquis added, "I did it by proving the negative."

Also weighing in on this issue was veteran prosecutor Norman Frink, of Multnomah County in Portland. Frink said that he'd prosecuted the disappearance of Tim Moreau, an employee of the Starry Night concert hall in Portland. Moreau had vanished in 1990. Ten years later, nightclub owner Larry Hurwitz pled no contest after another employee, George Castagnola, testified that he and Hurwitz had strangled Moreau to death to cover up a ticket-counterfeiting scam that Hurwitz had been part of.

Other lawyers, however, told Bennett Hall that prosecutors faced an uphill battle in the Wilberger case because it was a death penalty case. Sam Kauffman, a defense attorney with the law firm of Garvey Schubert Barer in Portland, said, "The state has the burden of proving a person died." The defense didn't have to prove a person was still alive.

Even Susan Rozelle said that the defense's best argument in the Wilberger case was that Brooke was not dead. If she wasn't dead Joel Courtney could *not* be prosecuted for her murder.

In May 2008, two stories dominated the headlines around Corvallis. One was that it was now the fourth anniversary of Brooke Wilberger's disappearance. The other headline was that in a short court appearance before Judge Locke Williams, both the prosecution and the defense were told by the judge that the trial was scheduled for February 2010. The

Wilberger family, who was in the audience, looked momentarily stunned. They had waited so long for justice for their daughter, and now they learned that they would have to wait a year and a half longer. Even then, the February 2010 date was just a "place-holder" on the court calendar. It could even be later than that.

Many of the local newspapers and television stations ran segments about Brooke, her family, and Joel Courtney. The *Oregonian* noted comments by Wilberger family spokesman Tom Sherry about the initial search for Brooke. "Everybody felt that everything that could be done was being done. The Wilbergers are an amazing family and remain committed to their religious faith and the principle of forgiveness. But the impact of Brooke's disappearance will be felt again when the case goes to trial. It will dredge up the worst feelings."

And then in July 2008, there was a short article that appeared in the *Salt Lake Tribune* in Utah. It simply stated: *Family of missing girl may support plea deal. The parents of Brooke Wilberger have signaled they would support a plea deal should the man accused of abducting and killing their daughter four years ago reveal the whereabouts of her remains.* As soon as this short article appeared, any other mention of plea deals disappeared from the press.

Of course, all of that depended upon Joel Courtney going along with a plea deal. So far, all of his actions had been ones of intransigence and contempt of the judicial system. He was still claiming he was innocent of all charges, and the chances of actually finding Brooke's remains seemed as remote as ever.

CHAPTER 22
OUT OF THE PAST

At least by the autumn of 2008, pretrial motions and hearings were moving ahead on the Brooke Wilberger case in Oregon. In September 2008, Joel Courtney's attorney Steven Krasik let the judge know that he and Steven Gorham were wading through twenty-six thousand pages of discovery documents, with still more to come. Neither the prosecution nor defense had as yet received documents from the FBI.

In November 2008, the issue of whether Joel would have to wear a stun belt while in court came up at a hearing. The judge had already ruled that Courtney could wear civilian clothes in court during trial. Steven Krasik, however, wanted to ensure that the jurors never saw Courtney wearing handcuffs, stomach chain, and restraints around his legs. Krasik told the judge, "It's important the jury can't see those shackles. Any kind of indication that he's not innocent, especially with chains, would indicate to people that there's some concern for this person."

Krasik added that Courtney had not been disruptive in any of his previous court hearings in Corvallis and that he didn't need to be overly restrained. DA John Haroldson countered that this was a death penalty case, and shackles were a well-established fact in Oregon.

There was a long hiatus in significant pretrial hearings until the spring of 2009. In March, DA Haroldson fought for a couple of issues on the case. The one case was, of course, the Brooke Wilberger disappearance and presumed murder. The other cases concerned the charges against Joel in the attempted kidnapping of the two OSU female students a few blocks away from where Brooke disappeared.

Haroldson told the judge, "There was a common scheme and plan in all of these actions. The plan was the abduction and sexual abuse of a young female." Haroldson wanted all three cases joined into one.

Even more important, Haroldson wanted a lot of Joel Courtney's previous history to be heard by jurors. The list included the details of the 1984 kidnapping and attempted rape of Sue McDonald, Joel's failure to appear at a Lincoln County court on the morning of May 24, 2004, Joel's drug and alcohol abuse, and the planned abduction of the other two female OSU students. The kidnapping and rape of Natalie Kirov in New Mexico was also part of the list.

DA Haroldson knew that without Brooke's body he was going to have to convince the jurors of Joel's guilt by other means. And the best way of doing that was by adding one issue at a time until there was a pile of issues against Joel. Even Haroldson admitted that the bulk of the state's case was subject to "OEC 404," which basically cited that *a defendant's propensity to act in a certain way may be used for other purposes, including proof of motive, opportunity, intent, plan and preparation.*

A lot was riding on Judge Locke Williams's decision to allow the matters that Haroldson wanted to be presented to jurors. If Williams ruled against most of these, then Haroldson was going to have a very, very difficult time convincing the jurors that Joel Courtney had abducted and murdered Brooke Wilberger. All he had was circumstantial evidence, with very little physical evidence.

And then in May 2009, Judge Williams heard some very powerful and detailed testimony. The testimony came from witnesses that DA Haroldson wanted the jurors to hear. If they were allowed to go on the stand during a trial, their testimony was going to be very damning against Joel Courtney.

DA Haroldson was not taking on this important matter alone. In fact, he had called upon the services of veteran Benton County DDA prosecutor Karen Kemper to argue most of the proceedings before Judge Williams and to question witnesses as well. One of the first was the powerful story of Natalie Kirov, once again telling of her evening of terror at the hands of Joel Courtney.

Even before matters got under way with Natalie, there were arguments between DA Haroldson and defense attorney Steven Gorham about the term "victim." Haroldson said at one point, "I use the word 'victim' because there is an interest by the state to shield those victims' names from any media exposure. I note there is a pool camera in the courtroom."

The defense didn't have any objection to keeping the witnesses' names out of the media, but Gorham added, "Concerning the term 'victim,' except for the individuals that Mr. Courtney has been convicted in relation to, we ask that the term not be used. Instead, we would like the term 'witness' used."

DA Haroldson agreed that the word "victim" might influence jurors, but there weren't any jurors there that day. This wasn't a trial, just a preliminary hearing. Judge Williams agreed with Haroldson and said that the witnesses could be referred to as "victims."

The next issue was that DA Haroldson wanted more than just the audio turned on to record what was transpiring in court that day. He wanted a video camera running the whole time as well.

Haroldson argued, "If someone is convicted in a capital case, there is an automatic appeal. I've had experiences where those cases come back, and witnesses are no longer available. It becomes even more significant than ever to preserve the testimony of that individual." Haroldson said that audio and video not only recorded what the witness said on the stand, but he claimed it preserved their manner of speaking as well.

Steven Gorham, on the other hand, replied, "Excuse my language, if it goes too far, but this is kind of a setup. Here we are at a motion hearing. And if we do cross-examine any of these witnesses, it is only to help decide on these motions. The trial is about guilt or innocence of Mr. Courtney. These proceedings are not. They are about prior acts and to consolidate. There should be no video camera now."

Haroldson objected to the word "setup" used by Gorham, and told the judge that he'd given the defense prior warning that he was going to ask for a video camera in the present proceedings. In the end, however, Judge Williams sided with Gorham and denied the use of a video camera in court.

With that done, Haroldson introduced his co-counsels that day—Karen Kemper, who was a Benton County DDA, and Stephanie Tuttle, a prosecutor from the Oregon Department of Justice (DOJ).

The first witness on the stand was Natalie Kirov. Once again she told of her evening of terror at the hands of Joel Courtney in Albuquerque, New Mexico. For the first time the Wilberger family got to see Natalie in person. By now, Natalie seemed much more calm and self-assured. This, after all, was her third time in being on a witness stand.

Karen Kemper asked Natalie, "Is English your first language?"

Natalie replied, "No."

"Your first language is Russian?"

"Yes."

Nonetheless, Natalie's command of English was now better and less accented than in her New Mexico testimony. In very graphic terms Natalie answered questions about her abduction, kidnapping at knifepoint, and being sexually abused. Natalie also gave a detailed description of the man who had attacked her—a man who matched the description of the way Joel Courtney had looked in the autumn of 2004. She said he was about six feet tall, had blue eyes, and wore a silver earring in his left ear. He was driving a red Honda two-door sedan, the type of car that Joel Courtney had at the time.

About being sexually abused at his hands, Natalie said that he had forced her to take off her clothes in the car. "He was touching me all over. My vagina. He wouldn't let me take my coat off my face. He parked the car and put his penis in my mouth."

Kemper asked, "Was there some difficulty when he was trying to make you perform oral sex?"

"Yes," Natalie responded. "I put his penis in my mouth. And he asked me if I knew how to do it, and I said no. His penis was soft."

Kemper queried, "What was his mood like?"

Natalie replied, "He seemed nervous."

"Was there any kind of sex act?"

Natalie said, "Right before that, he blew smoke into my mouth, and he was on top of me. He was kissing my neck and my breasts."

"Did he ask you how old you were?"

"I don't remember."

Kemper next had Natalie tell of her miraculous escape, and her account of running down the street clad only in a coat, which came down five inches below her waist. Kemper asked, "What can you tell us about the people who helped you?"

Natalie replied, "The girl who walked into the restaurant said, 'Do you want my pants?' They were in her car. A woman and maybe three girls were with her."

Kemper asked, "As you got into the car with them, what were you saying to them?"

"They were already on a cell phone. To 911. So

they gave me the phone, and I described the person and then I described the car."

"As you were there with the people who were helping you, did you see the man again?"

"I saw the red Honda drive away from the parking lot."

"Did you watch the car?"

"Yes."

"What did you think might happen?"

"I don't know."

"Were you afraid?"

"Yes."

At the end of this impassioned testimony, Kemper said to Natalie, "I know you said you were afraid. What did you think might happen?"

After a long pause Natalie replied, "I was afraid he would never let me go."

When DDA Kemper was done, there were no questions to her from the defense side of the courtroom.

Evidence that Joel had a court appointment that he missed on May 24, 2004, in Lincoln County came in via Lincoln County court clerk Nancy Jo Katner, who was now Nancy Jo Mitchell. Mitchell had made notes about Joel Courtney's reasons why he could not be in court on May 24. Kemper also asked about all the phone calls that had come in from Joel Courtney on May 24. In one of the phone calls, he had said he was on his way from Montana. In a later phone call, he actually said he was in Corvallis.

Then an audiotape of the Lincoln County courtroom on May 24, 2004, was played. On it, Judge Littlefield's voice can be heard saying the name of Joel

Courtney, and there was no response. A short time later, Judge Littlefield's voice could be heard again as he spoke to a court clerk. Littlefield said, "There is a matter of Joel Courtney, who is on his way from Montana." Later, when an ADA asked about Courtney, Judge Littlefield made his quip, "I think he took a boat with the Lewis and Clark expedition. He probably won't get here until 2005."

Then an audiotape of May 25, 2004, was played. On it could be heard a judge in the Lincoln County courtroom say, "The last call we got from Mr. Courtney, he said he was in Corvallis. Mr. Courtney was supposed to be here yesterday at eight-thirty. So I assume he's still around Corvallis."

Kemper once again asked Mitchell, "Based upon your knowledge, did Joel Patrick Courtney appear in the Lincoln County court on May 24, 2004?"

Mitchell replied, "No, he did not."

One interesting thing came up when the defense questioned Mitchell. She was asked, "Did Mr. Courtney ever show up at court?"

Mitchell looked at her records and noted that Courtney did appear for an arraignment on the DUI in Judge Huckleberry's courtroom on June 7, 2004. Which meant that if he did kidnap and murder Brooke Wilberger on May 24, 2004, he had the nerve to be in Oregon on June 7.

Taking this a step further, Kemper on redirect asked Mitchell if Joel Courtney made any more court appearances on the DUI matter. Mitchell looked at her files and said that Joel was supposed to attend a June 21, 2004, court date. When he did not do that, a "failure to appear" warrant was issued.

* * *

The next set of witnesses was very important for the prosecution. Not only was DA John Haroldson trying to get the cases of Diane Mason and Jade Bateman tied in with the Brooke Wilberger case, but he was also attempting to show that there was a pattern by Joel Courtney in all three cases. In Joel's attempts toward Diane and Jade, they had survived, and Brooke had not.

On the stand Diane Mason said that she was twenty years old in May 2004 and about five-three. She noted that she lived off campus and had a class at Shepard Hall at OSU at 10:00 A.M. on May 24, 2004. She had cut through the Oak Park Apartments parking lot that morning and noticed a green minivan there. She had then walked out onto Thirtieth Street toward campus and the green minivan had pulled up near her, partially blocking her path.

To avoid it, Diane had to walk out into the street. When she passed the open window on the driver's side of the minivan, a man sitting at the wheel spoke to her and said that he was lost and that he needed help with directions. He said that he was looking for a certain fraternity near campus. Diane noticed that the man was in his late thirties or forties, had light-colored eyes, light-colored hair, and a goatee. He was wearing a "hoop-type earring" in one ear.

Diane gave him directions, but he got out of the minivan, anyway, and said that he had a map of Corvallis in the back of the minivan. Once he slid the side door of the minivan open, Diane got nervous and left the scene. She said that she was aware of how alone she was in that location, and that she felt very vulnerable.

Kemper had Diane mark on a map where all of this had occurred. It was not far from the OSU Reser Stadium, less than two blocks from where Brooke Wilberger had disappeared.

Steven Gorham did not cross-examine Diane Mason.

Jade Bateman was another important witness in the prosecution's scenario to link Joel Courtney to three kidnapping attempts near the OSU campus on May 24, 2004—two of them unsuccessful and the third being that of Brooke Wilberger. Jade testified about being approached by a man in a green mini-van while she walked through the Reser Stadium parking lot on the morning of May 24, 2004. Jade basically reiterated all the things she had told investigators about that morning and her interactions with the man in the green minivan. Jade had been concerned for her safety at the time. In fact, she told her mother, whom she was talking to on a cell phone, not to hang up.

Bob Clifford was also part of this scenario. In May 2004, he had been an associate athletic director on the OSU campus. Clifford told Karen Kemper that he had to use a listening device because of a hearing impairment. Asked how long he had been using a listening device, Clifford said that he'd done so all of his life. In fact, there was a titanium screw in his skull, and the device was attached to that.

Clifford said that on May 24, 2004, he'd left his office around 9:30 A.M. and was driving out of the parking lot, which was dirt and gravel at the time.

"Halfway around a bend I noticed one of our female student employees walking across the parking lot. I recognized her. She was a student manager in women's basketball. Then a green minivan pulled over and the man started talking to her. It did not seem like a normal situation to me, so I drove over and pulled up to the passenger side of the van and tried to get the driver's attention. He kept his hands attached to the steering wheel and would not acknowledge my presence."

Clifford said that he then pulled around directly in front of the minivan, and the man gave him a quick glance. At that point, Jade started to walk away and the minivan driver pulled away onto Western Avenue and then onto Twenty-sixth Street. Clifford noted that the minivan had Minnesota license plates, and the man was wearing a baseball cap and sunglasses.

On cross-examination Gorham asked if Clifford had been questioned immediately after the Brooke Wilberger disappearance. Clifford said that he had been interviewed by a detective sometime in May 2004.

Gorham then queried, "How about at the time of the throw down (photo lineup) of 2006?"

"After the initial interview at OSU, there were follow-up interviews with the Corvallis PD."

"How many times were you interviewed about this?"

"I'd say about three or four different times."

"If I say the name 'John Chilcote' (a Benton County DA Office investigator), do you know who I'm talking about?"

"Yes, I do."

"Did you talk to him about this?"

"No."

* * *

Phillip Zerzan had been a sergeant with the OSU Police Department in 2004. Karen Kemper had him respond to questions about how well he knew the OSU campus, and Zerzan said he knew it very well. As far as traffic flows onto campus, Zerzan stated, "Normal traffic flow on a school day would come in from the east and would come up Monroe and access the northern border. Or it would come in from South Philomath Boulevard. If it was coming from the coast, it would come up Philomath Boulevard."

Zerzan said he had become involved in the Brooke Wilberger case on May 24, 2004, because the incident had occurred only about fifty yards off campus. Zerzan added, "We recognized this would have a significant impact on the campus community. Even though it was off campus, we often responded to that area as well. It was very near the parking lot for Reser Stadium. My involvement was to ensure we provided whatever resources were necessary to the Corvallis PD. And to act as a liaison to those aspects of the investigation that involved the campus and campus community."

On a different set of questions about the investigation, Zerzan said, "On December 1, 2004, I was contacted by Lieutenant Keefer, of the Corvallis PD, who wanted assistance in locating and interviewing a couple of people who had association with the campus. So I assisted him with that, and in addition there was a location where a vehicle had been reported sighted at Reser Stadium on May 24, 2004. I took Lieutenant Keefer out and showed him specifically where that location was. There had been a report he was investigating that a vehicle coming from the northwest corner of the parking lot had traveled across the lot in a southeasterly direction. And as we stood there, just kind of looking over the scene, you could see the rooftops of the Oak Park Apartments. It was a direct line. It was kind of an 'aha' moment for me. This was where the van was, and a short distance away is where the crime occurred."

Lieutenant John Keefer also testified about the location where Jade Bateman and Bob Clifford said they had seen the green minivan in the Reser Stadium parking lot. By May 2004, Keefer had been with the Corvallis Police Department for eight years. About his meeting with Zerzan, Keefer said, "You could see the Oak Park Apartments from there. Mr. Clifford remembered a green van in the parking lot. The driver was speaking with Jade there. It had Minnesota plates."

DDA Kemper then took Keefer back to the "throw down" he had conducted with Bob Clifford. Kemper asked, "Before you showed the photo lineup to Mr. Clifford, had there been extensive publicity about Joel Courtney?"

Keefer replied, "No, ma'am."

"To the best of your knowledge, had Joel Courtney's photograph been disseminated to the public at the time you showed the photo lineup?"

"It had not been."

This photo lineup was important, and Steven Gorham, on cross, queried Lieutenant Keefer more vigorously than had been done to some of the other witnesses.

Gorham asked, "Where was the throw down conducted?"

Keefer responded, "I believe it was in the sports complex. A conference room."

"How many throw downs have you done in your career?"

Keefer said, "I can guess it would be about thirty or so."

"What do they tell you in your training about throw downs?"

"In essence, we want images that are similar. Nothing that makes the suspect stand out. Position needs to rotate if different people look at it. We give an admonishment that a person can change their looks through a haircut, moustache, et cetera."

Gorham asked, "When Mr. Clifford looked at the photos, what comments did he make?"

Keefer looked at his report and said, "Mr. Clifford was concerned about the red hat the suspect had worn."

Gorham then asked, "Did you suggest Mr. Clifford do something?"

"I suggested that he cover the top half of the photos' heads, to see if someone looked familiar."

"He only did that with the top row of photos?"

Keefer stated, "No, I believe he did it with both rows."

"You asked him on a scale of one to ten, one being he wasn't sure, and ten that he was very sure, how he felt that photo number three was the person he had seen. Well, I'll ask a more direct question. Did he say he was certain it was not one, two, four, or six?"

"Yes."

"He told you number three had the right look?"

"Yes, sir."

"He didn't identify number three, did he?"

"At the end he did."

"But not verbally?"

"No, sir. But when he was about to leave, I left the number off the photograph. And he wrote down the number three."

"There was some discussion about high cheekbones?"

"Not to my recollection."

"Well, did he tell you that number five had high cheekbones?"

"Yes, he did."

"What was the context of that?" Gorham wondered.

Keefer replied, "He basically just said that. I don't know if he was looking for high cheekbones or not."

"So you don't remember him talking about the person he saw at the parking lot as having high cheekbones?"

"I do not."

On redirect Kemper asked Lieutenant Keefer to look at an admonition statement that Clifford used. Keefer looked at the statement and said that since Bob Clifford had a hearing impairment, it was important to have given him a written statement.

Kemper then asked, "Did he read the instructions carefully?"

Keefer said, "Yes, he did."

Jade Bateman's mother also took the stand, speaking of the phone call she had made to her daughter that morning. Jade had been very concerned about the man in the green van; she told her mother to stay on the phone. Jade's mother said that it was more of a demand than a request.

Lending weight to what Diane Mason and Jade Bateman had to say was John Chilcote, an investigator for the Benton County DA's Office. In a turnabout of questioning, it was Steven Gorham who wanted Chilcote on the stand so that he could question him. Gorham asked on direct if Chilcote was involved with the two indictments brought forth that day by John Haroldson on the Mason and Bateman matters. Chilcote said that he was the DA's investigator on the Brooke Wilberger case, and that he did know about the Mason and Bateman indictments.

Gorham asked, "When did you start working on the Brooke Wilberger case?"

Chilcote answered that he had begun on the day after she went missing.

Asked if he knew that a tip hotline had been set up about Brooke, Chilcote said that he did.

So Gorham showed Chilcote a police document that stated: *Bateman asked the driver if he was looking for something.* Gorham then said, "It seems that she made contact with him first, and not the other way around."

Chilcote replied, "No. There were many people on this case and sharing information. What is correct is that she indicated that he spoke to her first."

Gorham came back with, "This report is from a person named Stauder?"

"Yes, she is a detective with the Corvallis PD."

"Do you know if anything was done with this tip (by Bateman) until December 2004?"

Chilcote replied, "No, I don't know the specifics of how they responded to that tip."

"You were on the major task force on this case. Do you remember anything about this tip or any other tip concerning a green van from May to December 2004?"

Chilcote said, "I remember a lot of information coming after May about two OSU students who had been contacted by a person in a van."

Kemper, on cross, asked Chilcote, "Roughly, when did the green van become a point of interest to law enforcement?"

Chilcote responded, "A van was of interest to us relatively soon in the investigation, because we were receiving information about these reports about a van not far from the scene of the abduction of Brooke Wilberger. It was a van of a certain color and certain size. The tips came from Diane Mason and Jade Bateman."

DDA Kemper wanted to know, "Was Bob Clifford someone who came to your attention?"

"Yes," Chilcote said. "He came to my attention about the same time through investigators."

"Was Mr. Clifford able to give more information about the van?"

"Yes. He was able to give more details about the driver of that van, and he also was able to identify the license plate on that van as being from Minnesota."

Kemper asked, "Was Mr. Clifford able to pick an individual out of a photo lineup?"

"Yes," Chilcote responded. "He picked out Mr. Courtney."

On redirect Gorham asked, "Would it be fair to say that [the] focus of the investigation was not on Ms. Mason's tip, or Ms. Bateman's tip, or Mr. Clifford's tip, or the green van, until you already were looking at Mr. Courtney as a suspect?"

Chilcote replied, "It really refocused us. And the task force was about fifty people at that point."

Because John Chilcote had mentioned Detective Karen Stauder as the one who had written a report that it was Jade Bateman who first spoke with Joel Courtney, and not the other way around, Steven Gorham had Stauder testify.

Karen Stauder said that she was a detective with the Corvallis PD in 2004 and had been a part of the Brooke Wilberger Task Force.

Gorham had Stauder look at a report she had made and asked, "That report, did you submit it to anyone?"

"Yes, to my police department," she said.

Gorham had Stauder read the report and then had her read something written by some other officer, which was termed a "tip slip."

What Gorham was getting at was that Detective Stauder's report was somewhat different from the wording of the tip slip. The tip slip may have come from Detective Sarah Fontaine, because Gorham asked Detective Stauder who Fontaine was. Stauder said that Fontaine was a member of the Oregon State Police.

Gorham asked, "Did you see Ms. Bateman in person?"

"No," Stauder replied, "I spoke to her on the phone."

"Did Ms. Bateman say she approached the person in the van?"

Stauder said, "Yes and no. If I may elaborate on that."

"Sure," Gorham responded.

So Stauder explained, "She told me that a person in a van was driving by very slowly and staring at her. It was at that point that she initiated contact with that person."

"So she initiated that contact," Gorham said.

Stauder gave the same reply she had just mentioned.

Not letting her off the hook on this, Gorham added, "What did she tell you she asked him?"

Stauder said, "She asked if he was looking for something."

Apparently, Gorham was reasoning that if Jade Bateman first made verbal contact with Joel Courtney, then he couldn't have been too threatening to her. Otherwise, she would have simply run away rather than sticking around and talking to him.

Karen Kemper, on cross, wanted to get to the bottom of why Detective Stauder would make a comment as to whether Jade Bateman first made contact with the suspect, as being "Yes and no." To get to this point, Kemper first asked Detective Stauder how long she had been in law enforcement. Stauder replied that she had been a police officer for sixteen years and a detective for the last five years. She said she had trained in defensive tactics, body language, and many other things of that nature.

Kemper asked Stauder what she meant about "body language."

Stauder replied that if someone was staring at her, that was a form of unspoken contact.

Kemper asked, "From your experience, how might you counter that nonverbal contact?"

Stauder began to answer, "For me as a woman, I—"

This brought an immediate objection from Gorham. "What her thoughts are on something like this is irrelevant."

Judge Williams sustained the objection.

So Karen Kemper tried again. "Ms. Stauder, you're a female, and you weren't always an officer. Correct?"

"Yes."

"You live in the city."

"Yes."

"You walk around."

"Yes.

"Did you ever have anyone stare at you?"

"Yes, I have."

Gorham objected once again to this line of questioning. He said, "Maybe these questions aren't objectionable, but they are leading to something that is."

Kemper, on the other hand, claimed, "This officer has testified that she's taken specialized training in behavior and mannerisms. Therefore, she is qualified as an expert to talk about nonverbal situations, both as an officer and a female."

Gorham disagreed and said, "Then the argument is that every female is an expert in being female. I guess that would make me an expert in not being female. She's not an expert in anything except in being who she is. It's not relevant. What is relevant is what occurred between Ms. Bateman and somebody in a green van. If you listened to Ms. Bateman on the stand, it would seem that the person in the van initiated contact. Now we learn that is not accurate."

Judge Williams sustained the objection once again.

Kemper kept trying, however. She had Detective Stauder tell about her training and experience. While doing this, Karen Stauder said, "Actions of people who are nonverbal are very important. A person who is driving slowly by you and staring, that is a prime example. In law enforcement we are trained that nonverbal contact can be very important. We are trained to watch people's movements. Even if someone is just staring at you—we are trained to notice that they are staring at us. A nonverbal thing like that cannot be ignored."

In the end all that Detective Stauder was able to get in was that she was a trained officer who thought nonverbal communication was important. It was her belief that when Jade Bateman was walking alone through a large parking lot, and a man drove slowly by her, staring at her, it was appropriate for Jade to make the first spoken contact. It was not because she was happy to see the man there—rather, it was because she was worried for her own safety and wanted to know what was going on.

These witnesses had been bad enough for Joel Courtney's case. However, there were four others who were absolutely devastating, and they would box him into a very tight corner.

CHAPTER 23

"I STARTED SCREAMING AND CRYING."

One of these witnesses was Jesus Ordaz, Joel's brother-in-law. Since Spanish was Ordaz's first language, an interpreter was called in just in case that route would be easier to follow. Ordaz said that he had been married for eighteen years. His wife's sister, Rosy, was Joel Courtney's wife. Ordaz said that he had known Joel for seventeen years.

In April and May 2004, Joel, Rosy, and their kids were living at the Ordaz residence in the southeast section of Portland. Jesus was working for CBM, which did janitorial work in many Western states. A calendar of May 2004 was produced in court, and it proved that no one except Joel Courtney had driven that green van for the company in that month. During the early part of May, Joel drove the van, with Minnesota plates, to Montana and Idaho on a job. On a return trip to Oregon, Joel got a ticket for speeding.

Later that same month, on May 23, 2004, a friend invited Jesus and his family to a First Communion party. Jesus and his wife invited Rosy and her kids to come as well, and they did so. It was a Sunday, so they all went to church before the Communion. It was a full mass, and they were there from noon until one-thirty. The party started around two, and Joel didn't arrive until some time later, since he'd been working on a janitorial job. Jesus seemed to think that Joel didn't get there until 6:00 P.M.

As Jesus recalled, he and Joel stayed late at the party, after their wives left. In fact, both Jesus and Joel stayed there all through the night, drinking beers and tequila. Jesus also recounted that Joel went a few times into a room, where Jesus suspected illegal drugs were being used.

When Jesus and Joel got home, it was around six-thirty in the morning on Monday, May 24. Joel said he had to use the phone to make a long-distance call, and Jesus let him do so. The prosecution brought out a document concerning Jesus Ordaz's phone number and phone calls to the court in Lincoln County, Oregon. Ordaz said that the document was correct about his phone number. It was noted that phone calls to the court in Lincoln County were made at 7:21, 7:22, and 7:27 A.M.

Ordaz continued, "Joel left my house right after his last phone call. He was driving the green van. The van was clean on the outside at the time he left. Joel would usually take some clothes with him when he went on a trip. On that day he was wearing the same clothes he had worn at the party. And he wore a baseball cap and some dark sunglasses.

"Joel did not come back to our house for some time. I'm not sure, but I think it was either late on May twenty-fifth or early on May twenty-sixth. I wasn't home at the time. I was working, because I normally work from five-thirty P.M. until two A.M. the next morning. When I got home on May twenty-sixth, the green van was outside and all dirty on the outside. Like when you drive a van up in the mountains. It was muddy. I knew when I saw the van, my supervisor wouldn't like seeing it like that. So I took it to work, where there was good water pressure, and I washed it there."

Jesus added about going on vacation to Southern California in early June 2004. When he got home, Joel was gone, and so was the green van. Jesus discovered that Joel had driven the green Dodge van to New Mexico, without permission. A short time later, Jesus Ordaz's superior at CBM phoned and had Jesus go to New Mexico and retrieve the green van, which he did.

Even more damaging to Courtney than Jesus Ordaz was the testimony of several women who had been sexually molested by Joel Courtney. One of these was Sue McDonald, who had been eighteen years old in 1984. She spoke of hanging out with teenage friends, "watching television and doing regular teenage stuff." One of the teenagers there was Joel Courtney. Once again, McDonald told her story of being in a car with Joel after getting

together with the others, and being out on an isolated road alone with him.

"There were no streetlights and very few houses
on the road. I was driving and Joel started putting
his hand on my leg. Making advances. I asked him,
'What are you doing?' He kept at it and I had to stop
driving. When I stopped, he climbed on top of me.
He hit me in the face with his fist.

"He got out of the car and dragged me out. He
pulled my pants down. I was sitting in the gravel by
the side of the road. I asked him to stop. I asked if
we could go back to Vickie's house if he wanted to
do it. I thought maybe I could convince him to go
back where people were. I was scared."

At this point in her testimony, Sue broke down
crying. She asked for a moment to collect herself
and have a drink of water. After she had done that,
Sue continued. "At some point he stopped and kind
of agreed with me. We got back in the car. And then
he changed his mind and said for me to just take
him home."

It was this incident that eventually led to a conviction of Joel Courtney for sexual molestation.

Karen Kemper asked if Sue saw Joel Courtney in
the courtroom. She pointed to Joel, who was sitting
at the defense table.

DDA Kemper said, "Understanding that many
years have intervened, do you recall his height back
then?"

Sue answered, "He was about six feet tall."

"And what was your height then?"

"I was about five foot three."

Gorham, on cross, asked, "After that night, did
you ever see Mr. Courtney again?"

Sue replied, "I think I saw him again a year or two later. I don't remember where."

Gorham then queried, "Could it have been hanging out with other friends?"

Sue responded, "It probably was with mutual friends."

Possibly even more damaging to Joel Courtney than Sue McDonald was the testimony of his own sister, Dina McBride. Dina was not able to take the actual witness stand because of recent leg surgery, so she was sworn in lower down in the courtroom. Once she began to testify, Dina said that she was two and a half years older than Joel.

Karen Kemper asked her, "Is coming here today difficult for you?"

Dina replied, "I guess I'm glad to have the opportunity to see him. But it's a sad occasion."

"How do you feel about the defendant?"

Dina responded, "I love my brother. I love his family. But I'm sad because of what we're here for."

DDA Kemper wanted to know where she and Joel were raised. Dina said they were raised in Beaverton, Oregon.

"In the spring of 1993, where was your brother living?" (This mention of the year 1993 didn't mean much in the way of previous testimony. But it soon would have a very important connotation.)

Dina said, "I think in North Portland or over by Multnomah. There was an apartment up in the hills. I think he and Rosy were living there at the time."

"Was he working then?"

Dina responded, "I think he was a mechanic then."

"Do you know what kind of mechanic?"

"I remember someone saying a Honda-certified mechanic."

Kemper asked, "Do you remember what your brother looked like in the spring of 1993?"

Dina said, "He was tall. He had kind of long hair in the back. It was kind of gelled on top. Maybe kind of spiky. When he was fairly young, he was given a very light prescription of reading glasses. He didn't wear them often. But he would wear sunglasses when it was sunny outside."

DDA Kemper produced a photo of Dina at her wedding in November 1993. In the photo was Joel, his wife, Rosy, and their first son. Dina said, yes, that was the way Joel looked in 1993.

Switching to a different year, Kemper asked about June 2004. Kemper asked if there was a time during that June 2004, when Joel showed up at their grandmother's house. Dina replied, "Yes, there were actually four generations living in that house. My husband and I, my mom, my children and grandmother. It was a little before noon when Joel arrived. It was around the same time I was coordinating a large children's event at church. I actually sent an e-mail right around that time to my husband, because I was so concerned about Joel. I asked my husband to pray for Joel.

"I was at home with my grandma. My mom was at work. The house was pretty quiet, and I had just finished getting Grandma lunch. Grandma wasn't feeling good, so she went to lay down. It was around eleven forty-five A.M. when Joel came in. I hadn't seen him in a while and he seemed—not exactly agitated, but like he was on edge. A little, not quite hyper but—well, he walked through the door and he said, 'You won't believe where I've been for the last three days.' His conversation was very animated.

"I said, 'Well, what went on?' And he said, 'I was kidnapped for three days, and there were guys there with guns and knives. There was a kind of a party at first, and people were there, but later they were gone. I was hiding in the bushes, and it rained part of the time, and I was naked part of the time. I was freezing and hungry, and I haven't had anything to eat.'

"It was a lot of information coming from him in [a] very disjointed manner. And he mentioned there was a girl there, but there wasn't a lot of description about her. There was even some information about the proximity of where this had all occurred."

Dina started to say, "The implication was—"

Gorham objected and was sustained. There wasn't going to be any testimony about "implications."

So Karen Kemper asked, "What did the girl look like?"

Dina said, "He didn't give any specifics about short, tall, thin, fat, whatever. There was a mention that there was a blond girl in the group."

"Did he tell you about blood?"

"He did mention blood and guns and knives. Someone had an automatic firearm and it was frightening."

"Did he tell you where the blood was?"

"No, he did not."

"Did he tell you what happened to the girl?"

"No, he didn't."

Kemper then wanted Dina to look at a document

that concerned her interview by Detective Houck in September 2008. Dina looked at the document of what she had said to Houck, and now added, "Joel said that he had been sleeping outdoors. Somehow I thought he meant in the woods somewhere. Joel talked about it starting at a party and there was a progression of movement. I don't know where the girl came into the story line. She was a blond girl, and he said there was blood on her. And then she died."

Gorham had no cross-examination of Dina McBride, but he said that he might when it came to trial.

Many of the witnesses who had just testified had done so before, and their stories were known to one degree or another by the media. That was not the case with the next witness. She was new to the stories about Joel Courtney, and what she had to say added one more huge nail to his coffin. The woman was Sandy Vargas.

Even before Sandy began to testify, Karen Kemper told the judge, "She remembers things in pictures more than words." Kemper asked the judge to allow Sandy to close her eyes at times while testifying to remember things.

Judge Locke Williams asked for more of an explanation, so Sandy told him, "I have a photographic memory. I can remember things much better when I close my eyes." There was no objection coming from the defense table, so Judge Williams allowed it.

Sandy said that in 1993 she was fourteen years old, five-one, and weighed about 105 pounds. Close to Easter, 1993, she was a runaway and living on the streets of Portland. Sandy testified, "One day after Easter, I gave my heart to the Lord at church. I left that church in Northeast Portland and in the afternoon I was sitting on a curb in a residential neighborhood. I went to a grocery store and bought some potato chips. I was in the deodorant aisle and I stole a deodorant. There was a man in the deodorant aisle in a long black coat and he saw me steal it. I saw that he noticed me doing it.

"I went out and sat on a bench, and at first I thought it was cool that he didn't give me away. But then he came over, and I was afraid that he might be a security guard. I put the deodorant in my bag of chips and began walking down a side street. And the man who had worn the black coat pulled up in a white car. He didn't have the black jacket on anymore. He asked me if I needed help, if I was okay. I thought how nice this was. He seemed like a safe person. Maybe he was a guy from church who wanted to help me.

"He had a square kind of face, bluish eyes, and his blond hair was kind of spiky. He looked like he was in his thirties. He had kind of a baby face and good teeth. He asked me where I was coming from, and I told him I was coming from church. He asked me what my name was, and I gave him a fake name. I didn't want to be turned in as a runaway. I asked him what his name was, and he said that it was 'Dave.' I told him that was my father's name.

"He asked me if I needed a ride. I thought about it. He seemed really nice and I felt at ease with him. But I told him no, and said that I needed to go home. I lied that my parents were waiting for me. He drove away and I was going to walk back where there were people and stores. But then I thought, he might not think I was going home if I did that. So I turned back and started walking in the direction I had been walking.

"I heard a noise behind me. Somebody running, and it was the guy himself. The one who said he was Dave. He said, 'Wait! Wait!' And I thought he was still trying to help me. He was wearing his long black coat again.

"He pulled out a gun and pointed it at me. There was another guy walking by, but Dave pulled out the gun, anyway. It was just getting dark around then. He put the gun on me and covered me with his coat, and told me where we were going to walk. He said something like, 'Don't say anything!' My head only came up to about his chest. He was about six feet tall. We walked by a couple. The girl had curly hair. She was with her boyfriend. I was scared. I looked into her eyes and I wanted to tell her something was wrong. But I didn't want to hurt her or see her get hurt.

"I just gave her a look like I was okay. We turned left and walked down a road. I saw his car. I also saw that there was nobody around anymore. I walked past the car, because there was no one around, and I was going to keep walking. But he showed me the gun again and shoved it against my stomach. He opened the door and forced me in.

"We drove somewhere. It wasn't a very far drive. There was nobody around and he parked the car. We just sat there for a while. He had me move closer to him, and he told me he just wanted to hold me. 'I'm not gonna hurt you,' he said. 'I'm just gonna hold you.'

"So I moved over and he felt me up. I was cringing and moving around. Then he asked me to take off my clothes. And I started to take my shoe off and [I] started crying. And I think I was asking for my mom. And then I thought, no, I'm not going to do this.

"He had some handcuffs and he pointed at them. He told me to put the handcuffs on myself. He didn't want to put them on me. But I wouldn't do it. I started screaming and crying. He got real upset and put his hand to his forehead, like an adult would with a crying child. He was frustrated with me.

"I was screaming uncontrollably and I started praying out loud. 'Our Father who art in Heaven. Hallowed be thy name. Thy Kingdom come, thy will be done, on earth as it is in Heaven. Give us this day, our daily bread, and forgive [us] our trespasses as we forgive those who trespass against us. Lead us not into temptation, and deliver us from evil. For thine is the Kingdom, and the power, and the glory, Forever. Amen.'

"And then I prayed for him. I said, 'Father, forgive him of his sins, because he knows not what he does.'

"He started to freak out. I looked at him, and he looked so scared. He looked out the window, and he had his hands on the wheel. His hands were like at the two and eleven positions. I looked at him again and at the gun on his lap. I was praying and God was speaking to me. God said, *'Get out of the car.'* Not in a loud voice, but in a quiet one.

"And I asked God when to do it. And he said, *'Now.'*

"I looked at the gun, and then at the door, which was unlocked. I opened it, got out, and ran. I ran all the way up the street and then down the next street. There were cars going by, but not many. I saw only one lit place nearby, so I went there and stood under a light. And his car came up and drove back and forth right by me. Back and forth.

"I was scared. I went inside the café and the cashier asked me if I was all right. I said I was okay because I didn't want to go home. I thought maybe he really was a policeman. He had a gun and handcuffs. They looked like police things. I was a child. Nobody would believe me.

"I finally hid in the bathroom for about fifteen minutes. When I came out of the bathroom, I saw him drive by one more time. I went outside to call a friend of mine from a pay phone. It was either a friend named Diana or Heather. And the parents answered the phone."

Sandy's story ended there, and tears were running down her face by the time she stopped her long monologue.

DDA Kemper asked what happened next.

Sandy said that the police eventually picked her up as a runaway, and she told them the story of what had happened with the man in the black coat.

The policeman told her, "See, that's what happens when you run away from home."

Kemper approached Sandy with a photo of Joel Courtney and the way he looked in 1993. Sandy said that the person in the photo looked like the man who had pulled a gun on her and forced her into his car.

As to why she was bringing all of this up now, Sandy said, "A friend of mine was dating and doing it by the Internet. I didn't think that was safe, and I went online to tell her about that. It was in February 2009. I was looking under 'serial killers,' and that kind of thing. And the name Joel Courtney popped up. I saw that he had blue eyes and blond hair. It also said that he was in Oregon from 1991 to 1993. It spoke of the kind of girls he would take. Their age, height, and weight. And I thought I would check this out because it had happened to me.

"The first picture I looked at was him with a mullet! And I thought that maybe it could be the man who attacked me. But I wasn't sure. So I called a contact number. It was either the Corvallis Police Department or Benton County Sheriff's Office. I just wanted to know. Around that time I was having a garage sale. And my boyfriend came over and I told him about this for the first time. Then I looked on the computer again that day. And I said, 'He didn't wear his hair like that back then. And he didn't wear glasses.' Then I looked up one more thing. And it was about a trial of him in New Mexico. And it was a video of him moving and walking in court. And then I was one hundred percent sure. My body started shaking all over. It was horrible."

Kemper asked Sandy, "You're aware there have been television reports and newspaper articles about Joel Courtney with photos, correct?"

"Yes, but I didn't see any newspaper articles about him until last week."

DDA Kemper wanted to know if the incident that happened to her still bothered her.

Sandy shut her eyes again and replied, "I get flashbacks a lot. When I see a car like his, it scares me. I can still remember the license plate he had. The first numbers were either three-four-one or two-three-one. There were letters near the end of the alphabet on the plate."

When she opened her eyes, sitting across the courtroom was the man who was like a ghost from her past—Joel Patrick Courtney.

CHAPTER 24

"I'M READY TO TRY THIS CASE IN ANY COUNTY IN THE STATE!"

After all the witnesses had been heard, the prosecution knew that their summation to Judge Locke Williams was vitally important. Not only were they trying to consolidate the trials of Brooke Wilberger, Diane Mason, and Jade Bateman, but they also were attempting to get into an upcoming trial all the damning testimony of the witnesses who had just been on the stand. Just because they had said all those things now did not mean that the judge would ever allow jurors to hear the information.

Karen Kemper began by saying that sometime between 10:00 and 10:30 A.M. on May 24, 2004, was the last time that anyone—except Joel Courtney—saw Brooke Wilberger alive. Kemper pointed out that Courtney left that morning from Jesus Ordaz's home, and they knew that because he had phoned the Lincoln County court three times, saying he was going there and he would be late. "We listened to those tapes. We know that he did not appear for court. He even called from Corvallis, saying that he was en route. But he never made it there."

Kemper spoke of Diane Mason's interaction with a man driving a green minivan near Thirtieth Street on the morning of May 24, 2004. And she gave a description that matched that of Joel Courtney and the green Dodge van he had been driving at the time. Jade Bateman and Bob Clifford also gave detailed descriptions about the green van and the man driving it. Clifford even remembered that the green van had Minnesota license plates—just like the Minnesota license plates that were on Joel Courtney's green van.

Kemper said, "We know that all of this took place in a small perimeter of the Oregon State University campus, not far from the Oak Park Apartments. And it all took place just prior to ten A.M. on May 24, 2004. Lieutenant Zerzan and Lieutenant Keefer stood where Jade Batman had stood, and they could see the rooftops of the Oak Park Apartments. They weren't using binoculars or anything else. They could plainly see the apartments."

Kemper spoke of how similar Natalie Kirov's incident was to what had occurred with Brooke, and had almost occurred with Diane and Jade. And Kemper brought up the situation with Sue McDonald: "Suddenly the defendant was on her, with the steering wheel at his back, forcing himself on her. He struck her in the temple with his fist and then dragged her out of the car."

Kemper then brought up about Sandy Vargas and

her ordeal. Kemper said, "Your Honor, the case law says similarity, timing, and repetition. Weighing that there is undue prejudice—and it must be remembered that evidence is always prejudicial to the defendant—we all know this is a no-body homicide case. Brooke Wilberger's remains have never been recovered. The state does not have the usual information that would be brought to a jury in the form of forensic evidence. And that must be considered as part and parcel of the state's need in this circumstance."

Kemper told Judge Locke Williams that the state's need was "narrowly focused." Limiting instructions would ensure just that sort of thing. Kemper then cited *State* v. *Hampton* and *State* v. *Brown* and said that those cases were a template on how the judge should rule now.

Kemper even used an ELMO (an overhead projection device) and showed both of those cases side by side.

Kemper asked a rhetorical question: "Do those cases ask whether the evidence is logically relevant?" Yes, she replied to her own question, they did. Then she asked, "Is the evidence relevant for a noncharacter purpose? We are not suggesting, once a bad person, always a bad person. That is not the point of this evidence. Once again, it is the repetition and similarity of these acts."

Highlighting sections, Kemper pointed out that Sue McDonald was eighteen years old, height five-three, weight 130 pounds. Sandy Vargas, fourteen years old, height five-one, weight 105 pounds. Diane Mason—twenty years old, height five-seven, weight 125 pounds. Jade Bateman—twenty-one years old, five-seven, 130 pounds. Natalie Kirov—twenty-two years old, five-four, 125 pounds. Brooke Wilberger—nineteen years old, five-four, 105 pounds. In every case, the women and girls were much younger than Joel Courtney, much shorter and weighed much less.

Kemper said, "Your Honor, each of these victims are relevant. There is no prejudice that substantially outweighs the relevance of these victims. This evidence goes to plan, opportunity, and intent. The state urges this court to deem all of this evidence to be admissible."

Steven Gorham, of course, was just as adamant that everything that had been said by the witnesses be excluded as evidence, and that Diane Mason's case and Jade Bateman's case not be combined with that of Brooke Wilberger. Gorham said, "I'll use a colloquial term—what the state is trying to do is throw mud at Mr. Courtney, and have as much of that mud stick as possible. Then they'll use what mud is there to try and convict Mr. Courtney on the Wilberger case."

Gorham said that the Dina McBride and Jesus Ordaz so-called evidence wasn't relevant at all. Gorham claimed that the prosecution was just restating things that had occurred around the time of May 24, 2004. He said there was no connection to Brooke Wilberger.

As to the prosecutions' major purpose, Gorham related, "You've heard what they've said their purpose is. Their purpose is about plan, opportunity, and intent. Every safe robber may know the same technique, but it doesn't mean that one person did similar safe robbing. In this case the prosecution is saying, 'Once a rapist, always a rapist.' And that is not legal."

As far as Diane Mason and Jade Bateman went, Gorham said that Joel Courtney never attempted to kidnap them—all he had done was ask them for directions. Then Gorham pointed out dissimilarities in what the prosecution was bringing in now. With Sandy Vargas, the man in question had used a gun and handcuffs. That had not been the case with Joel Courtney with either Sue McDonald or Natalie Kirov. "And the fact that they are saying that Natalie and Brooke were both near stadiums—there was no campus or stadium with Sue McDonald and Sandy Vargas."

John Haroldson had his say after Steven Gorham. Haroldson told the judge, "It has been the practice in this state to enhance the evidence that is known. Then the court can evaluate the witnesses that might be in a trial. This is a clear analysis about other acts and admissibility. If it's prejudicial, that is not enough. It must substantially outweigh the probative value."

Haroldson brought up as an example another case he had prosecuted in that same court. The defendant had been charged with murder, and five years previously the defendant had been convicted of a fourth-degree assault in Alaska. There was a disparity in the victims' ages in those cases. One was a young teenager and the other was twenty-eight years old. Using the same structure as he was doing with those cases with Joel Courtney, Haroldson said that in the previous case the judge, an appeals court, and the state supreme court all said he was correct and upheld his conviction.

"It boils down to this," Haroldson said. "This so-called mud is relevant. It's incriminating evidence. And it is not in the defendant's interest to have relevant, incriminating evidence offered against him. And that's why a zealous defense attorney doesn't want it to come in.

"We have never made the argument that this is a signature crime (a crime that is patterned exactly like other crimes). Our argument has been to the similarities that exist. The theory of the state is that Joel Courtney arrived in Corvallis on the morning of May 24, 2004, to abduct, sexually assault, and kill a young woman. The Oregon State University campus was a target-rich environment for him."

Haroldson told the judge that all three contacts by Courtney were made within an hour, and all were in proximity to one another. "His intent was to perpetrate the same crime. The difference is how far along he got in his plan. Jade Bateman and Diane Mason saw the defendant in a green van—a green van that later proved to have Brooke Wilberger's DNA in it."

As an example Haroldson brought up a situation about a bank robber who robs a bank. Witnesses see the man in a café across the street from the bank a half hour before he robs it. They don't actually see the man rob the bank, but the witnesses' testimony about seeing him in the café is admissible by law.

Steven Gorham had one last shot to convince the judge not to allow all this evidence in. Gorham argued, "These cases have been cross-pollinated." Then Gorham noted that one of the cases that Haroldson had cited concerned traffic citations. "To decide a death penalty issue on traffic citations in a joinder case—that's where our due process argument comes in. Those things are different! Death penalty cases are different than other minor cases. Ms. Wilberger's case should rise and fall on Ms. Wilberger's case."

Now it was Stephanie Tuttle's turn. She was an expert in Oregon state law and she told the judge, "I disagree that we're just trying to pile on. And as far as the traffic citation case goes—the law is what the law is. It doesn't change case by case. The statute is the same whether it is for a traffic citation or an aggravated murder case.

"Even if there was some prejudice against the defendant in this case, that could be taken care of at a later time by jury instructions. Right now all we want to do is join these cases. And they have met the criteria to do so."

Judge Locke Williams took all of this under advisement and said that he would rule on it later. His rulings would have a profound effect upon how Joel Courtney and his lawyers would proceed toward their defense at trial.

Joel Courtney's defense team soon had a motion of their own. They wanted Courtney's trial moved out of Benton County, citing all the publicity that had occurred there since May 2004. Then, in a surprise move, DA Haroldson conceded the move to another county without an argument.

Perhaps stunned by this unexpected turn of events, Steven Krasik told Judge Locke Williams that the request for a move out of Benton County was just a tactic. Krasik added, "It's quite possible that this county would have been our choice."

DA Haroldson was not pleased with all this flip-flopping on the defense's part. Haroldson said, "The motion has been made and conceded." And yet, being pragmatic, he added, "I'm ready to try this case in any county in the state! I have confidence in our Benton County jurors, but believe that the truth will not change—no matter which county we're in."

Judge Williams had to go on the assumption that the trial would be moving to another county, and to that end he said he would find out what districts could hold the trial, which promised to be a lengthy one.

Even Sheriff Diana Simpson chimed in on this matter of flip-flopping by the defense. She told reporters that there were going to have to be a lot of logistics set up for the move to another county and would include high security. She added, "Wherever the trial is held, that's where Courtney will be held."

One thing that no one counted on in all of this was Joel Courtney himself. Always contrary when it came to legal matters, he was staying true to form once again. For some unknown reason Courtney now did not want the trial to leave Benton County. And his sudden turnabout made his attorneys look like fools.

Steven Krasik and Steven Gorham had to write a

motion to Judge Williams why they no longer wanted a change of venue. In part they said that Joel Courtney wanted time to consider if he could get a fair trial in Benton County, based upon a survey of potential jurors. And in a sentence that must have been hard to swallow for the attorneys, they wrote, *The defendant asserts that his attorneys did not give him adequate time to reflect on the ramifications of the decision.*

The *Gazette-Times* noted, *Changing stances is not new to Courtney. In 2004, he was arrested for the rape and kidnap of a college student in New Mexico. Just before the start of the 2007 trial, he pleaded guilty to the charges. He then tried to withdraw the plea at the sentencing hearing.*

The Benton County prosecutors must have also been irritated by Courtney's constant disruptions. DDA Karen Kemper told reporters, "The defendant's complaint is that he apparently wanted to change the venue, but when he got what he wanted, he doesn't want it anymore."

Soon thereafter, Judge Locke Williams made his decisions on the important matters that had been brought up by the various witnesses during the previous hearing. The prosecution got most of what it wanted, as far as joining the cases of Diane Mason, Jade Bateman, and Brooke Wilberger. Judge Locke Williams let it be known that the cases "were similar in character, and occurred within minutes of each other and within a remarkably limited geographical area. The separately charged offenses are part of a common scheme or plan."

Judge Williams ruled on the testimony of Sue McDonald and Sandy Vargas, and he noted that they occurred in 1985 and 1993. These, according to the judge, were too remote, and he would not allow this evidence at trial.

The evidence about Joel Courtney drinking and using cocaine at the party on May 23, 2004, and his failure to appear at Lincoln County court on May 24, 2004, were going to be allowed in as evidence. And most important of all, the testimony of Diane Mason, Jade Bateman, and Bob Clifford was going to be allowed at trial. These three could put a man matching Joel Courtney's description, driving a green van, within blocks of the spot where Brooke Wilberger was abducted. A green van that just happened to contain DNA evidence that Brooke had been inside it.

Steven Krasik and Steven Gorham must have known they were in for a very tough legal battle on the Joel Courtney case. And in a short time, Courtney was about to make their job a lot harder for them.

CHAPTER 25
CRIMINAL MISCHIEF

On July 21, 2009, Joel Courtney was in a medical room at the Benton County Jail with psychiatrist Jon Sobotka. For whatever reason, shortly after 2:00 P.M., Courtney went berserk. He grabbed a fax machine from a desk and threw it at Dr. Sobotka. Then he damaged medical records that pertained to himself and other inmates. The uproar caused a major disturbance in the entire jail as officers came running to Sobotka's aid.

Sheriff Diana Simpson said about the incident that doctors and psychiatrists would have extra security in the jail after this fracas. Simpson added that she couldn't recall the last time a psychiatrist, doctor, or nurse had been assaulted in the jail.

Once again, defense lawyers had to try to clean up a mess that Joel Courtney had created. The best Steven Krasik could do was tell reporters that jails were stressful places. Krasik said, "Sometimes people respond to stress in ways that create additional problems."

The "additional problem" for Courtney was that he now faced more criminal charges. DA John Haroldson brought charges of second-degree-assault, unlawful use of a weapon, menacing, and second-degree criminal mischief. And all of this ended up in Judge Janet Holcomb's courtroom. The same judge whom previous Benton County DA Scott Heiser said he would not allow to preside over the Brooke Wilberger case.

With the latest assault in mind, the prosecution asked Judge Williams to make sure that Courtney wore a stun belt when the Wilberger case came to trial. DDA Karen Kemper told the judge, "The safety of courtroom personnel, lawyers, jury, and spectators must be considered in light of Courtney's alleged assault on Dr. Sobotka. That assault demonstrates his likelihood for violence. During Mr. Courtney's sentencing in New Mexico, he told the judge he would spit on him if he was close enough."

Steven Gorham countered that there would be plenty of deputies in the courtroom at trial, so that Courtney did not need to wear a stun belt. And Gorham added that the injury to Dr. Sobotka was very minor. "It wasn't like a broken bone or something like that."

Judge Locke Williams, however, sided with the prosecution after this latest outburst by Joel Courtney. Williams said that a stun belt was appropriate under the circumstances and Courtney would have to wear a Band-it stun belt device beneath his clothing. The jurors would not be able to see the stun belt.

* * *

In the weeks before trial, the defense peppered the court with an array of motions, most of which the prosecution was against. In one motion the defense wanted individual jurors questioned in voir dire outside the presence of other jurors. This would make the process a very lengthy one. The DA's office retorted, "To the extent the court is concerned that the entire panel would have to sit in the same room for days on end during voir dire, this problem can be alleviated by separate and smaller panels. There is no need to individually voir dire each juror in seclusion on every issue, as the defendant proposes. This will lengthen the process immeasurably."

Already it was a case that had occurred in May 2004 and was still going through the system in 2009. And if anything, the long process of picking jurors in Natalie Kirov's New Mexico case showed how long voir dire could take, in a case that had even less media exposure.

In another defense motion they asked the court to bar the prosecution from challenging jurors based on their religious beliefs. Obviously, the defense thought that some jurors' religious beliefs would not allow them to vote for a death penalty. The prosecution countered that the Oregon Supreme Court and United States Supreme Court both allowed prosecutors to exclude potential jurors based upon their religious beliefs concerning the death penalty. Stephanie Tuttle wrote, *The defendant's proposal denies the state the right to challenge jurors that cannot or will not follow the law.*

Not surprisingly, in light of Joel Courtney having assaulted Dr. Sobotka in a jail office, the defense wanted the judge to exclude expert testimony on issues of Courtney's future dangerousness. The outbursts that Joel Courtney had engaged in could definitely come back to haunt him if a trial ever got to the death penalty stage.

Stephanie Tuttle disagreed and wrote to the judge on this: *Defendant's risk to commit future acts of violence is a fact of consequence in any death penalty case. An expert who testifies about risk factors and ways of evaluating future dangerousness offers testimony that helps a jury understand the evidence in the case.* Tuttle stated that under Oregon law, expert testimony in this area was legal and used often, especially during a sentencing phase.

DDA Karen Kemper was busy on all of this as well. She responded to a defense motion to suppress samples of Joel Courtney's hair, saliva, and prints from his fingers and palms. The thrust of this motion was that law enforcement had obtained these samples illegally.

Kemper wrote back that during Courtney's arrest and incarceration in New Mexico, for the abduction and rape of Natalie Kirov, Corvallis PD detective Shawn Houck had drafted an affidavit in support of a search warrant on Joel Courtney. Detective Hughes, a detective with the Albuquerque Police Department, wrote up his own search warrant on Courtney, based upon Houck's warrant. Detective Hughes noted that he reviewed Houck's search warrant request and *found that it contains sufficient probable cause for the issuance of this search warrant.*

The New Mexico search warrant asked that the

home that Joel Courtney and his wife, Rosy, shared in Rio Rancho, New Mexico, be searched for biological specimens. During that search the detectives noted that string, duct tape, shoestrings, and a rope tied into a noose had been collected. So had a duffel bag identified as belonging to Joel Courtney, a hair tie with blond hair in it, and a floorboard mat with blond hair on it. Because of all of this evidence, Bernalillo County District Court Judge James Blackmer had allowed officers to take four buccal swabs from Joel Courtney, fifty hairs from his head, pubic hairs, and a set of major case prints, including palm prints. DDA Kemper wrote that all of that was legal in New Mexico, and it was now legal in Oregon.

One of the more unusual motions coming from the defense side was one to require separate juries for the guilt and penalty phases of a trial. As Stephanie Tuttle pointed out, *There is no legal authority for this proposition or even authorized by law. The Oregon and United States courts have never held this to be an improper process.* The DOJ attorney was referencing the time-honored tradition of one jury for both phases.

There were other matters percolating along at that time as well that concerned Joel Courtney and the Wilberger family. In the Wilberger civil suit against the company Courtney had been working for when he kidnapped Brooke, the Wilbergers were suing CBM for millions of dollars.

In response, Jose Lomeli, who had been the regional manager of CBM in May 2004, stated that Joel had been terminated on May 15, 2004—nine days before Brooke was abducted. Lomeli in an affidavit stated that he had personally supervised Joel for a week on a training trip. Lomeli wrote, *On the training trip, we stayed at the same motel at night and were together for a week. Mr. Courtney appeared to be very normal in all his interactions with me and our customers and crews. He appeared to drive normally, and did not show any violent behavior to anyone. He did not use the van in any illegal way.*

Lomeli's opinion of Joel soon changed, however. He wrote in the affidavit that Joel missed appointments, couldn't be reached on the company cell phone, and would not return calls. There were several complaints from customers. Based on this, Lomeli decided to terminate Courtney on May 15, 2004. Yet even then, Joel Courtney did not return the van or the company cell phone.

Lomeli stated that he went to Jesus Ordaz's home in Portland to get the green company van. When he got there, no one was home, and the van was in the driveway. Lomeli had no way of driving the van away without its keys, though. When he made a second trip to the Ordaz home, he noticed the green van was gone.

Lomeli eventually learned that the company van had been driven to New Mexico by Joel Courtney. Lomeli sent Jesus Ordaz there to retrieve the van, which he did, and Ordaz continued to use the green van on company business until it was seized by authorities several months later.

Even as the motions and countermotions went back and forth like shuttlecocks in a game of badminton, the all-important trial date crept closer and closer. And as always, Joel Courtney would prove to have an unexpected trick up his sleeve.

CHAPTER 26
A BODY IN THE WOODS

It looked as if after five years, the trial of Joel Courtney for the abduction and murder of Brooke Wilberger was actually going to take place. That was the common consensus in the legal arena and community at large. But there was always one unknown factor in the equation—Joel Courtney. He had shown in past court actions that he was always unpredictable, and he would show that once again in a very dramatic fashion in September 2009.

Even members of the local media, who had been intently following this story for more than five years, were not aware what was going on behind closed doors in a neighboring county courthouse. Then on September 21, 2009, Joel Courtney was sitting down with his defense lawyers, DA John Haroldson, and Judge Locke Williams; and just as in New Mexico in the Natalie Kirov case, Courtney was about to hammer out a plea deal. What was at stake this time was his very life.

After intense discussions Joel Courtney put his pen to a document. The document began: *I am the defendant in this proceeding, and I hereby withdraw my plea of not guilty. I waive my right to trial, and I choose to plead guilty to the following charge: Count 1—Aggravated Murder—Concealing the commission of the crime of kidnapping in the second degree.*

Courtney then noted that he was forty-three years old, had completed school up to fourteen years of age, and could read, speak, and understand English. He stated that he had fully discussed the plea deal with his attorneys and had been advised by them on the matter. He had also discussed with them the sentence he would receive for signing the document.

Courtney noted that he was not under the influence of drugs or alcohol while signing the document, and that he took the medications of Atenolol, Lisinopril, and Prilosec.

Then Courtney initialed three very important statements: *(1.) I know that if I plead guilty to the charge, I cannot challenge on appeal any of the trial court's earlier rulings in this case. (2.) I agree to a sentence of life imprisonment without the possibility of release or parole. (3.) I agree that my criminal history is accurately set forth as an attachment to the plea agreement.*

In a separate document to the judge, DA Haroldson noted that Brooke Wilberger's parents, Diane Mason, and Jade Bateman were all in agreement with the plea deal. They were not standing in the way of it, and the matter would not be taken to trial where Joel Courtney could possibly receive the death penalty.

After the signing of the documents, Haroldson had one more very important matter to take care of—a press conference that was about to reveal something everyone in the area wanted to know. For in this complicated plea agreement, Joel Courtney had to reveal where Brooke Wilberger's remains were, in order to spare his life.

The press conference that ensued was absolutely jammed with reporters, law enforcement personnel, OSU students, former volunteers in the hunt for Brooke, and ordinary citizens. DA John Haroldson began by telling the throng, "I'd like to take a moment and reflect on the great loss and protracted grief that the Wilbergers have had to endure at having to face a parent's absolute worst nightmare. On May 24, 2004, Joel Courtney abducted Brooke Wilberger, the daughter of Greg and Cammy Wilberger. He abducted her. He raped her. He murdered her and left her body in the woods. And not until this weekend did we begin to recover the remains, and were able to confirm with absolute certainty that we had recovered the remains of Brooke Wilberger."

Haroldson said that the recovery of Brooke's remains came after a long effort to settle the case outside of a jury trial. Haroldson then related that through the plea agreement, Joel Courtney was now sentenced to life in prison without parole. In return, Haroldson said, the Wilbergers now had a chance to lay Brooke to rest "in a proper and honorable fashion."

Haroldson related that Joel Courtney disclosed that on May 24, 2004, he was driving a van and pulled into a parking lot where Brooke was cleaning lampposts. Joel said that he made a U-turn with the van as to block the view of Brooke so that she could not be seen from the apartments. He exited the van with a FedEx envelope in his hand, as if he was a delivery person. He then pretended to be looking for an address in the apartment complex. By that means he was able to get close to Brooke.

Joel said that he abducted her at knifepoint and forced her into the van. In the struggle she screamed and lost her flip-flops on the pavement. Once they were both in the van, he drove a short distance and bound her with duct tape.

"What followed was twenty-four hours of an isolated situation where Brooke was kept in the woods. There Mr. Courtney raped Brooke Wilberger and finally caused her death by bludgeoning her skull."

Haroldson noted that investigators in the case had taken many, many tips from the community. And that over the years, Brooke Wilberger had become an "icon" to Corvallis. "And in that sense, we, as a family, all felt the loss. And we will all remember Brooke Wilberger."

Haroldson reiterated about the immense amount of tips coming in, but no viable suspects emerged from those tips. It was Courtney's abduction of Natalie Kirov, and her escape, that had been Joel's undoing. It was Albuquerque PD's background search on Courtney that led in a line to Joel's DUI arrest in Lincoln County, Oregon, and his failure to show up for court there. And it was APD detectives contact with the Corvallis Police Department that began the threads that would tie together and lead back to Joel Courtney and Brooke Wilberger.

Haroldson said that investigators began an exhaustive search on where Joel Courtney had lived, where he had worked, and what vehicles he had driven. And this investigation eventually led to the green Dodge van owned by the CBM company and Joel's employment with them. Then Haroldson stated that once the investigators searched the van, they discovered a blond hair in the van. The blond hair had come from Brooke Wilberger.

Haroldson spoke of the other two OSU female students who had come in contact with a man in a green van on the morning of May 24, 2004. Haroldson added that by their suspicion of the man and by good luck, they had escaped what was soon to befall Brooke Wilberger.

Haroldson ended his presentation by saying, "This is a case which has tested many of us, and yet, we have never given up on seeking justice or holding on to the value of family and community. We sought a just result to ensure that Joel Courtney would be imprisoned for the rest of his life. I realize there have been some questions about where the exact remains were recovered, and I would share with you that the recovery process is not yet complete. And for that reason, out of respect for the integrity of the process, and in order to completely recover the existing remains of Brooke Wilberger, we are attempting not to draw public attention to that area until the entire recovery is complete."

After DA Haroldson was done, Cammy Wilberger approached the microphone. She told the assembled gathering, "Thank you for coming. Thank you for being so supportive these last five and a half years. It's been a long haul for all of us. Today we're grateful. We're grateful to all of the law enforcement people who have searched so diligently for so long, and who never gave up hope. And we are thankful for the district attorney's office, and all of those who have worked so faithfully in that office. We feel a true closeness with them and I appreciate so much their kindness to us. And their willingness to keep us in the loop, every step of the way."

Cammy said that her family likened the whole process to an iceberg. What the public saw so often in newspapers and on television was only the tip of the iceberg. And what the public felt was only a portion of what the Wilberger family felt on the inside. In the newspapers and on television, there was only glimpses and fragments of what was occurring behind the scenes in law enforcement and at the DA's office.

Cammy once again said that the family was grateful for all the hard work everyone had done on behalf of their daughter. Then she unexpectedly added, "It may be hard for you to understand, but at this time we really feel gratitude, even to Mr. Courtney, that he could see fit to tell us where he left Brooke. And for our family, we are thankful that justice was served and that he will not have an opportunity for parole. Now he can go on with what's left of his life. We want to strengthen our family, and go on with our life. We're just grateful to all of you, and want you to know that."

After Cammy Wilberger spoke, the floor was opened up to questions.

One person asked, "How long will the recovery effort take?"

Haroldson answered, "My best estimate—it may be completed in a week."

Another person asked, "Were the remains in Corvallis?"

Haroldson replied, "No. They are in Benton County, but not in Corvallis."

"Who provided you information as to where the remains were?"

Haroldson said, "Joel Courtney provided us details that led us to the remains."

Someone wanted to know why the plea deal was offered now, and why Courtney accepted it.

Haroldson replied, "Our position never changed. It takes two to make an agreement work. The question becomes, when does an opportunity present itself in an accelerated fashion? We did not want to let this opportunity pass by. I believe our decision was the right one. We were successful in recovering her remains and successful in bringing a resolution to the case."

"He didn't take a deal last time. Why did he do it now?"

The answer was "There are a number of layers influencing that. You'd be best to ask him. But we can point to rulings and motions—a decision made in New Mexico on an appeal to the conviction of the crime he had committed there. Sometimes you reach a crossroads where it appears this is the time to resolve the case. Ultimately that's defined by the individual and what triggers them to act. We at the DA's office must always be prepared to try the case, but also to find the best resolution."

There was a question, "Is the state disappointed that the death penalty is now out?"

Haroldson replied, "Under these circumstances, no. I say that because the death penalty in Oregon presents a lengthy process, involving appeals, and draws out closure for a family that has suffered as the Wilberger family has. And one must take into consideration what it means to recover remains and bring closure under those circumstances. It is not an easy decision. But in this case I stand by that decision."

Someone wanted to know what changes Haroldson had seen in Joel Courtney from the time he arrived from New Mexico until the present day. Haroldson said, "Most recently the changes that I saw were reflected in Courtney's willingness to disclose where the remains were. Courtney's willingness to admit the rape. To admit the murder. To admit the kidnapping. Those were signs he was assuming a different posture than contesting everything that was put before him."

"Did Courtney lead investigators to the scene?"

The answer was "No. He did not go out with investigators to the scene."

A follow-up question was "Where is Courtney now?"

"He is in transport or may have already been transported to New Mexico. He has an eighteen-year prison sentence, which he has to serve in New Mexico first. After that, the matter will be managed in the Department of Corrections to determine if they want to bring him back."

"Has Courtney expressed any remorse to the family?"

"No."

The next question brought a long answer from Haroldson. The question was "What agencies did your office collaborate with?"

Haroldson replied, "The lead investigating agency in this case, of course, was the Corvallis Police Department, since the case originated in the city of Corvallis. The supporting agencies included the FBI, Oregon State Police, Benton County Sheriff's Office, the DA office investigators, the Oregon Department of Justice, the Philomath Police Department, and Benton County Search and Rescue. They literally went out on their hands and knees and covered every inch at prospective sites we looked at.

"We received additional important support from Governor Ted Kulongoski and Governor Bill Richardson. We had the support of Attorney General John Kroger, who made available to us the Department of Justice. In addition, we had the support of the Benton County commissioners, who worked with me and were able to ensure that we would have the funding to see this through from start to finish. No matter whether it required litigating the case through to the death penalty, having to repeat the case in appellate fashion—they would stand with us and support us in that effort.

"I specifically have to commend my senior prosecutor Karen Kemper and also Stephanie Tuttle, from the Department of Justice. I'm proud of the manner in which Benton County and the Corvallis PD have been able to work in a multiagency fashion to create the type of synergy that ensures success."

Someone wanted to know what areas has been searched and why the searchers had come up empty there. Haroldson replied, "There were numerous areas that were searched based upon leads that we received. There were incredible efforts in that regard. One of the benefits in going through those exercises is that it really prepared us all for the day when it came, where we would be at the right place at the right time. A very methodical approach helped in going to recover her remains in a very careful and respectful manner.

"Before, it was really like a needle in a haystack, unless you had somebody telling you, 'Go look at such-and-such a place.' We had information ranging through all areas of the state from Mount Hood down to the southern area of the state. I can tell you, after five years the amount of growth that can occur can make it particularly challenging, because it's not self-evident for a person to simply be passing by through an area and spot something."

Someone wanted to know how compliant Harold-son thought Brooke Wilberger was when she had been kidnapped.

Haroldson replied, "The information that we have received through Joel Courtney's attorneys provides Joel Courtney's account of what happened. Some of that account I will submit is a romanticized version of what really happened. I say that with a caveat as to how much weight to give to some of the representations he gave. Joel Courtney's account was that he had abducted Brooke Wilberger and he used duct tape to bind her. He said he went into the woods with her and spent some time with her. He said he was using drugs and that at one point he got hungry. He bound her, went back into town for some food, then drove back out to the woods.

"Joel said that he spent the night in his vehicle and that she was still alive at that point. The following morning was when the sexual assault took place, according to Courtney. He said that Brooke Wilberger reacted very strongly—and her reaction was so strong, it was then that he thought he'd better do something. That's when he ended her life. He commented, 'I was surprised that she fought so hard.'"

A person asked, "How long was it from the time you got the information until her remains were discovered?"

Haroldson replied, "In the recovery process, unless you have a body that is contained in some fashion, you simply don't find the person. There are many processes that may cause remains to move via gravity or otherwise. We found in the forest some remains, and have continued to recover remains, even as we speak."

"Why do you not want any publicity about where the remains have been found?" another person asked.

Haroldson stated, "The reason it was done with little or no publicity was foremost preserving the integrity of the recovery of the remains. The probability that could have arisen would have been individuals going out there to explore an area that we needed to be able to go in with professionals. It would have significantly compromised the process. Secondly, [we] were directed in the court not to discuss the settlement until we reached the plea and sentencing. Our interest was in preserving the opportunity to successfully recover the remains in a manner that would not have to contend with others who were curious and looking at the area."

Chapter 27
Recovery

DA John Haroldson, of course, had not revealed the location where some of Brooke Wilberger's remains had been found, and where work on finding more of her remains was still in progress. However, there were plenty of people in that area who were very aware about what and where that had occurred and was still occurring. It was a small town in the Oregon Coast Range, and the advent of so many law enforcement personnel near their town was not something that could easily be hidden. Incredibly, in Bonnie Wells's vision clear back in 2004, she had predicted that Brooke would be found in that direction, and her admonition to Shawna to search in that area was very close to where the remains were found.

Brooke's remains were discovered near Blodgett, Oregon, a town of only a few hundred people, situated along Highway 20 in the Coast Range. And in a strange twist of events, it was near the Blodgett Country Store, where onetime Brooke Wilberger suspect Loren Krueger had parked his vehicle, after wearing a ski mask, to do a Peeping Tom episode upon a young woman resident of the area. Even though Krueger had nothing to do with Brooke Wilberger's abduction, it was strange that so many things were coming full circle.

In fact, one of the few businesses in town was the Blodgett Country Store, where locals gathered, and they started sharing their stories with inquisitive journalists. Store owner Mark Scacco told a reporter interested in the developments of the Brooke Wilberger case that the area in the hills was heavily wooded and crisscrossed by dirt logging roads. Scacco added one more thing. He said that many residents of the area always thought that Brooke Wilberger's remains might be found back in that wild area. Scacco related, "With the timeline the authorities gave, we've always thought she was out here somewhere. A couple of us actually searched in that area."

Katie Davis, a local resident, told a reporter, "It was kind of shocking to hear about this at first. We hunt out here, and you wonder. All this time she was in the area. It's a bittersweet thing finding her."

Tina Nunn, an employee at the store, expressed her admiration for Cammy Wilberger. "She was so strong throughout the whole thing. And at the press conference, she was so lovely. She's at peace with it."

Asked if they now had fears about where they lived, because of what had happened there, both Nunn and Scacco said that it could have happened anywhere and that they weren't afraid to live in such an isolated area. Scacco related, "I still feel real safe and secure in my community because we all look after each other."

A reporter wanted to know how Scacco felt about Joel Courtney's plea deal and how others in the area felt about it. Scacco responded, "A lot of them are saying he should still get the death penalty. Life in prison is too good for him."

After the authorities scoured the area as thoroughly as possible for Brooke Wilberger's remains and her personal possessions, DA John Haroldson finally let the press know exactly where the location was. He said that Joel Courtney had taken pride in being able to find remote locations and was extremely detailed when he explained to authorities where Brooke's remains were. The remains were on an abandoned logging road off Highway 20, twelve miles west of Corvallis, not far from Blodgett. Brooke's body was about five hundred yards up the logging road on private property. Joel had concealed her body beneath a fallen log, using ferns and moss to cover her. She had been hidden so well that a search team had passed right past her remains in the week after she had disappeared.

A few more details started making their way into the press as well as to why Joel Courtney had made a 180-degree turn from his previous stance of not taking a plea deal. Much of it had to do with Judge Locke Williams's order to allow evidence in about Diane Mason, Jade Bateman, and Bob Clifford. Those three individuals could place Courtney and the green van within blocks of where Brooke had been kidnapped on May 24, 2004. And testimony about Natalie Kirov was going to be heard by jurors as well.

In September 2009, a change of venue was in the

works, either to Marion County or Multnomah County, and the judge ordered DA John Haroldson and defense attorney Steven Gorham to meet at a conference in Marion County. Joel Courtney was secretly transported to the Marion County Courthouse on various occasions. And, for whatever reason, Judge Williams included information to the prospective parties that Polk County Judge Charles Luukinen was willing and able to preside over ongoing talks about a plea deal. Just why this Polk County judge became involved was not stated.

Perhaps because Judge Luukinen was a third party who had never made any rulings in relation to Joel Courtney, he was acceptable to all sides. Whatever the reason, both DA John Haroldson and defense attorney Steven Gorham later said that Judge Luukinen had been instrumental in helping all parties reach an agreement on the plea deal.

And KVAL-TV added, through its investigation, that a prime motivator in the deal for Joel Courtney was not only that his life would be spared, but a provision that he would be allowed to serve prison time near his family in New Mexico. In fact, Steven Gorham stressed this point.

Gorham said, "The plea bargain was much more to do with Courtney's assurance, in writing, that he would stay in New Mexico, rather than his desire to avoid the death penalty. I think they're as much as any family is together."

Gorham also said that there had been talks in the works for a long time from DA Haroldson that if Joel Courtney came clean about all other victims, a deal could be made for life without parole. Courtney, however, always insisted that there were no other victims. Finally it got down to revealing where Brooke Wilberger's remains were.

Gorham also added some information that had never been revealed about the actual kidnapping. According to Courtney, after he had snatched Brooke from the parking lot in the Oak Park Apartments, he had transported her to a McDonald's restaurant in Philomath. There he had bound her in the back of the green van. From the McDonald's, he drove to the isolated woods near Blodgett.

Courtney said that he had gone on walks in the woods with her on May 24 and talked to her, trying to calm her down. Gorham said that he didn't know if Courtney had gagged Brooke at that point. And Gorham added, "I'm sure she was trying her best to talk him out of whatever he might be thinking of doing, and trying to talk him into letting her go."

Before nightfall, according to Courtney, he placed Brooke back in the van and drove to Philomath once again to the same McDonald's. He ordered them both something to eat and then drove back to the woods near Blodgett. Gorham said that Courtney had been doing cocaine, and at some point he ran out, which only made him more irritable and unstable. And according to Courtney, he sexually assaulted Brooke for the first time on the following morning, May 25. When he was done, he took either a large piece of wood or a tree branch and beat her in the head until she was dead. Then he concealed her body beneath a fallen log and covered that up with ferns and moss.

* * *

There were victims in all directions from this murder. Obviously, the Wilberger family was the most prominent. But Dina McBride, Joel's sister, was a victim as well by her association to him. Dina sent a statement to media outlets, letting everyone know just how sorry she was for what her brother had done:

> *I am the eldest sister of Joel Patrick Courtney. I am currently hospitalized for a lengthy ongoing health problem, and am unable to make a statement in person. I would, however, like to make a brief statement. During the early morning hours of November 30, 2004, a phone call awakened our family. Information was given that informed us that my younger brother, Joel Patrick Courtney, had been arrested in New Mexico. We did not know what the charge was at that point in time. It was later in the evening when we learned that he had been accused of kidnpping and sexually assaulting a young college co-ed at knifepoint.*
>
> *That evening began a conversation amongst my husband and I that started with the half-posed questions, "Do you think . . ." Pause. "He couldn't be involved with . . ." and then finally, "It's impossible to think it's possible."*
>
> *Those phrases came because as soon as we heard of the details of the case in New Mexico—we couldn't help but wonder at the similarities related to the disappearance of Brooke Wilberger.*
>
> *We talked at length. We tried to reconstruct events from several months earlier. We came up with a basic idea of a timeline, and then we went to our family datebook and compared notes.*
>
> *With dawning realization, we dreaded that there*

*was, perhaps, a chance that Joel was somehow in-
volved in the abduction of beautiful, vivacious, pre-
cious Brooke Wilberger.*

*What do you do when you are faced with the
thought that someone whom you love is capable of
something so inexplicably evil? Who do you call? We
wondered if we were just being paranoid. We wondered if we were not paranoid enough.*

*After a great deal of time communicating about it,
well into the early hours of the morning, we concluded
that we would pray, sleep on it, and then if we still
felt that there was any chance of Joel's involvement,
we should contact law enforcement.*

*As it turned out, we didn't have time. Law enforce-
ment contacted us. Early December 2004 began a
working relationship between my mother, now deceased, myself, and the various law enforcement agencies involved with the pursuit of truth and justice
for Brooke Wilberger and her loving family.*

*From the very first inkling of a possible connection,
the core of our family has stood with the solid conviction that while we love Joel, we answer to God first
and foremost, and would commit to making ourselves
available to the pursuit of clarification of facts and
events.*

*This has been a long and difficult season for all
concerned. Our hearts continue to weep for the
Wilberger family. We weep for Joel's family—two of
whom are young children who have suffered losses
that continue to break our hearts. There are countless
other family members and friends who have suffered
in one way or the other for the Wilberger family, and
our own.*

Our first prayer from November 30, 2004, was,

"Father God, we ask, if Joel is responsible for this that he would tell the truth, and please let Brooke be found." This is a prayer that has oft been repeated. We'd go so far as to say it daily. When we learned that the truth had been revealed and Brooke's body had been recovered, I wept. The emotions are so bittersweet, but I am thankful that the Wilberger family can have the resolution that they have so diligently sought.

As a family, we want to express our love and continued support for the Wilberger family. Their unswerving devotion has been an inspiration and encouragement to us. We also wish to thank the various law enforcement agencies that have been involved, the Assistant District Attorney and District Attorney of Benton County. Their commitment to excellence, attention to detail, kind and compassionate interaction with our family has been a blessing.

Lastly, if I could ask anything of you, the media, and those who hear or read these words, to remember that these actions taken by my brother have deeply impacted, and will continue to do so, several extended families. We as a family continue to ask that you respect our privacy and honor our need to mourn and heal.

On October 10, 2009, there was a final memorial service for Brooke Wilberger at the LaSells Stewart Center on the OSU campus. The LaSells Stewart Center was only a few blocks from where Brooke had been abducted on May 24, 2004. The center had also been a command center during the fevered search for her during May and June 2004. Now the entire region was invited to the memorial service to remember what had been lost.

Hundreds of people attended as DA John Haroldson and the Wilberger family were on stage to remember Brooke. A slide show was presented about Brooke growing up. Then there were speeches by Haroldson, Benton County Emergency Services coordinator Peggy Pierson, and the Reverend John Dennis, of Corvallis's First Presbyterian Church. A community choir sang, and then a solo hymn was sung by LDS member Valerie Steig. She sang "I Am a Child of God."

Many people who had been volunteers in the months and months of searching for Brooke attended the event. Two of them were Dale and Bonnie Romrell, who were there to remember Brooke and to remember all the people who had given up their ordinary lives to search for the girl whom they came to think of as their daughter.

Cammy Wilberger took the stage. Bathed in a glow of spotlights, she was gracious as she had always been.

Cammy said to the audience, "We loved Brooke. You grew to love her like we did. Now we've grown to love you all."

In some ways things had come full circle. It was near the LaSells Stewart Center where Joel Courtney had tried abducting Diane Mason and Jade Bateman on May 24, 2004. And not far away, he eventually succeeded in abducting Brooke Wilberger. By his rash and thoughtless act, Joel had ended her young life. And in time he also ensured that he would never see the light of day beyond prison walls for the rest of his life.